REMAINS IN VERSE AND PROSE.

REMAINS IN VERSE AND PROSE

OF

ARTHUR HENRY HALLAM

WITH A PREFACE AND MEMOIR

Vattene in pace, alma beata e bella. — ARIOSTO

BOSTON
TICKNOR AND FII
1863

RIVERSIDE, CAMBRIDGE:
STEREOTYPED AND PRINTED BY H. O. HOUGHTON.

CONTENTS.

ADVERTISEMENT.

THE Editor of the following Poems has been induced, after the lapse of many years, to reprint a limited number of copies. Arthur Henry Hallam had the happiness to possess the friendship of one, then as young as himself, whose name has risen to the highest place among our living poets. What this distinguished person felt for one so early torn from him, has been displayed in those beautiful poems, intitled "In Memoriam," which both here and in America have been read with admiration and delight. The image of Arthur hovers, like a dim shadow, over these; and as the original copies of his own productions, given solely to his friends, are not easily to be procured, it has been thought by the Editor, after much deliberation, that others may be interested in possessing them. A few have not been reprinted in this Edition.

Another great calamity fell on the Editor about two years since; a second time he was bereaved of a son, whose striking resemblance in character to Arthur had long been his consolation and his pride. It is, therefore, appropriate on the present occasion to subjoin a short memoir of Henry Fitzmaurice Hallam, drawn up soon after his death by two very intimate friends, Henry Sumner Maine and Franklin Lushington. Never were brothers more akin in every moral excellence of disposition, or in their habitual pursuits, or in a depth of thought which did not exclude a lively perception of what was passing before them, and an entire enjoyment of friendly intercourse.

March, 1853.

PREFACE.

THE writer of the following Poems and Essays was so well known to the greater part of those into whose hands they are likely to come, that it may seem almost superfluous to commemorate a name little likely to fade from their recollection. Yet it is a pious, though at the same time, a very painful office, incumbent on the Editor, to furnish a few notices of a life as remarkable for the early splendor of genius, and for uniform moral excellence, as that of any one who has fallen under his observation; especially as some there must probably be, who will read these pages with little previous knowledge of him to whom they relate.

Arthur Henry Hallam was born in Bedford Place, London, on the 1st of February, 1811.

Very few years had elapsed before his parents observed strong indications of his future character, in a peculiar clearness of perception, a facility of acquiring knowledge, and above all, in an undeviating sweetness of disposition, and adherence to his sense of what was right and becoming. As he advanced to another stage of childhood, it was rendered still more manifest that he would be distinguished from ordinary persons, by an increasing thoughtfulness, and a fondness for a class of books, which in general are so little intelligible to boys of his age that they excite in them no kind of interest.

In the summer of 1818, he spent some months with his parents in Germany and Switzerland, and became familiar with the French language, which he had already learned to read with facility. He had gone through the elements of Latin before this time; but that language having been laid aside during his tour, it was found upon his return, that a variety of new scenes having effaced it from his memory, it was necessary to begin again with the first rudiments.

He was nearly eight years old at this time; and in little more than twelve months he could read Latin with tolerable facility. In this period his mind was developing itself more rapidly than before; he now felt a keen relish for dramatic poetry, and wrote several tragedies, if we may so call them, either in prose or verse, with a more precocious display of talents than the Editor remembers to have met with in any other individual. The natural pride, however, of his parents did not blind them to the uncertainty that belongs to all premature efforts of the mind; and they so carefully avoided everything like a boastful display of blossoms, which, in many cases have withered away in barren luxuriance, that the circumstance of these compositions was hardly ever mentioned out of their own family.

In the spring of 1820, Arthur was placed under the Rev. W. Carmalt, at Putney, where he remained nearly two years. After leaving this school, he went abroad again for some months; and in October, 1822, became the pupil of the Rev. E. C. Hawtrey, an assistant master of Eton College. At Eton he continued till the summer of 1827. He was now become a good, though not perhaps a first-rate scholar, in the Latin and Greek languages. The loss of time, relatively to this object, in travelling, but far more, his increasing avidity for a different kind of knowledge, and the strong bent of his mind to subjects which exercise other faculties than such as the acquirement of languages calls into play, will sufficiently account for what might seem a comparative deficiency in classical learning. It can only however be reckoned one, comparatively to his other attainments, and to his remarkable facility in mastering the modern languages.

The Editor has thought it not improper to print in the following pages an Eton exercise, which, as written before the age of fourteen, though not free from metrical and other errors, appears, perhaps, to a partial judgment, far above the level of such compositions. It is remarkable that he should have selected the story of Ugolino, from a poet with whom, and with whose language he was then but very slightly acquainted, but who was afterwards to become, more perhaps than any other, the master mover of his spirit. It may be added that great judgment and taste are perceptible in this translation, which is by no means a literal one; and in which the phraseology of Sophocles is not ill substituted, in some passages, for that of Dante.

The Latin poetry of an Etonian is generally reckoned at that school the chief test of his literary talent. That of Arthur was good without being excellent; he never wanted depth of thought, or truth of feeling; but it is only in a few rare instances, if altogether in any, that an original mind has been known to utter itself freely and vigorously, without sacrifice of purity, in a language the capacities of which are so imperfectly understood; and in his productions there was not the thorough conformity to an ancient model which is required for perfect elegance in Latin verse. He took no great pleasure in this sort of composition; and perhaps never returned to it of his own accord.

In the latter part of his residence at Eton, he was led away more and more by the predominant bias of his mind from the exclusive study of ancient literature. The poets of England, especially the older dramatists, came with greater attraction over his spirit. He loved Fletcher and some of Fletcher's contemporaries, for their energy of language and intenseness of feeling; but it was in Shakspeare alone that he found the fulness of soul which seemed to slake the thirst of his own rapidly expanding genius for an inexhaustible fountain of thought and emotion. He knew Shakspeare thoroughly; and indeed his acquaintance with the early poetry of this country was very extensive. Among the modern poets, Byron was at this time far above the rest and almost exclusively his favorite; a preference which in later years he transferred altogether to Wordsworth and Shelley.

He became, when about fifteen years old, a member of the debating society established among the elder boys, in which he took great interest; and this served to confirm the bias of his intellect towards the moral and political philosophy of modern times. It was probably however of important utility in giving him that command of his own language which he possessed, as the following Essays will show, in a very superior degree, and in exercising those powers of argumentative discussion which now displayed themselves as eminently characteristic of his mind. It was a necessary consequence that he declined still more from the usual parts of study, and abated perhaps somewhat of his regard for the writers of antiquity. It must not be understood, nevertheless, as most of those who read these pages will be aware, that he ever lost his sensibility to those ever-living effusions of genius which the ancient languages preserve. He loved Æschylus and Sophocles (to Euripides he hardly did justice), Lucretius and Virgil; if he did not seem so much drawn to Homer as might at first be expected, this may probably be accounted for by his increasing taste for philosophical poetry.

In the early part of 1827, Arthur took a part in the "Eton Miscellany," a periodical publication, in which some of his friends in the debating society were concerned. He wrote in this, besides a few papers in prose, a little poem on a story connected with the Lake of Killarney. It has not been thought by the Editor advisable, upon the whole, to reprint these lines; though, in his opinion, they bear very striking marks of superior powers. This was almost the first poetry that Arthur had written, except the childish tragedies above mentioned. No one was ever less inclined to the trick of versifying. Poetry with him was not an amusement, but the natural and almost necessary language of genuine emotion ; and it was not till the discipline of serious reflection, and the approach of manhood gave a reality and intenseness to such emotions, that he learned the capacities of his own genius. That he was a poet by nature these Remains will sufficiently prove ; but certainly he was far removed from being a versifier by nature; nor was he probably able to perform, what he scarce ever attempted, to write easily and elegantly on an ordinary subject. The lines in p. 125, on the story of Pygmalion, are so far an exception, that they arose out of a momentary amusement of society ; but he could not avoid, even in these, his own grave tone of poetry.

Upon leaving Eton in the summer of 1827, he accompanied his parents to the Continent, and passed eight months in Italy. This introduction to new scenes of nature and art, and to new sources of intellectual delight, at the very period of transition from boyhood to youth, sealed no doubt the peculiar character of his mind, and taught him, too soon for his peace, to sound those depths of thought and feeling, from which, after this time, all that he wrote was derived. He had, when he passed the Alps, only a moderate acquaintance with the Italian language ; but during his residence in the country, he came to speak it with perfect fluency, and with a pure Sienese pronunciation. In his study he was much assisted by his friend and instructor, the Abbate Pifferi, who encouraged him to his first attempts at versification. The few sonnets which are now printed were, it is to be remembered, written by a foreigner, hardly seventeen years old, and after a very short stay in Italy. The Editor might not, probably, have suffered them to appear, even in this private manner, upon his own judgment. But he knew that the greatest living writer of Italy, to whom they were shown some time since at Milan, by the author's excellent friend, Mr. Richard Milnes, had expressed himself in terms of high approbation ; and he is able to confirm this by the testimony of Mr. Panizzi, which he must take the liberty to insert in his own words: —

"My dear Sir, — I do not know how to express myself respecting the Italian sonnets which I have had the pleasure to read several times, lest I might appear blinded by my affection for the memory of their lamented author. They are much superior not only to what foreigners have written, but to what I thought possible for them to write in Italian. I have formed this opinion after having perused the poems repeatedly last evening as well as this morning, and tried (although in vain) to forget by whom they were written."

The growing intimacy of Arthur with Italian poetry, led him naturally to that of Dante. No poet was so congenial to the character of his own reflective mind; in none other could he so abundantly find that disdain of flowery redundance, that perpetual reference of the sensible to the ideal, that aspiration for somewhat better and less fleeting than earthly things, to which his inmost soul responded. Like all genuine worshippers of the great Florentine

Poet, he rated the "Inferno" below the two later portions of the "Divina Commedia;" there was nothing even to revolt his taste, but rather much to attract it, in the scholastic theology and mystic visions of the "Paradiso." Petrarch he greatly admired, though with less idolatry than Dante; and the sonnets here printed will show to all competent judges how fully he had imbibed the spirit, without servile centonism, of the best writers in that style of composition who flourished in the 16th century.

But Poetry was not an absorbing passion at this time in his mind. His eyes were fixed on the best pictures with silent, intense delight. He had a deep and just perception of what was beautiful in this Art; at least in its higher schools; for he did not pay much regard or perhaps quite do justice, to the masters of the 17th century. To technical criticism he made no sort of pretension; painting was to him but the visible language of emotion; and where it did not aim at exciting it, or employed inadequate means, his admiration would be withheld. Hence he highly prized the ancient paintings, both Italian and German, of the age which preceded the full development of Art. But he was almost as enthusiastic an admirer of the Venetian, as of the Tuscan and Roman, Schools ; considering these Masters as reaching the same end by the different agencies of form and color. This predilection for the sensitive beauties of painting is somewhat analogous to his fondness for harmony of verse, on which he laid more stress than poets so thoughtful are apt to do. In one of the last days of his life, he lingered long among the fine Venetian pictures of the Imperial Gallery at Vienna.

He returned to England in June, 1828 ; and in the following October went down to reside at Cambridge ; having been entered on the boards of Trinity College before his departure to the Continent. He was the pupil of the Rev. Wm. Whewell. In some respects, as soon became manifest, he was not formed to obtain great academical reputation. An acquaintance with the learned languages, considerable at the school where he was educated, but not improved, to say the least, by the intermission of a year, during which his mind had been so occupied by other pursuits, that he had thought little of antiquity even in Rome itself, though abundantly sufficient for the gratification of taste and the acquisition of knowledge, was sure to prove inadequate to the searching scrutiny of modern examinations. He soon, therefore, saw reason to renounce all competition of this kind; nor did he ever so much as attempt any Greek or Latin composition during his stay at Cambridge. In truth, he was very indifferent to success of this kind; and conscious, as he must have been, of a high reputation among his contemporaries, he could not think that he stood in need of any University distinctions. The Editor became, by degrees, almost equally indifferent to what he perceived to be so uncongenial to Arthur's mind. It was, however, to be regretted, that he never paid the least attention to mathematical studies. That he should not prosecute them with the diligence usual at Cambridge, was of course to be expected; yet his clearness and acumen would certainly have enabled him to master the principles of geometrical reasoning; nor, in fact, did he so much find a difficulty in apprehending demonstrations, as a want of interest, and a consequent inability to retain them in his memory. A little more practice in the strict logic of geometry, a little more familiarity with the physical laws of the universe, and the phenomena to which they relate, would possibly have repressed the tendency to vague and mystical speculation which he was too fond of indulging. In the philosophy of the human mind, he was in no danger of the materializing theories of some ancient and modern schools; but in shunning this extreme, he might sometimes forget, that in the honest pursuit of truth, we can shut our eyes to no real phenomena, and that the physiology of man must always enter into any valid scheme of his psychology.

The comparative inferiority which he might show in the usual trials of knowledge sprung in a great measure from the want of a prompt and accurate memory. It was the faculty wherein he shone the least, according to ordinary observation; though his very extensive reach of literature, and his rapidity in acquiring languages, sufficed to prove that it was capable of being largely exercised. He could remember anything, as a friend observed to the Editor, that was associated with an idea. But he seemed, at least after he reached manhood, to want almost wholly the power, so common with inferior understandings, of retaining with regularity and exactness, a number of unimportant uninteresting particulars. It would have been nearly impossible to make him recollect for three days, the date of the battle of Marathon, or the names in order of the Athenian months. Nor could he repeat poetry, much as he loved it, with the correctness often found in young men. It is not improbable that a more steady discipline in early life would have strengthened this faculty, or that he might have supplied this deficiency by some technical devices; but where the higher powers of intellect were so extraordinarily manifested, it would have been preposterous to complain of what may perhaps have been a necessary consequence of their amplitude, or at least a natural result of their exercise.

But another reason may be given for his deficiency in those unremitting labors which the course of academical education, in the present times, is supposed to exact from those who aspire to its distinctions. In the first year of his residence at Cambridge, symptoms of disordered health, especially in the circulatory system, began to show themselves; and it is by no means improbable, that these were indications of a tendency to derangement of the vital functions, which became ultimately fatal. A too rapid determination of blood towards the brain, with its concomitant uneasy sensations, rendered him frequently incapable of mental fatigue. He had indeed once before, at Florence, been affected by symptoms not unlike these. His intensity of reflection and feeling also brought on occasionally a considerable depression of spirits, which had been painfully observed at times by those who watched him most from the time or his leaving Eton, and even before. It was not till after several months that he regained a less morbid condition of mind and body. The same irregularity of circulation returned again in the next spring, but was of less duration. During the third year of his Cambridge life, he appeared in much better health.

In this year (1831), he obtained the first College Prize for an English declamation. The subject chosen by him was the conduct of the

Independent party during the Civil War. This exercise was greatly admired at the time, but was never printed. In consequence of this success, it became incumbent on him, according to the custom of the College, to deliver an Oration in the Chapel immediately before the Christmas vacation of the same year. On this occasion, he selected a subject very congenial to his own turn of thought and favorite study, — the Influence of Italian upon English Literature. He had previously gained another prize for an English essay on the philosophical writings of Cicero. This Essay is, perhaps, too excursive from the prescribed subject; but his mind was so deeply imbued with the higher philosophy, especially that of Plato, with which he was very conversant, that he could not be expected to dwell much on the praises of Cicero in that respect.

Though the bent of Arthur's mind by no means inclined him to strict research into facts, he was full as much conversant with the great features of ancient and modern History, as from the course of his other studies and the habits of his life, it was possible to expect. He reckoned them, as great minds always do, the ground-works of moral and political philosophy, and took no pains to acquire any knowledge of this sort, from which a principle could not be derived or illustrated. To some parts of English history, and to that of the French Revolution, he had paid considerable attention. He had not read nearly so much of the Greek and Latin Historians, as of the Philosophers and Poets. In the history of literary, and especially of philosophical and religious opinions, he was deeply versed, as much so as it is possible to apply that term at his age. The following pages exhibit proofs of an acquaintance, not crude or superficial, with that important branch of Literature.

His political judgments were invariably prompted by his strong sense of right and justice. These, in so young a person, were naturally rather fluctuating, and subject to the correction of advancing knowledge and experience. Ardent in the cause of those he deemed to be oppressed, of which, in one instance, he was led to give a proof with more of energy and enthusiasm than discretion, he was deeply attached to the ancient institutions of his country.

He spoke French readily, though with less elegance than Italian, till from disuse he lost much of his fluency in the latter. In his last fatal tour in Germany, he was rapidly acquiring a readiness in the language of that country. The whole range of French literature was almost as familiar to him as that of England.

The society in which Arthur lived most intimately, at Eton and at the University, was formed of young men, eminent for natural ability and for delight in what he sought above all things, — the knowledge of truth and the perception of beauty. They who loved and admired him living, and who now revere his sacred memory, as of one to whom, in the fondness of regret, they admit of no rival, know best what he was in the daily commerce of Life; and his eulogy should, on every account, better come from hearts, which, if partial, have been rendered so by the experience of friendship, not by the affection of nature.

One of his most valued friends has kindly made a communication to the Editor, which he cannot but insert in this place.

"*March* 11, 1834.

"My dear Sir, — I have delayed writing longer than I thought to have done; but dwelling upon the pleasant hours of my intercourse with Arthur, has brought with it a sense of changes and losses which has, I think, taken away all my spirits. At best, I cannot pretend to give you anything like an adequate account of his habits and studies, even during the few years of our friendship. My own mind lagged so far behind his, that I can be no fit judge of his career; besides, the studies which were then my business, lay in a different direction; and we were seldom together, except in the ordinary hours of relaxation, or when a truant disposition stretched them later into the evening. I can scarcely hope to describe to you the feelings with which I regarded him, much less the daily beauty of his life out of which they grew. Numberless scenes, indeed, grave and gay, come back upon me, which mark him to me as the most accomplished person I have known or shall know.

But the displays of his gifts and graces were not for show; they sprang naturally out of the passing occasion, and being separated from it, would lose their life and meaning. And perhaps, the very brightness and gayety of those hours, would contrast too harshly with the shadow which has passed over them. Outwardly, I do not know that there was anything remarkable in his habits, except an irregularity with regard to times and places of study, which may seem surprising in one whose progress in every direction was so eminently great and rapid. He was commonly to be found in some friend's room, reading or conversing; a habit which he himself felt to be a fault and a loss; and he had occasional fits of reformation, when he adhered to hours and plans of reading, with a perseverance which left no doubt of his power to become a strict economiser of time. I dare say he lost something by this irregularity; but less, perhaps, than one would at first imagine. I never saw him idle. He might seem to be lounging or only amusing himself; but his mind, as far as I could judge, was always active, and active for good. In fact, his energy and quickness of apprehension did not stand in need of outward aids. He could read or discuss metaphysics as he lay on the sofa after dinner, surrounded by a noisy party, with as much care and acuteness as if he had been alone; and that on such subjects he could never have contented himself with idle or slovenly thinking, the writings he has left sufficiently prove. In other respects, his habits were like those of his companions. He was fond of society; the society (at least) which he could command at Cambridge. He moved chiefly in a set of men of literary habits, remarkable for free and friendly intercourse, whose characters, talents, and opinions of every complexion, were brought into continual collision, all license of discussion permitted, and no offence taken. And he was looked up to by all as the life and grace of the party. His studies again (though as I said, I am not the person best qualified to speak of them), were, upon the whole, desultory. He pursued all with vigor and effect; but I think none (while he was among us, at least,) systematically. His chief pleasure and strength lay certainly in metaphysical analysis. He would read any metaphysical book, under any circumstances, with avidity; and I never knew him decline a metaphysical discussion. He would always pursue the argument eagerly to the end, and follow his antagonist into the most difficult places. But indeed, nothing in the shape of literature or philosophy came amiss to him; there was no kind of intellectual power which did not seem native to him; no kind of discussion in which he could not take an active and brilliant part. If he had not as yet made the very most of his powers in any one path, that loss would have been amply made up in the end, by the fuller and more complete development of the whole mind. In the end, he would have found out his vocation; his other powers would have subsided into their natural subordination, and his range of thought in the chosen path would have been proportionably enlarged. As it is, the compositions which he has left (marvellous as they are) are inadequate evidences of his actual power, except to those who had watched the workings of his mind, and seen that his mighty spirit (beautiful and powerful as it had already grown) yet bore all the marks of youth, and growth, and ripening promise. His powers had not yet arranged themselves into the harmony for which they were designed.

He sometimes allowed one to interfere with the due exercise of another. Thus, his genius for metaphysical analysis, sometimes interfered with his genius for poetry; and his natural skill in the dazzling fence of rhetoric, was in danger of misleading and bewildering him in his higher vocation of philosopher. Moreover, he was not, it appeared to me, a very *patient* thinker. He read, thought, and composed with great rapidity; sometimes, as I used to tell him, with more haste than speed,—so that he did not always do full justice either to his author, or himself, or his reader. In anticipating his author's meaning too hastily, he sometimes misconceived. His own theories he was constantly changing and modifying; and he generally demanded from his reader, or hearer, a comprehension as quick and subtle as his own. Perhaps, I am speaking ignorantly;—this was an old subject of dispute between him and myself. But, if I am right, it seems due to his memory that it should be known how far what he had done falls short of what a few years hence he would have done,—how far his vast and various powers yet were from having attained their full stature and mature proportions. The distinctions which the

University holds out, he set little value on; or there is no doubt he might have distinguished himself without difficulty in either line. But in mathematics, for which he was in some respects singularly qualified, he declined the drudgery of the apprenticeship; and, as a scholar, he was content to feel and enjoy (which no man did with a finer relish) the classical writings, without affecting accurate or curious learning. For myself, I differed from him on many points, both of politics, literature, and philosophy; but our disputes never for a moment blinded me to the excellence of his gifts, and the weight of his opinion, and the light which his conversation threw on every subject, where we differed or where we agreed. I have met with no man his superior in metaphysical subtlety; no man his equal as a philosophical critic on works of taste; no man whose views on all subjects connected with the duties and dignities of humanity were more large, more generous, and enlightened. I have thus frankly given you my opinion of his intellectual powers; not because I can attach any value to it, nor, I think, would he have done so, but because it may be interesting to you to know the estimation he was held in by his companions, and the effect which his society produced upon their minds. Of his character as a friend and companion, I can speak with more confidence. While we were together, it left me nothing to desire; now that we are parted, there are but two things which I could wish had been otherwise, — that I had known him sooner, and that I had been a more careful steward of the treasure while it lasted. But how could I have guessed how soon it was to be withdrawn? For the rest, I look back upon those days with unmixed comfort; not a word ever passed between us that I need now wish unsaid. Perhaps I ought to mention that when I first knew him, he was subject to occasional fits of mental depression, which gradually grew fewer and fainter, and had at length, I thought, disappeared, or merged in a peaceful Christian faith. I have witnessed the same in other ardent and adventurous minds, and have always looked upon them as the symptom, indeed, of an imperfect moral state, but one to which the finest spirits, during the process of their purification, are most subject. I seldom saw him under these influences, and never talked with him on the subject. With me he was all summer, always cheerful, always kind, pleasant in all his moods, brilliant in all companies,—'a pard-like spirit, beautiful and swift.' No man tempered wit and wisdom so gracefully; no man was so perfectly made to be admired for his excellent accomplishments; to be revered for his true heart and chivalrous principle; to be delighted in for the sweetness, and gayety, and graciousness of his life and conversation; to be loved for all his qualities. When I think on these things, and look back on what I have written, I am ashamed to think how little I have been able to say of such a man, that is calculated to give even a faint notion of how he lived and what he was. But, perhaps, I shall not mend the matter by saying more. But do not think that the feelings which I have endeavored to express are exaggerated for the occasion. From the time that I became his familiar friend till the day of his death, I never regarded him with any other feelings. Though we lived on the freest and most careless terms, using daily all licence of raillery and criticism, he never caused in me a momentary feeling of displeasure, or annoyance, or even impatience; and, if I had drawn up an estimate of his character in our day of careless hope, when I little dreamed how soon his name might become a sacred one, I should have spoken of him in substance, even as I speak of him now."

The Editor is desirous to subjoin part of a letter from another of Arthur's earliest and most intimate friends, which displays much of his tastes in literature and poetry, as the last does of his philosophical pursuits: —

"*April* 12, 1834.

"I HAVE known many young men both at Oxford and elsewhere, of whose abilities I think highly, but I never met with one whom I considered worthy of being put into competition with Arthur for a moment: * * * * and myself have often talked together on this point, and we have invariably agreed that it was of him above all his contemporaries that great and lofty expectations were to be formed. I am the more anxious to express my strong conviction of his superiority, because it seems to me that if he is judged by the works which he has left behind him, the estimate formed of his powers, however high, will yet be completely inadequate. His poetical genius, to which I principally allude, as being the one among his many eminent gifts of which I can speak with the greatest confidence, was of too stately and severe a kind to be so soon matured. Intrinsically excellent as are many of his compositions, displaying, as everything which he has written abundantly does, the signs of intellectual power, there was yet wanting time and practice and meditation to clear away the occasional obscurities and hardnesses of his style, before it would have represented the intensity of his feelings and the loftiness of his conceptions with adequate harmony and truth. Had he been spared 'to fill,' as he himself beautifully expresses it,

> 'With worthy thought and deed
> The measure of his high desire ;'

had he chosen — which, however, from the tenor of his conversation latterly, I do not believe he would have done — to concentrate his genius upon poetry, any one who will examine candidly what he has left may easily perceive that the very highest rank among the Poets of thought and philosophy would have been at his command. As a critic there was no one upon whose taste and judgment I had so great a reliance. I never was sure that I thoroughly understood or appreciated any poem till I had discussed it with him. As was natural, the philosophical tendency of his own mind led him usually to prefer the poetry of thought to that of action; and in accordance with this preference, Wordsworth, among contemporary writers, was, upon the whole, his favorite; the splendor of Shelley's imagery, and the various melody of his versification, captivated him for a time, but I think that Wordsworth, whose depth and calmness was more congenial to the temper of his own mind than the turbulent brilliancy of Shelley, gradually regained his former ascendency. He also admired much of Keats, especially an Ode to Autumn, and one to the Nightingale; and entertained, as is, of course, well known to you, the highest opinion of his friend Alfred Tennyson as a rising poet. But though he admired these whom I have mentioned, and many others, Dante and Shakspeare were certainly the two whom he regarded as the highest and noblest of their class. I have often heard him complain that the former was not properly appreciated even by his admirers, who dwell only on his gloomy power and sublimity, without adverting to the peculiar sweetness and tenderness which characterize, as he thought, so much of his poetry. Besides Shakspeare, some of the old English dramatists were among his favorite authors. He has spoken to me with enthusiasm of scenes in Webster and Heywood, and he delighted in Fletcher. Massinger, I think, did not please him so much; I recollect his being surprised at my preferring that dramatist to Fletcher. He used to dwell particularly upon the grace of style and harmony of versification for which the latter is remarkable. Indeed, he was at all times peculiarly sensible of this merit, and was perhaps somewhat intolerant of the opposite fault, considering metrical harshness to indicate a defect rather in the soul than the ear of the poet. Of Milton he always spoke with due reverence; but I do not believe that he recurred to him with so much delight or rated him quite so high as his favorite Dante. Among the classical writers Æschylus and Sophocles, particularly the former, were those whom he used to mention most frequently. I do not at present recollect whether we ever conversed together about Homer; it is probable that we may have done so, but I cannot recall any of his opinions upon that subject. The short poems and fragments of Sappho interested him greatly; and I have heard him repeat frequently and dwell with deep feeling upon those beautiful and mournful lines of Bion, which begin *αἴ αἴ ταὶ μάλαχαι.* I do not think that either Euripides or Pindar were favorites in general, though he possessed too discriminating a taste, and too sincere an appreciation of what is beautiful wherever it existed, not to acknowledge and feel their many excellences. Of the Latin poets my impression is that he did not value any very highly, with the exception of Lucretius, and perhaps Catullus. Much of Virgil he undoubtedly admired, but I do not think that his own taste would have led him to place that poet in the prominent rank to which he has been elevated by general opinion.

"I have thus, my dear Mr. H——, endeavored to comply with your request; I have endeavored to place before you, as shortly and as clearly as I can, what I believe to have been the opinions entertained by the dearest and most valued of all my early friends upon that branch of literature which usually formed the subject of our conversations. I am ashamed of the slovenliness and insufficiency of the sketch which I venture to send to you, but it is all that I can furnish. Happily, however, for his fame — happily for your own feelings of proud though melancholy affection — his reputation is not left to depend upon the scanty reminiscences of one or two youthful friends: the memorials which he has bequeathed to us of his mental powers, together with the unanimous consent of all who had an opportunity of knowing and appreciating him as he deserved, are amply sufficient to secure to him that to which he is entitled — the sincere and lasting regret of all good men that such a mind should have been removed from among us at a time when the light of his matured genius, and the excellence of his moral nature, might have exercised so great and so beneficial an influence upon the happiness of mankind."

Arthur left Cambridge on taking his degree in January, 1832. He resided from that time with the Editor in London, having been entered on the boards of the Inner Temple. It was greatly the desire of the Editor that he should engage himself in the study of the law; not merely with professional views, but as a useful discipline for a mind too much occupied with habits of thought, which, ennobling and important as they were, could not but separate him from the every-day business of life, and might, by their excess, in his susceptible temperament, be productive of considerable mischief. He had during the previous long vacation read with the Editor the Institutes of Justinian, and the two works of Heineccius which illustrate them; and he now went through Blackstone's Commentaries, with as much of other law books, as in the Editor's judgment was required for a similar purpose. It was satisfactory at that time to perceive that, far from showing any of that distaste to legal studies which might have been anticipated from some parts of his intellectual character, he entered upon them not only with great acuteness but considerable interest. In the month of October, 1832, he began to see the practical application of legal knowledge in the office of an eminent conveyancer, Mr. Walters, of Lincoln's Inn Fields, with whom he continued till his departure from England in the following summer.

It was not, however, to be expected, or even desired, by any who knew how to value him, that he should at once abandon those habits of study which had fertilized and invigorated his mind. But he now, from some change or other in his course of thinking, ceased in a great measure to write poetry, and expressed to more than one friend an intention to give it up. The instances after his leaving Cambridge were few. The dramatic scene between Raffaelle and Fiammetta, which occurs in p. 151, was written in 1832; and about the same time he had a design to translate the "Vita Nuova" of his favorite Dante, a work which he justly prized as the development of that immense genius in a kind of autobiography which best prepares us for a real insight into the Divine Comedy. He rendered accordingly into verse most of the sonnets which the "Vita Nuova" contains; but the Editor does not believe that he made any progress in the prose translation. These sonnets appearing rather too literal, and consequently harsh, it has not been thought worth while to print.

In the summer of 1832 the appearance of Professor Rossetti's "Disquisizioni sullo Spirito Antipapale," in which the writings of Arthur's beloved masters, Dante and Petrarch, as well as most of the mediæval literature of Italy, were treated as a series of enigmas, to be understood only by a key that discloses a latent carbonarism — a secret conspiracy against the religion of their age — excited him to publish his own remarks in reply. It seemed to him the worst of poetical heresies to desert the Absolute, the Universal, the Eternal, the Beautiful and True, which the Platonic spirit of his literary creed taught him to seek in all the higher works of genius, in quest of some temporary historical allusion which could be of no interest with posterity. Nothing, however, could be more alien from his courteous disposition than to abuse the license of controversy, or to treat with intentional disrespect a very ingenious person, who had been led on too far in pursuing a course of interpretation which, within certain much narrower limits, it is impossible for any one conversant with history not to admit.

A very few other anonymous writings occupied his leisure about this time. Among these were slight memoirs of Petrarch, Voltaire, and Burke, for the "Gallery of Portraits," published by the Society for the Diffusion of Useful

Knowledge. His time was, however, principally devoted, when not engaged at his office, to metaphysical researches and to the history of philosophical opinions.

From the latter part of his residence at Cambridge, a gradual but very perceptible improvement in the cheerfulness of his spirits gladdened his family and his friends; intervals there doubtless were, when the continual seriousness of his habits of thought, or the force of circumstances, threw something more of gravity into his demeanor; but, in general, he was animated and even gay; renewing or preserving his intercourse with some of those he had most valued at Eton and Cambridge. The symptoms of deranged circulation which had manifested themselves before, ceased to appear, or, at least, so as to excite his own attention; and though it struck those who were most anxious in watching him, that his power of enduring fatigue was not quite so great as from his frame of body and apparent robustness might have been anticipated, nothing gave the least indication of danger, either to their eyes, or to those of the medical practitioners who were in the habit ot observing him. An attack of intermitting fever during the prevalent influenza of the spring of 1833, may, perhaps, have disposed his constitution to the last fatal blow. The Editor cannot dwell on anything later.

Arthur accompanied him into Germany in the beginning of August. In returning to Vienna from Pesth, a wet day probably gave rise to an intermittent fever, with very slight symptoms, and apparently subsiding, when a sudden rush of blood to the head put an instantaneous end to his life, on the 15th of September, 1833. The mysteriousness of such a dreadful termination to a disorder generally of so little importance, and, in this instance, of the slightest kind, has been diminished by an examination which showed a weakness of the cerebral vessels, and a want of sufficient energy in the heart. Those whose eyes must long be dim with tears, and whose hopes on this side the tomb are broken down forever, may cling, as well as they can, to the poor consolation of believing, that a few more years would, in the usual chances of humanity, have severed the frail union of his graceful and manly form, with the pure spirit that it enshrined.

The remains of Arthur were brought to England, and interred on the 3d of January, 1834, in the Chancel of Clevedon Church, in Somersetshire, belonging to his maternal grandfather, Sir Abraham Elton; a place selected by the Editor, not only from the connection of kindred, but on account of its still and sequestered situation, on a lone hill that overhangs the Bristol Channel.

More ought, perhaps, to be said; but it is very difficult to proceed. From the earliest years of this extraordinary young man, his premature abilities were not more conspicuous than an almost faultless disposition, sustained by a more calm self-command than has often been witnessed in that season of life. The sweetness of temper that distinguished his childhood, became, with the advance of manhood, an habitual benevolence, and ultimately ripened into that exalted principle of love towards God and man, which animated and almost absorbed his soul during the latter period of his life, and to which most of the following compositions bear such emphatic testimony. He seemed to tread the earth as a spirit from some better world; and in bowing to the mysterious will which has in mercy removed him, perfected by so short a trial, and passing over the bridge which separates the seen from the unseen life in a moment, and, as we believe, without a moment's pang, we must feel not only the bereavement of those to whom he was dear, but the loss which mankind have sustained by the withdrawing of such a light. But these sentiments are more beautifully expressed in a letter which the Editor has received from one of Arthur's earliest and most distinguished friends, himself just entering upon a career of public life, which, if in these times there is any field open for high principle and the eloquence of wisdom and virtue, will be as brilliant as it must, on every condition, be honorable: —

γενοῖ' ἀρ' εὐτυχέστερος
τὰ δ' ἄλλ' ὅμοιος.

. . . . "It was my happiness to live at Eton in habits of close intimacy with him; and the sentiments of affection which that intimacy produced, were of a kind never to be effaced. Painfully mindful as I am of the privileges which I then so largely enjoyed, of the elevating effects derived from intercourse with a spirit such as his, of the rapid and continued expansion of all his powers, of his rare and so far as I have seen unparalleled endowments, and of his deep enthusiastic affections both religious and human, I have taken upon me thus to render my feeble testimony to a memory, which will ever be dear to my heart. From his and my friend, D., I have learned the terrible suddenness of his removal, and see with wonder how it has pleased God, that in his death as well as in his life and nature, he should be marked beyond ordinary men. When much time has elapsed, and when most bereavements would be forgotten, he will still be remembered, and his place I fear will be felt to be still vacant, singularly as his mind was calculated by its native tendencies to work powerfully and for good in an age full of import to the nature and destinies of man."

A considerable portion of the poetry contained in this volume was printed in the year 1830, and was intended by the author to be published together with the poems of his intimate friend, Mr. Alfred Tennyson. They were, however, withheld from publication at the request of the Editor. The poem of "Timbuctoo" was written for the University Prize in 1829, which it did not obtain. Notwithstanding its too great obscurity, the subject itself being hardly indicated, and the extreme hyperbolical importance which the author's brilliant fancy has attached to a nest of barbarians, no one can avoid admiring the grandeur of his conceptions, and the deep philosophy upon which he has built the scheme of his poem. This is, however, by no means the most pleasing of his compositions. It is in the profound reflection, the melancholy tenderness, and the religious sanctity of other effusions, that a lasting charm will be found. A commonplace subject, such as those announced for academical prizes generally are, was incapable of exciting a mind, which, beyond almost every other, went straight to the furthest depths that the human intellect can fathom, or from which human feelings can be drawn. Many short poems of equal beauty with those here printed have been deemed unfit even for the limited circulation they might obtain on account of their unveiling more of emotion than, consistently with what is due to him and to others, could be exposed to view.

1834.

MEMOIR

OF

HENRY FITZMAURICE HALLAM.

BUT few months have elapsed since the pages of "In Memoriam" recalled to the minds of many, and impressed on the hearts of all who perused them, the melancholy circumstances attending the sudden and early death of Arthur Henry Hallam, the eldest son of Henry Hallam, Esq. Not many weeks ago the public journals contained a short paragraph announcing the decease, under circumstances equally distressing, and in some points remarkably similar, of Henry Fitzmaurice, Mr. Hallam's younger and only remaining son. No one of the very many who appreciate the sterling value of Mr. Hallam's literary labors, and who feel a consequent interest in the character of those who would have sustained the eminence of an honorable name; no one who was affected by the striking and tragic fatality of two such successive bereavements, will deem an apology needed for this short and imperfect Memoir.

Henry Fitzmaurice Hallam, the younger son of Henry Hallam, Esq., was born on the 31st of August, 1824; he took his second name from his godfather, the Marquis of Landsdowne. His health was somewhat delicate from infancy, and he displayed no great inclination for the ordinary games and pleasures of boyhood. A habit of reserve, which characterized him at all periods of life, but which was compensated in the eyes of even his first companions by a singular sweetness of temper, was produced and fostered by the serious thoughtfulness ensuing upon early familiarity with domestic sorrow. Even in its immaturity, his mind exhibited the germs of rare qualities. His great facility in learning, his quick appreciation of principles, and his tenacious memory, were remarked and encouraged by his earliest instructors; and on his entering Eton, in 1836, both his masters, and those of his schoolfellows who saw much of him, were struck with the general forwardness of his intellect, as well as the breadth and solidity with which the foundations of his education had been laid. His literary taste and information were uniformly recognized by his contemporaries as greatly in advance of their own. At the age when most boys are reading Scott or Byron, he studied Bacon and delighted in Wordsworth and Dante. Of school honors he was remarkably unambitious : a native serenity of temperament, and a love of literature for its own sake, which he very early manifested, may have made him indifferent to them ; but at the age of fifteen he entered the examination for the Newcastle scholarship, and obtained the medal or second prize, his performances indicating an extraordinary ripeness of thought in the judgment of the examiners, Lord Lyttelton and Mr. Gladstone. In all probability he would have won the scholarship in the following year ; but from weak health and other causes he never competed for it again.

Apart from his appearances at the debating club, where his speeches were already noted for ease and clearness, he was not conspicuous in what may be called the public life of Eton. Although generally respected, it was only by a few intimate friends that he was appreciated or understood. The impressions of his boyish character retained by these more familiar companions bear a signal resemblance to a large part of those which the associates of his later life received from intimacy of another kind. "He was gentle," writes one of his earliest and closest school-friends, "retiring, thoughtful to pensiveness, affectionate, without envy or jealousy, almost without emulation, impressible, but not wanting in moral firmness. No one was ever more formed for friendship. In all his words and acts he was simple, straightforward, true. He was very religious. Religion had a real effect upon his character, and made him tranquil about great things, though he was so nervous about little things."

He left Eton at the close of 1841, and in October, 1842, at the age of eighteen, he commenced his residence, as an undergraduate, at Trinity College, Cambridge, on the "side" of which the Rev. J. Heath and the Rev. W. H. Thompson were then the tutors. From the sketch of his boyhood given above, it will be divined that his earnest and energetic mind, which had always treated the actual school-work of Eton as slight exercise, while gratifying its intellectual cravings from other sources, would find but little inducement to spend its whole vigor in academical studies or in the pursuit of academical distinctions. It might almost be said, that he was inclined to undervalue both the one and the other: certainly he was indisposed to make any extraordinary efforts for university honors; and he was, at that time, too engrossingly occupied with subjects of more congenial interest, to appreciate altogether the worth of a scholarlike training. With all his remarkable clearness of perception, rapid classification of ideas, and excellent memory, it was not till a later period that he began practically to value delicate accuracy of detail as the groundwork of accurate induction. Neither at school nor at college did he ever spend upon his classical compositions, either in prose or verse, the time or labor requisite to make them severely correct, elegant, or strong: in metrical refinements especially he fell below the established standard of Etonians; though, at the same time, he translated into English most difficult historical or philosophical passages with great terseness and felicity of expression. He did not once compete for the annual university prizes; but in all the examinations which he underwent in the due course of his academical career, his natural ability and general attainments secured him a high position. In the Trinity examinations of June, 1843, he was among the very first of his year; at Easter, 1844, he obtained with ease a Trinity scholarship on the first trial: in his third year he gained the first prize for an English declamation, having selected as his thesis "The Influence of Religion on the various forms of Art;" and the oration which, as prizeman, he consequently delivered in the college hall, though occasionally vague and mystical in phraseology, contained abundant proofs both of the energy and the extent of his mental grasp. He took his degree in January, 1846; was among the Senior Optimes in the Mathematical Tripos; and second Chancellor's Medalist. He distinguished himself (especially for the clearness of his metaphysical papers) in the fellowship examination of his college in the ensuing October; and would, no doubt, have succeeded, without difficulty, in a second attempt. For various reasons, however, he never reëntered the lists—to the regret, not only of his contemporaries, but of many among the actual fellows, who had hoped to see a name of so much promise associated with their own. He finally quitted Cambridge at Christmas, 1846, to reside in London, and commence the study of the Law.

During all this time his mind never lay fallow. In the first year of his college-life he became the virtual founder of the "Historical" debating club, established to encourage a more philosophical habit in style, argument, and choice of subjects, than was in vogue in the somewhat promiscuous theatre of the Union. About the same time he entered a smaller and more intimate circle, where topics of the highest and deepest speculation were discussed orally and in writing. To this society he read many valuable and suggestive essays, and always took a principal share in its debates. Fluently and thoughtfully as he wrote, the natural and emphatic exponent of his ideas was his tongue and not his pen. He spoke quietly, earnestly, logically, and convincingly;

and though eager at the time to pursue an advantage to the utmost, to confound a fallacy, or expose a weak argument, he was so possessed with a spirit of candor and tenderness, as often afterwards to experience most serious uneasiness at the thought of having overstated the strength of his own positions, or pressed unfairly upon those of his adversary. He rarely attended the discussions of the Union ; but in May, 1845, when the question of an additional grant to Maynooth was attracting public notice, besides drawing up a very clearly worded and argued petition in favor of the measure, he spoke on the subject with so much strength, grace, fervor, and eloquence, as entirely to enchain the attention and subjugate the sympathies of an originally adverse audience, habituated to the excitements of far less chastened oratory. One who was his friend, but at the same time a very constant and skilful opponent of his views in general debate, observes, in describing him, that "he was the neatest extempore speaker I ever heard; his unprepared remarks were more precisely and elegantly worded than most men's elaborately written compositions. He had, too, a foresight and power of anticipation uncommon in such a youth, which enabled him to leave no salient points of attack, and made his arguments very difficult to answer. He was always most liberal in his concessions to the other side, and never committed the fault of claiming too much or proving too much. His was not a passionate oratory that carried his hearers away in a whirlwind, but a winning voice that stole away their hearts, the *ars celare artem*, the perfection of persuasiveness." *

What he might have proved in the full maturity of life and intellect may best be conjectured by the tastes and the cast of thought which he developed during his final residence in London. The professional education he commenced in 1846 exercised, on the whole, a very beneficial influence upon his mind. The constant contact with the facts and operations of every-day life, into which he was forced by his preparation for the bar, concurring, as it did, in time, with his permanent restoration to

* This is taken from an eulogy written with great discrimination, and with the warmth of friendship, which has appeared in the New York "Literary World," from the pen of Charles Astor Bristed, Esq., of that city, the contemporary of H. F. Hallam at Trinity College.

the sphere of his family, had the effect of completely correcting an undue preference for departments of study remote from popular interest which he had occasionally manifested at Cambridge. In certain favorite fields of investigation his curiosity had been apt to fasten most tenaciously, though by no means exclusively, on the obscure recesses which were chiefly remarkable for their disconnection from common associations. But, from the time of his leaving the University, he devoted his leisure hours almost entirely to the sciences which embrace the mechanism and growth of society. The study of English history he began upon a scale so vast, that the friend to whom he confided his design found it difficult to believe him serious. But within a few months of his death he was following out the plan he had formed with a patient elaborateness and attention to detail, which proved his sincerity, while it indicated an important improvement in the method of his intellectual exercises. About the same period he applied himself diligently to political economy, and bestowed much time latterly on the difficult problems which are furnished by the phenomena of currency and exchange.

It may here be added, that in the several tours which he had taken with his family on the Continent, as well as by other means, he had acquired a considerable acquaintance with modern languages and literature. He spoke French fluently and with a good accent, and could converse in Italian and German.

He was called to the bar in Trinity Term, 1850, and became a member of the Midland Circuit in the summer. Immediately afterwards he joined his family in a tour on the Continent. They had spent the early part of the autumn at Rome, and were returning northwards when he was attacked by a sudden and severe illness, affecting the vital powers, and accompanied by enfeebled circulation and general prostration of strength. He was able, with difficulty, to reach Siena, where he sank rapidly through exhaustion, and expired on Friday, October 25. It is to be hoped that he did not experience any great or active suffering. He was conscious nearly to the last, and met his early death (of which his presentiments, for several years, had been frequent and very singular) with calmness and fortitude. There is reason to apprehend, from medical examination, that his life would not have been of very long duration, even had this unhappy illness not occurred. But for some years past his health had been apparently much improved; and secured as it seemed to be by his unintermitted temperance and by a carefulness in regimen which his early feebleness of constitution had rendered habitual, those to whom he was nearest and dearest had, in great measure, ceased to regard him with anxiety. His remains were brought to England, and he was interred, on December 23d, in Clevedon Church, Somersetshire, by the side of his brother, his sister, and his mother.

His temper was cheerful and even. The reserve which has been before ascribed to him, belonged to his manner rather than his mind: it was bred by his habits and the circumstances of his life, and betrayed nothing like coldness or selfishness. Among intimate friends his conversation was critical, though rarely sarcastic; full of a quiet but penetrating and most various humor; revealing an inclination towards fanciful and even paradoxical tastes; occasionally scintillating with the purest wit. His diction was fluent and ready, abounding in felicities of idiom and phrase. In poetry his preferences were for depth, tenderness, and solemnity, rather than for brilliancy or passion; he was, however, exceedingly fond of the older English dramatists, frequently reading their works aloud, and delighting his hearers by his musical voice and graceful delivery. In painting he was attracted by all beautiful forms, but derived especial pleasure from the expression, through Art, of religious feeling. He was extremely quick to appreciate excellence of all kinds; particularly in accomplishments in which, during his boyhood, he had felt his own deficiency, — as, for instance, in athletic exercises. For continuous and sustained thought he had an extraordinary capacity, the bias of his mind being decidedly towards analytical processes, — a characteristic which was illustrated at Cambridge by his uniform partiality for analysis, and comparative distaste for the geometrical method, in his mathematical studies. His early proneness to dwell upon the more recondite departments of each science and branch of inquiry has been alluded to above. It is not to be inferred that, as a consequence of this tendency, he blinded himself at any period of his life to the necessity and the duty of practical exertion. He was always eager to act as well as speculate ; and, in this repect, his character preserved an unbroken consistency and harmony, from the epoch when, on commencing his residence at Cambridge, he voluntarily became a teacher in a parish Sunday-school for the sake of applying his theories of religious education, to the time when, on the point of setting forth on his last fatal journey, he framed a plan of obtaining access, in the ensuing winter, to a large commercial establishment, in the view of familiarizing himself with the actual course and minute detail of mercantile transactions.

He was full of kindness to his dependents ; very charitable ; generous to profusion where his sympathies were strongly engaged. In general society he was markedly courteous, and, though far from undemonstrative, he never gave offence : one has seldom been found who, with such strong opinions, ruffled so few susceptibilities. Insensibly and unconsciously, he had made himself a large number of friends and admirers in the last few years of his life. The painful impression created by his death in the circle in which he habitually moved, and even beyond it, was exceedingly remarkable both for its depth and its extent. For those united with him in a companionship more than ordinarily close, his friendship had taken such a character as to have almost become a necessity of existence. But it was upon his family that he lavished all the wealth of his disposition,—affection without stint, gentleness never once at fault, considerateness reaching to self-sacrifice.

Such is a faint outline of Henry Fitzmaurice Hallam. It is idle to speculate on the position which he might hereafter have taken in public life: for very different reasons, it is needless to speak of the influence which his memory will continue to exert upon all who knew him well. The friends of his Eton and Cambridge career will number their acquaintance with him among their most cherished reminiscences. Many among them will feel the imperfections of this hasty memoir, the want of happy and characteristic touches in the vain attempt to recall fully the features of the dead: —

> " Di ciò si biasmi il debole intelletto
> E' l' parlar nostro, che non ha valore
> Di ritrar tutte ciò che dice amore."

H. S. M.
F. L.

MEDITATIVE FRAGMENTS

IN BLANK VERSE.

I.

MY bosom friend, 'tis long since we have looked
Upon each other's face; and God may will
It shall be longer, ere we meet again.
Awhile it seemed most strange unto my heart
That I should mourn, and thou not nigh to cheer;
That I should shrink 'mid perils, and thy spirit
Far away, far, powerless to brave them with me.
Now am I used to wear a lonesome heart
About me; now the agencies of ill
Have so oppressed my inward, absolute self,
That feelings shared, and fully answered, scarce
Would seem my own. Like a bright, singular dream
Is parted from me that strong sense of love,
Which, as one indivisible glory, lay

On both our souls, and dwelt in us, so far
As we did dwell in it. A mighty presence!
Almighty, had our wills but been confirmed
In consciousness of their immortal strength
Given by that inconceivable will eterne
For a pure birthright, when the blank of things
First owned a motive power that was not God.
But thou — thy brow has ta'en no brand of grief,
Thine eyes look cheerful, even as when we stood
By Arno, talking of the maid we loved.
In sooth I envy thee; thou seemest pure:
But I am seared: He in whom lies the world
Is coiled round the fibres of my heart,
And with his serpentine, thought-withering gaze
Doth fascinate the sovran rational eye.
There is another world: and some have deemed
It is a world of music, and of light,
And human voices, and delightful forms,
Where the material shall no more be cursed
By dominance of evil, but become
A beauteous evolution of pure spirit,
Opposite, but not warring, rather yielding
New grace, and evidence of liberty.
Oh, may we recognize each other there,
My bosom friend! May we cleave to each other
And love once more together! Pray for me,
That such may be the glory of our end.

II.

A VALLEY — and a stream of purest white
Trailing its serpent form within the breast
Of that embracing dale — three sinuous hills
Imminent in calm beauty, and trees thereon,
Crest above crest, uprising to the noon,
Which dallies with their topmost tracery,
Like an old playmate, whose soft welcomings
Have less of ardor, because more of custom.
It is an English Scene: and yet methinks
Did not yon cottage dim with azure curls
Of vapor the bright air, and that neat fence
Gird in the comfort of its quiet walls,
Or did not yon gay troop of carollers
Press on the passing breeze a native rhyme,
I might have deemed me in a foreign land.
For, as I gaze, old visions of delight,
That died with th' hour their parent, are reflected
From the mysterious mirror of the mind,
Mingling their forms with these, which I behold.
Nay, the old feelings in their several states
Come up before me, and entwine with these
Of younger birth in strangest unity.

And yet who bade them forth? Who spake to
Time,
That he should strike the fetters from his slaves?
Or hath he none? Is the drear prison-house
To which, 'twould seem, our spiritual acts
Pass one by one, a phantom — a dim mist
Enveloping our sphere of agency?
A guess, which we do hold for certainty?
I do but mock me with these questionings.
Dark, dark, yea, "irrecoverably dark,"
Is the soul's eye: yet how it strives and battles
Thorough th' impenetrable gloom to fix
That master light, the secret truth of things,
Which is the body of the infinite God.

III.

DEEP firmament, which art a voice of God,
Speak in thy mystic accents, speak yet once:
For thou hast spoken, and in such clear tone,
That still the sweetness murmurs through my soul.
Speak once again: with ardent orisons
Oft have I worshipped thee, and still I bow,
With reverence, and a feeling, like to hope,
Though something worn in th' heart, by which we
 pray.
Oh, since I last beheld thee in thy pomp
Right o'er the Siren city of the south,
Rude grief and harsher sin have dealt on me
The malice of their terrible impulses;
And in a withering dream my soul has lived
Far from the love that lieth on thy front,
As native there; far from the poesies
Which are the effluence of thy holy calm.
Thou too art changed; and that perennial light
Which there a limitless dominion held,
In fitful breaks doth shoot along yon mist,
And trembles at its own dissimilar pureness.
Yet is thy bondage beautiful; the clouds

Drink beauty from the spirit of thy forms,
Yea, from the sacred orbits borrow grace,
To modulate their wayward phantasies.
But they are trifles: in thyself alone,
And the suffusion of thy starry light
Firmly abide in their concordant joy,
Beauty, and music, and primeval love:
And thence may man learn an imperial truth,
That duty is the being of the soul,
And in that form alone can freedom move.
Such is your mighty language, lights of heaven:
Oh, thrill me with its plenitude of sound,
Make me to feel, not to talk of, sovranty,
And harmonize my spirit with my God!

IV.

I LAY within a little bowered nook,
With all green leaves, nothing but green around
me,
And through their delicate comminglings flashed
The broken light of a sunned waterfall —
Ah, water of such freshness, that it was
A marvel and an envy! There I lay,
And felt the joy of life for many an hour.
But when the revel of sensations
Gave place to meditation and discourse,
I waywardly began to moralize
That little theatre with its watery scene
Into quaint semblances of higher things.
And first methought that twined foliage
Each leaf from each how different, yet all stamped
With common hue of green, and similar form,
Pictured in little the great human world.
Sure we are leaves of one harmonious bower,
Fed by a sap, that never will be scant,
All-permeating, all-producing mind;
And in our several parcellings of doom
We but fulfil the beauty of the whole.

Oh madness! if a leaf should dare complain
Of its dark verdure, and aspire to be
The gayer, brighter thing that wantons near.
Then as I looked
On the pure presence of that tumbling stream,
Pure amid thwarting stones and staining earth,
Oh Heaven! methought how hard it were to find
A human bosom of such stubborn truth,
Yet tempered so with yielding courtesy.
Then something rose within my heart to say —
"Maidenly virtue is the beauteous face
Which this clear glass gives out so prettily:
Maidenly virtue born of privacy,
Lapt in a still conclusion and reserve;
Yet, when the envious winter-time is come
That kills the flaunting blossoms all arow,
If that perforce her steps must be abroad
Keeps, like that stream, a queenly havior,
Free from all taint of that she treads upon;
And like those hurrying atoms in their fall,
A maiden's thoughts may dare the eye of day
To look upon their sweet sincerity."
With that I struck into a different strain: —
"O ye wild atomies, whose headlong life
Is but an impulse and coaction,
Whose course hath no beginning, no, nor end;
Are ye not weary of your mazed whirls,

Your tortuous deviations, and the strife
Of your opposed bubblings? Are there not
In you as in all creatures, quiet moods,
Deep longings for a slumber and a calm?
I never saw a bird was on the wing
But with a homeward joy he seem'd to fly
As knowing all his toil's o'er-paid reward
Was with his chirpers in their little nest.
Pines have I seen on Jura's misty height
Swinging amid the whirl-blasts of the North,
And shaking their old heads with laugh prolonged,
As if they joyed to share the mighty life
Of elements — the freedom, and the stir.
But when the gale was past, and the rent air
Returned, and the piled clouds rolled out of view,
How still th' interminable forest then!
Soundless, but for the myriad forest-flies,
That hum a busy little life away
I' th' amplitude of those unstartled glades.
Why what a rest was there! But ye, oh ye!
Poor aliens from the fixed vicissitudes,
That alternate throughout created things,
Mocked with incessantness of motion,
Where shall ye find or changement or repose?"
So spake I in the fondness of my mood.
But thereat Fancy sounded me a voice
Borne upward from that sparkling company:

"Repinement dwells not with the duteous free.
We do the Eternal Will; and in that doing,
Subject to no seducement or oppose,
We owe a privilege, that reasoning man
Hath no true touch of." At that reproof the tears
Flushed to mine eyes; and I arose, and walked
With a more earnest and reverent heart
Forth to the world, which God had made so fair,
Mired now with trails of error and of sin.

V.

WRITTEN IN VIEW OF BEN LOMOND.

MOUNTAIN austere, and full of kinglihood!
Forgive me if a child of later earth,
I come to bid thee hail. My days are brief
And like the mould that crumbles on thy verge
A minute's blast may shake me into dust;
But thou art of the things that never fail.
Before the mystic garden, and the fruit
Sung by that Shepherd-Ruler vision-blest,
Thou wert; and from thy speculative height
Beheld'st the forms of other living souls.
Oh, if thy dread original were not sunk
I' th' mystery of universal birth,
What joy to know thy tale of mammoths huge,
And formings rare of the material prime,
And terrible craters, cold a cycle since!
To know if then, as now, thy base was laved
With moss-dark waters of a placid lake;
If then, as now,
In the clear sunlight of thy verdant sides
Spare islets of uncertain shadow lay.

VI.

IT is a thing of trial to the heart,
Of trial and of painful wonderment,
To walk within a dear companion's voice
And hear him speak light words of one we hold
In the same compass of undoubting love.
"How is it that his presence being one,
His language one, his customs uniform,
He bears not the like honor in the thought
Of this my friend, which he hath borne in mine.
It minds me of that famous Arab tale
(First to expand the struggling notions
Of my child brain) in which the bold poor man
Was checked for lack of 'Open sesame.'
Seems it my comrade standeth at the door
Of that rich treasure-house, my lover's heart,
Trying with keys untrue the rebel wards,
And all for lack of one unsounded word
To open out the sympathetic mind."
Thus might a thoughtful man be eloquent,
To whom that cross had chanced: yet not such
The color, though the nature was the same,
Of the plain fact which won me to this muse.

One morn, while in * * * I sojourned,
That winsome Lady sitting by my side,
Whom still these eyes in every place desire,
We looked in quiet unison of joy
On a bright summer scene. Aspiring trees
Circled us, each in several dignity,
Yet taking, like a band of senators,
Most grandeur from their congregated calm.
Afar between two leafy willow stems
Visibly flowed the sunlit Clyde: more near
An infant sister frolicked on the lawn,
And in sweet accents of a far-off land,
Native to th' utterer, called upon her nurse
To help her steps unto us: nor delayed
Those tones to rouse within our inmost hearts
Clear images of a delightful past.
Capri's blue distance, Procida, and the light
Pillowed on Baiæ's wave: nor less the range
Of proud Albano, backed by Puglian snows,
And the green tract beside the Lateran
Rose in me, and a mist came o'er my eyes:
But I spoke freely of these things to her,
And for awhile we walked 'mid phantom shapes
In a fair universe of other days.
That converse passed away, and careless talk,
As is its use, brought divers fancies up,
Like bubbles dancing down their rivulet

A moment, then dilating into froth.
At last, a chance-direction being given,
I spake of Wordsworth, of that lofty mind,
Enthronized in a little monarchy
Of hills and waters, where no one thing is
Lifeless, or pulsing fresh with mountain strength,
But pays a tribute to his shaping spirit!
Thereat the Lady laughed — a gentle laugh;
For all her moods were gentle: passing sweet
Are the rebukes of woman's gentleness!
But still she laughed, and asked me how long since
I grew a dreamer, heretofore not wont
To conjure nothings to a mighty size,
Or see in Nature more than Nature owns.
Then taking up the volume, where it lay
Upon her table, of those hallowed songs,
I answered not but by their utterance.
And first the tales of quiet tenderness
(Sweet votive offerings of a loving life)
In which the feeling dignifies the fact,
I read; then gradual rising as that sprite
Indian, by recent fabler sung so well,*
Clomb the slow column up to Seva's throne,
I opened to her view his lofty thought
More and more struggling with its walls of clay,
And on all objects of our double nature,

* See Southey's "Kehama."

Inward, and outward, shedding holier light,
Till disenthralled at length it soared amain
In the pure regions of the eternal same,
Where nothing meets the eye but only God.
Then spoke I of that intimate belief
In which he nursed his spirit aquiline,
How all the moving phantasies of things,
And all our visual notions, shadow-like,
Half hide, half show, that All-sustaining One,
Whose Bibles are the leaves of lowly flowers,
And the calm strength of mountains; rippling lakes
And the irregular howl of stormful seas;
Soft slumbering lights of even and of morn,
And the unfolding of the starlit gloom;
But whose chief presence, whose imparted self,
Is in the silent virtues of the heart,
The deep, the human heart, which with the high
Still glorifies the humble, and delights
To seek in every show a soul of good.
Pausing from that high strain, I looked to her
For sympathy, for my full heart was up,
And I would fain have felt another's breast
Mix its quick heavings with my own: indeed
The lady laughed not now, nor breathed reproach,
Yet there was chillness in her calm approve,
Which with my kindled temper suited not.
Oh! there is union, and a tie of blood

With those who speak unto the general mind,
Poets and sages! Their high privilege
Bids them eschew succession's changefulness,
And, like eternals, equal influence
Shed on all times and places. I would be
A poet, were't but for this linked delight,
This consciousness of noble brotherhood,
Whose joy no heaps of earth can bury up,
No worldly venture 'minish or destroy,
For it is higher, than to be personal!
Some minutes passed me by in dubious maze
Of meditation lingering painfully,
But then a calm grew on me, and clear faith
(So clear that I did marvel how before
I came not to the level of that truth)
That different halts, in Life's sad pilgrimage,
With different minstrels charm the journeying soul.
Not in our early love's idolatry,
Not in our first ambition's flush of hope,
Not while the pulse beats high within our veins,
Fix we our soul in beautiful regrets,
Or strive to build the philosophic mind.
But when our feelings coil upon themselves
At time's rude pressure; when the heart grows dry,
And burning with immedicable thirst
As though a plague-spot seared it, while the brain
Fevers with cogitations void of love,

When this change comes, as come it will to most,
It is a blessed God-given aid to list
Some master's voice, speaking from out those depths
Of reason that do border on the source
Of pure emotion and of generous act.
It may be that this motive swayed in me,
And thinking so that day I prayed that she,
Whose face, like an unruffled mountain tarn,
Smiled on me till its innocent joy grew mine,
Might ne'er experience any change of mood
So dearly bought by griefs habitual;
Much rather, if no softer path be found
To bring our steps together happily,
Serve the bright Muses at a separate shrine.

1820.

TIMBUCTOO.

Be Yarrow stream unseen, unknown;
 It must or we shall rue it;
We have a vision of our own:
 Ah! why should we undo it. — WORDSWORTH.

THERE was a land, which, far from human sight,
 Old Ocean compassed with his numerous waves,
In the lone West. Tenacious of her right,
 Imagination decked those unknown caves,
And vacant forests, and clear peaks of ice
 With a transcendent beauty; that which saves
From the world's blight our primal sympathies,
 Still in man's heart, as some familiar shrine,
Feeding the tremulous lamp of love that never dies.
 Poets have loved that land, and dared to twine
Round its existence memories of old time,
 When the good reigned; and none in grief did pine.
Sages, and all who owned the might sublime
 To impress their thought upon the face of things,
And teach a nation's spirit how to climb,

Spake of long-lost Atlantis,* when the springs
Of clear Ilissus or the Tusculan bower
Were welcoming the pure rest which Wisdom brings
To her elect, the marvellous calm of power.
Oft, too, some maiden, garlanding her brow
With Baian roses, at eve's mystic hour,
Has gazed on the sun's path, as he sank low,
I' th' awful main, behind Inarime; †
And with clasped hands, and gleaming eye, "Shalt thou,
First-born of light, endure in the flat sea
Such intermission of thy life intense?
Thou lordly one, is there no home for thee?"
A Youth took up the voice: "Thou speedest hence,
Beautiful orb, but not to death or sleep,
That feel we; worlds invisible to sense,
Whose course is pure, where eyes forget to weep,
And th' earthly sisterhood of sorrow and love

* The legend of the lost continent Atlantis is so well known, and its derivation from an early knowledge of America seems so natural and probable, that, had not this Poem been pretty generally censured for its obscurity, I should have thought a note on the subject superfluous. In the beautiful opening of the "Timæus," Plato has alluded to a form of this legend highly creditable to the Athenians, which will serve to show the notions entertained of the extent and relative importance of Atlantis.

† Inarime, now the Island of Ischia.

Some god putteth asunder, these shall keep
  Thy state imperial now: there shalt thou move
Fresh hearts with warmth and joyance to rebound,
  By many a musical stream and solemn grove."
Years lapsed in silence, and that holy ground
  Was still an Eden, shut from sight; and few
Brave souls in its idea solace found.
  In the last days a man arose, who knew *
That ancient legend from his infancy.
  Yea, visions on that child's emmarvailed view
Had flashed intuitive science; and his glee
  Was lofty as his pensiveness, for both
Wore the bright colors of the thing to be!
  But when his prime of life was come, the wrath

* These lines were suggested to me by the following passage in Mr. Coleridge's "Friend." "It cannot be deemed alien from the purposes of this disquisition, if we are anxious to attract the attention of our readers to the importance of this speculative meditation, even for the worldly interests of mankind; and to that concurrence of nature and historic event with the great revolutionary movements of individual genius, of which so many instances occur in the study of history, how nature (why should we hesitate in saying, that which in nature itself is more than nature?) seems to come forward in order to meet, to aid, and to reward every idea excited by a contemplation of her methods in the spirit of a filial care, and with the humility of love." — "Friend," vol. iii. p. 190.

Mr. Coleridge proceeds to illustrate this by the very example of Columbus, and quotes some highly beautiful and applicable verses of Chiabrera.

Of the cold world fell on him ; it did thrill
  His inmost self, but never quenched his faith.
Still to that faith he added search, and still,
  As fevering with fond love of th' unknown shore,
From learning's fount he strove his thirst to fill.
  But alway Nature seemed to meet the power
Of his high mind, to aid, and to reward
  His reverent hope with her sublimest lore.
Each sentiment that burned ; each falsehood warrèd
  Against and slain ; each novel truth inwrought —
What were they but the living lamps that starred
  His transit o'er the tremulous gloom of Thought ?
More, and now more, their gathered brilliancy
  On the one master notion sending out,
Which brooded ever o'er the passionate sea
  Of his deep soul ; but ah ! too dimly seen,
And formless in its own immensity !
  Last came the joy, when that phantasmal scene
Lay in full glory round his outward sense ;
  And who had scorned before in hatred keen
Refuged their baseness now : for no pretence
  Could wean their souls from awe ; they dared not doubt
That with them walked on earth a spirit intense.
  So others trod his path : and much was wrought
In the new land that made the angels weep.
  That innocent blood — it was not shed for nought !

My God! it is an hour of dread, when leap,
  Like a fire-fountain, forth the energies
Of Guilt, and desolate the poor man's sleep.
  Yet not alone for torturing agonies,
Though meriting most, nor all that storm of Woe
  Which did entempest their pure fulgent skies,
Shall the deep curse of ages cling, and grow
  To the foul names of those who did the deed,
The lusters for the gold of Mexico!
  Mute are th' ancestral voices we did heed,
The tones of superhuman melody:
  And the "veiled maid" * is vanished, who did
      feed

* These lines contain an allusion to that magnificent passage in Mr. Shelley's "Alastor," where he describes "the spirit of sweet human love" descending in vision on the slumbers of the wandering poet. How far I have a right to transfer "the veiled maid" to my own Poem, where she must stand for the embodiment of that love for the unseen, that voluntary concentration of our vague ideas of the Beauty that ought to be, on some one spot, or country yet undiscovered, as in the instances I have chosen, on America or the African city; this the critics, if I have any, may determine. I shall, however, be content to have trespassed against the commandments of Art, if I should have called any one's attention to that wonderful Poem, which cannot long remain in its present condition of neglect, but which, when it shall have emerged into the light, its inheritance will produce wonder and enthusiastic delight in thousands, who will learn as the work, like every perfect one, grows upon them, that the deep harmonies and glorious imaginations in which it is clothed, are not more true than the

By converse high the faith of liberty
  In young unwithered hearts, and Virtue, and
    Truth,

great moral idea which is its permeating life. The lines alluded to are these: —

"The Poet wandering on, through Arabie
And Persia, and the wild Carmanian waste,
And o'er the aërial mountains which pour down
Indus and Oxus from their icy caves,
In joy and exultation held his way
Till in the vale of Cachmire, far within
Its loneliest dell, where odorous plants entwine
Beneath the hollow rocks a natural bower,
Beside a sparkling rivulet he stretched
His languid limbs. A vision on his sleep
There came, a dream of hopes that never yet
Had flushed his cheek. He dreamed a veiled maid
Sate near him, talking in low solemn tones.
Her voice was like the voice of his own soul,
Heard in the calm of thought: its music long,
Like woven sounds of streams and breezes, held
His inmost sense suspended in its web
Of many-colored woof and shifting hues.
Knowledge and Truth and Virtue were her theme,
And lofty hopes of divine liberty,
Thoughts the most dear to him, and poesy,
Herself a Poet. Soon the solemn mood
Of her pure mind kindled through all her frame
A permeating fire: wild numbers then
She raised with voice stifled with tremulous sobs
Subdued by its own pathos: her fair hands
Were bare alone, sweeping from some strange harp

And every thing that makes us joy to be!
  Lo! there hath passed away a glory of Youth
From this our world; and all is common now,
  And sense doth tyrannize o'er Love and Ruth.
What, is Hope dead? and gaze we her pale brow,
  Like the cold statues round a Roman's bier,
Then tearless travel on through tracts of human
      woe?
  No! there is one, one ray that lingers here,
To battle with the world's o'ershadowing form,
  Like the last firefly of a Tuscan year,
Or dying flashes of a noble storm.
  Beyond the clime of Tripoly, and beyond
Bahr Abiad, where the lone peaks, unconform
  To other hills, and with rare foliage crowned,
Hold converse with the Moon, a City stands
  Which yet no mortal guest hath ever found.
Around it stretch away the level sands
  Into the silence: pausing in his course,
The ostrich kens it from his subject lands.
  Here with faint longings and a subdued force
Once more was sought th' ideal aliment

Strange symphony, and in her branching veins
The eloquent blood told an ineffable tale,
The beating of her heart was heard to fill
The pauses of her music, and her breath
Tumultuously accorded with those fits
Of intermitted song."

Of Man's most subtle being, the prime source
Of all his blessings: here might still be blent
Whate'er of heavenly beauty in form or sound
Illumes the Poet's heart with ravishment.
Thou fairy City, which the desert mound
Encompasseth, thou alien from the mass
Of human guilt, I would not wish thee found!
Perchance thou art too pure, and dost surpass
Too far amid th' Ideas ranged high
In the Eternal Reason's perfectness,
To our deject and most embased eye,
To look unharmed on thy integrity,
Symbol of Love, and Truth, and all that cannot die.
Thy Palaces and pleasure-domes to me
Are matter of strange thought: for sure thou art
A splendor in the wild: and aye to thee
Did visible guardians of the Earth's great heart
Bring their choice tributes, culled from many a mine,
Diamond, and jasper, porphyry, and the art
Of figured chrysolite: nor silver shine
There wanted, nor the mightier power of gold:
So wert thou reared of gore, City divine!
And who are they of blisses manifold,
That dwell within thee? Spirits of delight,
It may be spirits whose pure thoughts enfold,

In eminence of Being, all the light
That interpenetrates this mighty all,
And doth endure in its own beauty's right.
And oh! the vision were majestical
To them, indeed, of column, and of spire,
And hanging garden, and hoar waterfall!
For we, poor prisoners of this earthy mire,
See little; they, the essence and the law
Robing each other in its peculiar tire.
Yet moments have been, when in thought I saw
That city rise upon me from the void,
Populous with men: and phantasy would draw
Such portraiture of life, that I have joyed
In over-measure to behold her work,
Rich with the myriad charms, by evil unalloyed.
Methought I saw a nation, which did heark
To Justice, and to Truth: their ways were strait,
And the dread shadow, Tyranny, did lurk
Nowhere about them: not to scorn, or hate
A living thing was their sweet nature's bond:
So every soul moved free in kingly state.
Suffering they had (nor else were virtue found
In these our pilgrim spirits): gently still
And as from cause external came the wound,
Not like a gangrene of soul-festering ill,
To taint the springs of life, and undermine
The holy strength of their majestic will.

Methought I saw a face whose every line
Wore the pale cast of Thought;* a good, old man,
Most eloquent, who spake of things divine.
Around him youths were gathered, who did scan
His countenance so grand and mild; and drank
The sweet, sad tones of Wisdom, which outran
The lifeblood, coursing to the heart, and sank
Inward from thought to thought, till they abode
'Mid Being's dim foundations, rank by rank
With those transcendent truths, arrayed by God
In linked armor for untiring fight,
Whose victory is, where time hath never trod.
Methought I saw a maiden in the light
Of beauty musing near an amaranth bower,
Herself a lordly blossom. Past delight
Was fused in actual sorrow by the power
Of mightiest Love upon her delicate cheek;
And magical was her wailing at that hour.
For aye with passionate sobs she mingled meek
Smiles of severe content: as though she raised
To Him her inmost heart, who shields the weak.

* These characters are of course purely ideal, and meant to show, by way of particular diagram, that right temperament of the intellect and the heart which I have assigned to this favored nation. I cannot, however, resist the pleasure of declaring, that in the composition of the lines "Methought I saw," &c., my thoughts dwelt almost involuntarily on those few conversations which it is my delight to have held with that "good old man, most eloquent," Samuel Coleridge.

She wept nor long in solitude : I gazed,
  Till women, and sweet children came, and took
Her hand, and uttered meaning words, and praised
  The absent one with eyes, which as a book
Revealed the workings of the heart sincere.
  In sooth, it was a glorious thing to look
Upon that interchange of smile and tear!
  But when the mourner turned, in innocent grace
Lifting that earnest eye and forehead clear,
  Oh then, methought, God triumphed in her face!
But these are dreams : though ministrant on good,
  Dreams are they ; and the Night of things their place.
So be it ever! Ever may the mood
  "In which the affections gently lead us on"*
Be as thy sphere of visible life. The crowd,
  The turmoil, and the countenances wan
Of slaves, the Power-inchanted, thou shalt flee,
  And by the gentle heart be seen, and loved alone.

June, 1829.

* Wordsworth's "Tintern Abbey."

SONNETS.

ALLA STATUA, CH' E A FIRENZE DI LORENZO DUCA D'URBINO, SCOLTA DA MICHEL ANGIOLO.

DEH, chi se' tu, ch' in sì superba pietra
Guardi, e t' accigli, più che creatura?
La maestà della fronte alta, e pura,
L' occhio, ch' appena il duro marmo arretra
L' agevol man, da cui bel velo impetra
La mossa de pensier profonda, e scura,
Dicon: "Questi é Lorenzo, e se pur dura
Suo nome ancor, questo il Destino spetra"
Tosca magion — ahi vituperio ed onta
Della nobil città, che l' Arno infiora,
Qual danno fé de vostre palle il suono!
Pure innanzi a beltade ira tramonta:
E Fiorenza, ch' l giogo ange, e scolora,
Dice ammirando, "Oimè! quas' io perdono!"

ROME, *Dec.* 1827.

GENOVA bella, a cui l' altiera voce *
Di costanza e virtù feo grande onore,
Allorchè rosseggiò quel tristo albore,
Pien di spaventi, e gridi, e guasto atroce
E'l fiume ostil, che mai non mise foce
Nel dolce suol, che della terra è fiore,
Piagava sì, ma non vincea quel core.
Or che ti resta? Or dov' é la feroce
Antica mente? E Lei — tra pene, e guai
L' invitta Liberta — qual rupe or serba?
Forse (oh pensier!) qui volge il passo omai,
E freme, e tace; o con dolcessa acerba
Dice, oscurando del bel viso i rai,
"Com' è caduta la città superba!"

Dec. 1827.

* Alluding to the Sonnet of Passerini, beginning "Genova mia." It is in the "Componimenti Lirici" of Mathias.

TO AN ENGLISH LADY.

("TRA BELLA E BUONA NON SO QUAL FOSSE PIU,")

Who, not having fulfilled her promise to meet me at a Roman festival, sent me a note requesting pardon.

AHI vera donna! or dal tessuto inganno
Riconosco, chi sei: la gran vaghezza
Ch' angelica mi parve, or fugge, e spezza
Quel caro laccio di soave affanno.
Collo, ch' i neri anelli un marmo fanno,
Trecce, che più di sè l' anima apprezza,
E voi, begli occhi di fatal dolcezza,
Che feci io mai per meritar tal danno?
Tu pur, notte spietata, or vieni, e dille
(Chè senza testimon nol crederia)
Com' io guardava a mille visi, e mille,
E dicea, sospirando, in fioco suono,
"Mille non sono, quel ch' una saria"—
Va, traditrice, e non sperar perdono.

ROME, *Jan.* 1828.

SCRITTE SUL LAGO D'ALBANO.

SOAVE venticel ch' intorno spiri,
Or cogli elci scherzando, or sulle sponde
Destando il mormorar di lucid' onde,
Deh non tardar, non più frenar tuoi giri.
Vattene innanzi, e là 've giuso ammiri
Un fiorellin, che dall' amena fronde
Gioia, e dolcezza in ogni seno infonde,
China le piume, e dille i miei sospiri.
Quanta invidia ti porto! In sul bel volto
Lente isvolazzi, e baci quel natio
Aureo sorriso, cui veder m' è tolto!
Fossi pur teco! Ahi quale tremolio
Al cor darebbe il trastullarmi avvolto
Ne' cari lacri, e il susurrar "Sonio!"

March, 1828.

ON A LADY SUFFERING SEVERE ILLNESS.

(IMITATED FROM THE ENGLISH.)

PIETA! Pieta! gran Dio! deh, volgi omai
L'impietosito sguardo: il bel sembiante
Le luce giovanette, e vaghe, e sante,
Non mertan, no, soffrir dell' empio i guai.
"Mortal, mortal, che derilando vai,"
Rispose quel del trono sfolgorante,
"Ve' com' ogni dolor par che si schiante
A' puri di gran Fede augusti rai"
"Alma beata è questa! E se pur l'ange
Nel fior degli anni suoi cotanta pena,
To la sostengo; e questa man la mena!"
Cosi lo spirto umil, cui nulla frange,
(O speme di virtù salda, e serena!)
Beve l'amaro nappo, e mai non piange.

ROME, *April*, 1828.

ALLA SIRENA, NUME AVITO DI NAPOLI,

(SCRITTO IN TIROLO.)

DONNA di gran poter, ch' il colle adorno
  Molci regina, u' sospirar non lice,
Fuori ch' ai dolce lai, che d'ogni intorno
  S'odon nell' ombra de' gran vati altrice,
Deh vieni, oh tu si bella — e senza scorno
  (Pietà per fermo a niuna dea disdice)
Favellami di lei, ch'il tuo soggiorno
  Par faccia più ridente, e più felice.
Misero, che ragiono? il suon risponde
  D'Euro ululando tra l'Alpina foglia;
Tu pur ti stai lontana — e fai gran senno;
Che se'l tuo vol piegassi ad ogni cenno
  Ch' ad or, ad or, manda l'atroce doglia,
Lungi da lei verresti a torbid' onde!

May, 1828.

ON THE PICTURE OF THE THREE FATES IN THE PALAZZO PITTI, AT FLORENCE.

USUALLY ASCRIBED TO MICHEL ANGIOLO.

NONE but a Tuscan hand could fix ye here
In rigidness of sober coloring.
Pale are ye, mighty Triad, not with fear,
But the most awful knowledge, that the spring
Is in you of all birth, and act, and sense.
I sorrow to behold ye: pain is blent
With your aloof and loveless permanence,
And your high princedom seems a punishment.
The cunning limner could not personate
Your blind control, save in th' aspect of grief;
So does the thought repugn of sovran fate.
Let him gaze here who trusts not in the love
Toward which all being solemnly doth move:
More this grand sadness tells, than forms of fairest life.

TO MALEK.

MALEK, the counsel of thine amity
I slight not, kindly tendered, but rejoice
To hear or praise or censure from thy voice
Both for thy sake, and hers, whose spirit in thee
Indwelleth ever, starlike Poesy!
Woe, if I pass the temple of her choice
With reckless step, or th' unexpressive joys
Disdain of fancy, pure to song, and free!
Yet deem not thou thy friend of early days
So lost to high emprize: trust me, his soul
Sleeps not the dreamless sleep, which thou art fearing.
No! still on lights the love of noble praise,
His pilgrim bark, like a clear star appearing:
And oh, how bright that beam, where storm-waves roll!

June, 1828.

OH blessing and delight of my young heart,
  Maiden, who was so lovely and so pure,
I know not in what region now thou art,
  Or whom thy gentle eyes in joy assure.
Not the old hills on which we gazed together,
  Not the old faces which we both did love,
Not the old books, whence knowledge we did gather,
  Not these, but others now thy fancies move.
I would I knew thy present hopes and fears,
  All thy companions, with their pleasant talk,
And the clear aspect which thy dwelling wears:
  So, though in body absent, I might walk
With thee in thought and feeling, till thy mood
Did sanctify mine own to peerless good.

April, 1829.

WRITTEN IN EDINBURGH.

EVEN thus, methinks, a city reared should be,
Yea, an imperial city, that might hold
Five times a hundred noble towns in fee,
And either with their might of Babel old,
Or the rich Roman pomp of empery
Might stand compare, highest in arts enroll'd,
Highest in arms; brave tenement for the free,
Who never crouch to thrones, or sin for gold.
Thus should her towers be raised — with vicinage
Of clear bold hills, that curve her very streets,
As if to vindicate, 'mid choicest seats
Of art, abiding Nature's majesty,
And the broad sea beyond, in calm or rage
Chainless alike, and teaching Liberty.

TO AN ADMIRED LADY.

WHEN thou art dreaming, at the time of night
  That dreams have deepest truth, comes not the
      form
Of th' ancient poet near thee? Streams not light
  From his immortal presence, chasing harm
From thy pure pillow, and each nocturnal sprite
  Freighting with happy fancies to thy soul?
  Says he not, "Surely, maiden, my control
Shall be upon thee, for thy soul is dight
In a most clear majestic tenderness,
  And natural art springs freshly from its deeps."
Then as he clasps his reverend palms to bless,
  Out from the dark a gentle family leaps,
Juliet and Imogen, with many a fere,
Acclaiming all "Welcome, our sister dear!"

STANZAS.

WRITTEN AFTER VISITING MELROSE ABBEY IN COMPANY OF SIR WALTER SCOTT.

I.

I LIVED an hour in fair Melrose;
It was not when "the pale moonlight"
Its magnifying charm bestows;
Yet deem I that I "viewed it right."
The wind-swept shadows fast careered,
Like living things that joyed or feared,
Adown the sunny Eildon Hill,
And the sweet winding Tweed the distance crownèd well.

II.

I inly laughed to see that scene
Wear such a countenance of youth,
Though many an age those hills were green,
And yonder river glided smooth,
Ere in these now disjointed walls
The Mother Church held festivals,

And full-voiced anthemings the while
Swelled from the choir, and lingered down the
echoing aisle.

III.

I coveted that Abbey's doom;
For if I thought the early flowers
Of our affection may not bloom,
Like those green hills through countless hours,
Grant me at least a tardy waning,
Some pleasure still in age's paining;
Though lines and forms must fade away,
Still may old Beauty share the empire of Decay!

IV.

But looking toward the grassy mound
Where calm the Douglas chieftains lie,
Who, living, quiet never found,
I straightway learnt a lesson high:
For there an old man sat serene,
And well I knew that thoughtful mien
Of him whose early lyre had thrown
Over these mould'ring walls the magic of its tone.

V.

Then ceased I from my envying state
And knew that awless intellect

Hath power upon the ways of fate,
And works through time and space uncheckt.
That minstrel of old chivalry
In the cold grave must come to be,
But his transmitted thoughts have part
In the collective mind, and never shall depart.

VI.

It was a comfort too to see
Those dogs that from him ne'er would rove,
And always eyed him rev'rently
With glances of depending love.
They know not of that eminence
Which marks him to my reasoning sense;
They know but that he is a man,
And still to them is kind, and glads them all he can.

VII.

And hence their quiet looks confiding,
Hence grateful instincts seated deep,
By whose strong bond, were ill betiding,
They'd risk their own his life to keep.
What joy to watch in lower creature
Such dawning of a moral nature,
And how (the rule of things obey)
They look to a higher mind to be their law and stay!

August, 1829.

WRITTEN AT CAUDEBEC IN NORMANDY.

I.

WHEN life is crazy in my limbs,
  And hope is gone astray,
And in my soul's December fade
  The love-thoughts of its May,
One spot of earth is left to me
  Will warm my heart again:
'Tis Caudebec and Mailleraie
  On the pleasant banks of Seine.

II.

The dark wood's crownal on the hill,
  The river curving bright,
The graceful barks that rest, or play,
  Pure creatures of delight, —
Oh, these are shows by nature given
  To warm old hearts again,
At Caudebec and Mailleraie
  On the pleasant banks of Seine.

III.

The Tuscan's land, I loved it well,
  And the Switzer's clime of snow,
And many a bliss me there befell
  I never more can know;
But for quiet joy of nature's own
  To warm the heart again,
Give me Caudebec and Mailleraie
  On the pleasant banks of Seine.

June, 1829.

A FAREWELL TO GLENARBAC.*

I.

WHEN grief is felt along the blood,
And checks the breath with sighs unsought,
'Tis then that Memory's power is wooed
To soothe by ancient forms of thought.
It is not much, yet in that day
Will seem a gladsome wakening;
And such to me, in joy's decay,
The memory of the Roebuck Glen.

II.

Nor less, when fancies have their bent,
And eager passion sweeps the mind;
'Twill bless to catch a calm content
From happy moment far behind.
Oh, it is of a heavenly brood
That chast'ning recollection!
And such to me, in joyous mood,
The memory of the Roebuck Glen.

* The Glen of the Roebuck.

III.

I grieve to quit this lime-tree walk,
  The Clyde, the Leven's milder blue
To lose, yon craigs that nest the hawk
  Will soar no longer in my view.
Yet of themselves small power to move
  Have they: their light's a borrowed thing
Won from her eyes, for whom I love
  The memory of the Roebuck Glen.

IV.

Oh dear to nature, not in vain
  The mountain winds have breathed on thee!
Mild virtues of a noble strain,
  And beauty making pure and free,
Pass to thee from the silent hills:
  And hence, where'er thy sojourning,
Thine eye with gentle weeping fills
  At memory of the Roebuck Glen.

V.

Thou speedest to the sunny shore,
  Where first thy presence on me shone;
Alas! I know not whether more
  These eyes shall claim thee as their own:
But should a kindly star prevail,
  And should we meet far hence again,

How sweet in other lands to hail
  The memory of the Roebuck Glen.

VI.

Oh, when the thought comes o'er my heart
  Of happy meetings yet to be,
The very feeling that thou art
  Is deep as that of life to me;
Yet should sad instinct in my breast
  Speak true, and darker chance obtain,
Bless with one tear my final rest,
  One memory from the Roebuck Glen.

July, 1829.

WRITTEN ON THE BANKS OF THE TAY.

I.

I SAW a child upon a Highland moor
  Playing with heath-flowers in her gamesome mood,
And singing snatches wild of Gaelic lore
  That thrilled like witch-notes my susceptive blood.
I spake a Southern word, but not the more
  Did she regard or move from where she stood.
It seemed the business of her life to play
With euphrasies and bluebells day by day.

II.

Then my first thought was of the joy to grow
  With her, and like her, as a mountain plant,
That to one spot attached doth bud and blow,
  Then, in the rains of autumn, leaves to vaunt
Its fragrance to the air, and sinks, till low
  Winter consign it, like a satiate want,
To the earth's endearment, who will fondly nourish
The loosed substance, until spring reflourish.

III.

"To be thy comrade, and thy brother, maiden,
  To chaunt with thee the antique song I hear:

Joying the joy that looks not toward its fading,
  The sweet philosophy of young life's cheer!
We should be like two bees with honey laden,
  Or two blithe butterflies a rose-tree near!"—
So I went dreaming how to play a child
Once more with her who 'side me sang and smiled.

IV.

Then a stern knowledge woke along my soul,
  And sudden I was sadly made aware
That childish joy is now a folded scroll,
  And new ordainments have their several fair:
When evening lights press the ripe greening knoll,
  True heart will never wish the morning there:
Where arched boughs enlace the golden light,
Did ever poet pray for franchised sight.

V.

When we were children, we did sigh to reach
  The eminence of a man; yet in our thought,
And in the prattled fancies of our speech,
  It was a baby-man we fashioned out;
And now that childhood seems the only leech
  For all the heartaches of a rough world caught,
Sooth is, we wish to be a twofold thing,
And keep our present self to watch within.

July, 1829.

ON MY SISTER'S BIRTHDAY.

WRITTEN AT CALLANDER, NEAR LOCH KATRINE.

I.

FAIR fall the day! 'Tis thirteen years
Since on this day was Ellen born:
And shed the dark world's herald tears
On such another summer's morn.
I may not hear her laughter's flow,
Nor watch the smile upon her face,
But in my heart I surely know
There's joy within her dwelling-place.

II.

Oh, at the age of fair thirteen
A birthday is a thing of power:
The meadows wear a livelier green,
Be it a time of sun, or shower;
We scarce believe the robin's note
Unborrowed from the nightingale,
And when the sweet long day is out,
Our dreams take up the merry tale.

III.

That pleasure being innocent,
  With innocence alone accords;
The souls that Passion's strife has rent
  Have other thoughts and other words;
They cannot bear that meadow's green;
  Strange grief is in the robin's song;
And when they hope to shift the scene,
  Their dreams the anguish but prolong.

IV.

Oh, pray for them, thou happy child,
  Whose souls are in that silent woe;
For once, like thee, they gayly smiled,
  And hoped, and feared, and trusted so!
Pray for them in thy birthday mood,
  They may not pass that awful bar,
Which separates the early good
  From spirits with themselves at war.

V.

Their mind is now on loves grown cold,
  On friendships falling slow away,
On life lived fast, and heart made old
  Before a single hair was gray.
Or should they be one thought less sad,
  Their dream is still of things forgone,

Sweet scenes that once had made them glad,
  Dim faces seen, and never known.

VI.

My own dear sister, thy career
  Is all before thee, thorn and flower;
Scarce hast thou known by joy or fear
  The still heart-pride of Friendship's hour:
And for that awful thing beyond,
  The first affections going forth,
In books alone thy sighs have owned
  The heaven, and then the hell, on earth.

VII.

But time is rolling onward, love,
  And birthdays are another chase;
Ah, when so much few years remove,
  May thy sweet nature hold its place —
Who would not hope, who would not pray,
  That looks on thy demeanor now?
Yet have I seen the slow decay
  Of many souls as pure as thou.

VIII.

But there are some whose light endures —
  A sign of wonder, and of joy,
Which never custom's mist obscures,

Or passion's treacherous gusts destroy.
God make with them a rest for thee!
For thou art turned toward stormy seas,
And when they call thee like to me,
Some terrors on my bosom seize.

IX.

Yet why to-day this mournful tone,
When thou on gladness hast a claim?
How ill befits a boding moan
From one who bears a brother's name!
Here fortune, fancifully kind,
Has led me to a lovely spot,
Where not a tree or rock I find,
My sister, that recalls thee not!

X.

Benan is worth a poet's praise;
Bold are the cairns of Benvenue;
Most beautiful the winding ways
Where Trosachs open on the view;
But other grace Loch Katrine wears,
When viewed by me from Ellen's Isle;
A magic tint on all appears;
It comes from thy remembered smile!

XI.

'Twas there that Lady of the Lake,
  Moored to yon gnarled tree her boat;
And where Fitz James's horn bade wake
  Each mountain echo's lengthened note;
'Twas from that slope the maiden heard:
  Sweet tale! but sweeter far to me,
From dreamy blendings of that word,
  With all my thoughts and hopes of thee.

FROM SCHILLER.

WRITTEN AT MALVERN.

I.

To yonder vale where shepherds dwell,
  There came with every dawning year,
Ere earliest larks their notes did trill,
  A lady wonderful and fair.

II.

She was not born within that vale,
  And none from whence she came might know,
But soon all trace of her did fail,
  Whene'er she turned her, far to go.

III.

But blessing was when she was seen:
  All hearts that day were beating high:
A holy calm was in her mien,
  And queenly glanced her maiden eye.

IV.

She brought with her both fruits and flowers
  Were gathered in another clime,

Beneath a different sun from ours,
  And in a nature more sublime.

V.

To each and all a gift she gave,
  And one had fruit, and one had flower;
Nor youth, nor old man with his stave,
  Did homeward go without his dower.

VI.

So all her welcome guests were glad —
  But most rejoiced one loving pair,
Who took of her the best she had,
  The brightest blooms that ever were!

LINES

SPOKEN IN THE CHARACTER OF PYGMALION.

WRITTEN ON THE OCCASION OF A REPRESENTED CHARADE.

'TIS done, the work is finished — that last touch
Was as a God's! Lo! now it stands before me,
Even as long years ago I dreamed of it,
Consummate offspring of consummate art;
Ideal form itself! Ye Gods, I thank you,
That I have lived to this: for this thrown off
The pleasure of my kind; for this have toiled
Days, nights, months, years; — am not I recompensed?
Who says an artist's life is not a king's?
I *am* a king, alone among the crowd
Of busy hearts and looks — apart with nature
I sit, a God upon the earth, creating
More lovely forms than flesh and blood can equal.
Jove's workmanship is perishable clay,
But mine immortal marble; when the proudest
Of our fair city dames is laid i' the dust
This creature of my soul will still be lovely.
Let me contemplate thee again. That lip —

How near it wears the crimson ! and that eye —
How strives it with the marble's vacancy !
Methinks if thou wert human, I could love thee ;
But that thou art not, nor wilt ever be —
Ne'er know and feel how beautiful thou art.
O God, I am alone then — she hears not —
And yet how like to life ! Ha — blessed thought,
Gods have heard prayers ere now, Hear me, bright
Venus,
Queen of my dreams, hear from thy throne of light,
Forgive the pride that made my human heart
Forget its nature. Let her live and love !
I dare not look again — my brain swims round —
I dream — I dream — even now methought she
moved —
If 'tis a dream, how will I curse the dawn
That wakes me from it ! There — that bend again —
It is no dream — Oh, speak to me and bless me.

1832.

TO TWO SISTERS.

Love thoughts be rich when canopied with flowers. — SHAKSPEARE.

In Leigh Hunt's "Indicator," it is stated that the name "Mary" has its origin in a Hebrew word, signifying "exalted;" and a suggestion occurs in the same book, that "Emily" may possibly come from some element akin to "Amo."

WELL do your names express ye, sisters dear,
In small clear sounds awaking mournful thoughts,
Mournful, as with the refluence of a joy
Too pure for these sad coasts of human life.
Methinks had not your happy vernal dawn
Ever arisen on my trancèd view,
Those flowing sounds would syllable yourselves
To my delighted soul, or if not so,
Yet when I traced their deeper meaning out,
And fathomed his intent, who in some hour,
Sweet from the world's young dawn, with breath of life
Endowed them, then your certain forms would come,
Pale but true visions of my musing eye.
For thee, oh! eldest flower, whose precious name

Would to inspired ears by Chebar once,
Or the lone cavern hid from Jezabel,
Sound as "Exalted"—fitliest therefore borne
By that mysterious Lady who reposed
In Egypt far, beyond the impious touch
Of fell Herodes, or the unquiet looks
Of men, who knew not Peace to earth was born,—
There happily reposed, waiting the time
When from that dark interminable day
Should by God's might emerge, and Love sit throned,
And Meekness kiss away the looks of Scorn;
Oh Mary! deem that Virgin looks on thee
With an especial care; lean thou on her,
As the ideal of thy woman's heart;
Pray that thy heart be strengthened from above
To lasting hope, and sovran kindliness;
That conquering smiles and more than conquering tears
May be thy portion through the ways of life:
So walk thou on in thy simplicity,
Following the Virgin Queen for evermore!
Thou other name, I turn with deepest awe
To think of all thou utterest unto me.
Oh Emily! how frail must be my speech,
Weighed with the thought that in my spirit burns,
To find no rest until 'tis known by thee,

Till our souls see each other face to face.
Thou hearest not, alas! thou art afar,
And I am lone as ever, sick and lone
Roaming the weary desert of my doom
Where thou art not, altho' all speaks of thee,
All yearns for thee, my love: each barren wold
Would teem with fruitful glory at thy smile.
But so—'twas of thy name that I would speak,
And thus I will not lend me to that lie,
That from the old and proud Æmilian clan
Thy name was brought, the famous Roman dames
Who, in a sweeping stole, broad-zoned and full,
With solemn brows and settled eyes severe,
Tended the household glory of their lords.
Ah, no! a sweeter birth, fair name, is thine!
Surely some soul born in the tender light
Of golden suns and deep-starred night divine,
Feeling the want of some far gentler word
Than any speech doth own, to slake the thirst
Of his impetuous heart, and be at once
The symbol and relief of that high love
Which made him weary and faint even unto death,
He gathering up the wasted energies
For a last work, and breathing all his life
Into a word of love, said "Amelie,"
Meaning "Beloved;" and then methinks he died,
And the melodious magic of his voice

Shrank in its fulness; but the amorous air
And the blue sea close murmuring to the shore
With a sweet regular moan, the orange grove
Rising from that slope shore in richest shade,
Blent with the spiked aloe, and cactus wild,
And rarer growth of the luxuriant palm,
Lived in that word, and echoed "Emily,"
Tempering the tone with variation sweet.
Thou seest it, maiden: if the fairest things
Of this fair world, and breathing deepest love,
Sang welcome to the name then framed for thee,
And such as thee, the gentlest of the earth,
Should I, to whom this tale was whispered
By some kind Muse in hours of silent thought,
Look on thy face and call thee not "Beloved,"
It were in me unmeasured blasphemy.
Oh! envy not thyself thy station high:
Consent to be "Beloved;" I ask no more
Than to fulfil for thee thy warning name
And in a perfect loving live and die.

Nov. 1830.

THIS was my lay in sad nocturnal hour,
What time the silence felt a growing sound
Awful, and winds began among the trees,
Nor was there starlight in the vaulted sky.
Now is the eyelid of the jocund sun
Uplifted on the region of this air;
And in the substance of his living light
I walk enclosed, therefore to matin chaunts
Of all delighted birds I marry a note
Of human voice rejoicing unto thee
Ever-loved, warbling my rapture now,
As erst to thee I made melodious moan.
Then I believed thee distant from my heart;
Thou hadst not spoken then, I had not heard:
And I was faint, because I breathed not
Breath of thy love, wherein alone is life;
But at this hour my heart is seen, my prayer
Answered and crowned with blessing; I have looked
Into thine eyes which have not turned awry,
But rested all their lavish light upon me,
Unutterably sweet, till I became
Angelic in the strength of tenderness,
And met thy soul down-looking into mine

With a responsive power; thy word hath passed
Upon my spirit, and is a light forever,
High o'er the drifting spray of circumstance.
Thy word, the plighted word, the word of promise,
And of all comfort! In its mighty strength
I bid thee hail, not as in former days,
Not as my chosen only, but my bride,
My very bride, coming to make my house
A glorious temple! Be the seal of God
Upon that word until the hour be full!

Feb. 1831.

TO THE LOVED ONE.

MY heart is happy now, beloved,
Albeit thy form is far away;
A joy that will not be removed
Broods on me like a summer's day.
Whatever evil Fate may do,
It cannot change what has been thine;
It cannot cast those words anew,
The gentle words I think divine.

No touch of time can blight the glance
That blest with early hope my love;
New years are dark with fearful chance,
That moment is with God above:
And never more from me departs
Of that sweet time the influence rare,
When first we looked into our hearts
And told each other what was there.

Yes, I am happy, love; and yet
Long cherished pain will keep a strife;

Something half fear and half regret
  Is lingering at the seat of life.
But now in seasons of dismay
  What cheering hope from thoughts of thee!
And how will earnest fancy stray
  To find its home where thou mayst be!

Sometimes I dream thee leaning o'er
  The harp I used to love so well;
Again I tremble and adore
  The soul of its delicious swell;
Again the very air is dim
  With eddies of harmonious might,
And all my brain and senses swim
  In a keen madness of delight.

Sometimes thy pensive form is seen
  On the dear seat beside the fire;
There plainest thou with Madeline
  Or Isabella's lone desire.
He knows thee not, who does not know
  The tender flashing of thine eye
At some melodious tale of woe,
  And the sweet smile and sweeter sigh.

How oft in silent moonlight air,
  When the wide earth is full of rest,

And all things outward seem more fair
  For the inward spirit less opprest,
I look for thee, I think thee near,
  Thy tones are thrilling through my soul,
Thy dark eyes close to mine appear,
  And I am blest beyond control!

Yet deem not thou my absent state
  Is measured all by amorous moan;
Clear-voiced Love hath learned of Fate
  New harmonies of deeper tone.
All thoughts that in me live and burn,
  The thirst for truth, the sense of power;
Freedom's high hope — to thee they turn;
  I bring them as a precious dower!

The beauty which those thoughts adore
  Diffused through this perennial frame
Centres in thee; I feel it more
  Since thy delivering presence came:
And with a clearer affluence now
  That mystic spirit fills my heart,
Wafts me on hope's enthusiast flow,
  And heals with prayer the guilty smart.

Oh! best beloved, it were a bliss
  As pure as aught the angels feel,

To think in after days of this,
  Should time a strength in me reveal
To fill with worthy thoughts and deed
  The measure of my high desire;
To thee were due the glorious meed,
  Thy smiles had kindled first the fire.

But if the starry courses give
  No eminence of light to me,
At least together we may live,
  Together loved and loving be;
At least what good my spirit knows
  Shall seek in thee a second birth,
And in thy gentle soul's repose
  I'll wean me from the things of earth.

Even now begins that holy life,
  For when I kneel in Christian prayer
Thy name my own, my promised wife,
  Is blent with mine in fondest care.
Oh pray for me that both may know
  That inward bridal's high delight,
And both beyond the grave may go
  Together in the Father's sight.

Jan. 1831.

TO MY MOTHER.

WHEN barren doubt like a late-coming snow
Made an unkind December of my spring,
That all the pretty flowers did droop for woe,
And the sweet birds their love no more would
sing;
Then the remembrance of thy gentle faith,
Mother beloved, would steal upon my heart;
Fond feeling saved me from that utter scathe,
And from thy hope I could not live apart.
Now that my mind hath passed from wintry gloom,
And on the calmed waters once again
Ascendant Faith circles with silver plume,
That casts a charmed shade, not now in pain,
Thou child of Christ, in joy I think of thee,
And mingle prayers for what we both may be.

Jan. 1831.

A LOVER'S REPROOF.

WHEN two complaining spirits mingle,
Saintly and calm their woes become:
Alas the grief that bideth single,
Whose heart is drear, whose lips are dumb!

My drooping lily, when the tears
Of morning bow thy tender head,
Oh scatter them, and have no fears:
They kill sometimes if cherished.

Dear Girl, the precious gift you gave
Was of *yourself* entire and free.
Why front *alone* Life's gloomy wave,
Why fling the brilliant foam to me?

Am I the lover of thy mirth,
A trifling thing of sunny days,—
A soul forbid for want of worth,
To tread with thee th' unpleasant ways?

No — trust me, love; if I delight
  To mark thy brighter hour of pleasure,
To deep-eyed Passion's watchful sight
  Thy sadness is a costlier treasure.

July, 1831.

A MELANCHOLY thought had laid me low;
 A thought of self-desertion, and the death
Of feelings wont with my heart's blood to flow,
 And feed the inner soul with purest breath.
 The idle busy star of daily life,
Base passions, haughty doubts, and selfish fears,
 Have withered up my being in a strife
Unkind, and dried the source of human tears.
 One evening I went forth, and stood alone
With Nature: moon there was not, nor the light
Of any star in heaven: yet from the sight
 Of that dim nightfall better hope hath given
Upon my spirit, and from those cedars high
Solemnly changeless, as the very sky.

Sept. 1830.

A SCENE IN SUMMER.

ALFRED, I would that you behold me now,
Sitting beneath a mossy ivied wall
On a quaint bench, which to that structure old
Winds an accordant curve. Above my head
Dilates immeasurable a wild of leaves
Seeming received into the blue expanse
That vaults this summer noon: before me lies
A lawn of English verdure, smooth and bright,
Mottled with fainter hues of early hay,
Whose fragrance, blended with the rose perfume
From that white flowering bush, invites my sense
To a delicious madness — and faint thoughts
Of childish years are borne into my brain
By unforgotten ardors waking now.
Beyond, a gentle slope leads into shade
Of mighty trees, to bend whose eminent crown
Is the prime labor of the pettish winds,
That now in lighter mood are twirling leaves
Over my feet, or hurrying butterflies,

And the gay humming things that summer loves,
Thro' the warm air, or altering the bound
Where yon elm-shadows in majestic line
Divide dominion with the abundant light.

June, 1831.

OH Poetry, oh rarest spirit of all
 That dwell within the compass of the mind,
Forsake not him, whom thou of old didst call:
 Still let me seek thy face, and seeking find.
Some years have gone about since I and thou
 Became acquainted first: we met in woe;
Sad was my cry for help as it is now;
 Sad too thy breathed response of music slow;
 But in that sadness was such essence fine,
So keen a sense of Life's mysterious name,
 And high conceit of natures more divine,
That breath and sorrow seemed no more the same.
 Oh let me hear again that sweet reply!
 More than by loss of thee I cannot die.

June, 1831.

ALAS! that sometimes even a duteous life,
  If uninspired by love, and love-born joy,
Grows fevered in the world's unholy strife,
  And sinks destroyed by that it would destroy!
Beloved, from the boisterous deeds that fill
  The measure up of this unquiet time,
  The dull monotonies of Faction's chime,
And irrepressible thoughts foreboding ill,
  I turn to thee as to a heaven apart —
Oh! not apart, not distant, near me ever,
So near my soul that nothing can thee sever!
  How shall I fear, knowing there is for me
  A city of refuge, builded pleasantly
Within the silent places of the heart?

May, 1831.

WHY throbbest thou, my heart, why thickly
breathest?
I ask no rich and splendid eloquence:
A few words of the warmest and the sweetest
Sure thou mayst yield without such coy pretence:
Open the chamber where affection's voice,
For rare occasions is kept close and fine:
Bid it but say "sweet Emily, be mine,"
So for one boldness thou shalt aye rejoice.
Fain would I speak when the full music-streams
Rise from her lips to linger on her face,
Or like a form floating through Raffaelle's dreams,
Then fixed by him in everliving grace,
She sits i' the silent worship of mine eyes.
Courage, my heart: change thou for words thy
sighs.

STILL here — thou hast not faded from my sight,
Nor all the music round thee from mine ear:
Still grace flows from thee to the brightening year,
And all the birds laugh out in wealthier light.
Still am I free to close my happy eyes,
And paint upon the gloom thy mimic form,
That soft white neck, that cheek in beauty warm,
And brow half hidden where yon ringlet lies;
With, Oh! the blissful knowledge all the while
That I can lift at will each curved lid,
And my fair dream most highly realize.
The time will come, 'tis ushered by my sighs,
When I may shape the dark, but vainly bid
True light restore that form, those looks, that smile.

LADY, I bid thee to a sunny dome
  Ringing with echoes of Italian song;
  Henceforth to thee these magic halls belong,
And all the pleasant place is like a home.
Hark, on the right with full piano tone,
  Old Dante's voice encircles all the air;
  Hark yet again, like flute-tones mingling rare,
Comes the keen sweetness of Petrarca's moan.
Pass thou the lintel freely: without fear
  Feast on the music: I do better know thee,
  Than to suspect this pleasure thou dost owe me
Will wrong thy gentle spirit, or make less dear
  That element whence thou must draw thy life;—
  An English maiden and an English wife.

SPEED ye, warm hours, along th' appointed path,
  Speed, though ye bring but pain, slow pain to
      me;
I will not much bemoan your heavy wrath,
  So ye will make my lady glad and free.
What is't that I must here confined be,
  If she may roam the summer's sweets among,
See the full-cupped flower, the laden tree,
  Hear from deep groves the thousand-voiced song?
Sometimes in that still chamber will she sit
  Trim ranged with books, and cool with dusky blinds,
That keep the moon out, there, as seemed fit,
  To sing, or play, or read—what sweet hope finds
Way to my heart? perchance some verse of mine—
Oh happy I! speed on, ye hours divine!

WHEN gentle fingers cease to touch the string,
  Dear Charles, no music lingers on the lyre;
But the sea-shells from everlasting ring
  With the deep murmurs of their home desire;
Lean o'er the shell, and 'twill be heard to plain
  Now low, now high, till all thy sense is gone
Into the sweetness; then depart again,
  Still though unheard, flows on that inner moan;
Full oft like one of these our human heart
  Secretly murmurs on a loving lay,
  Though not a tone finds any outward way.
Then trust me, Charles, nor let it cause thee smart,
  That seldom in my songs thy name is seen —
  When most I loved, I most have silent been.

1831.

THE garden trees are busy with the shower
  That fell ere sunset; now methinks they talk,
Lowly and sweetly as befits the hour,
  One to another down the grassy walk.
Hark the laburnum from his opening flower
  This cherry-creeper greets in whisper light,
  While the grim fir, rejoicing in the night,
Hoarse mutters to the murmuring sycamore.
What shall I deem their converse? would they hail
The wild gray light that fronts yon massive cloud,
  Or the half bow, rising like pillared fire?
  Or are they sighing faintly for desire
That with May dawn their leaves may be o'erflowed,
And dews about their feet may never fail.

1831.

SCENE AT ROME.

RAFFAELLE *sitting in his Studio ;* FIAMMETTA *enters.*

R. DEAREST, I wished for thee a moment gone,
And lo, upon the wish thou art here.
F. Perhaps
It was thy wish that even now as I entered,
Gleamed through the citron-shadow, like a star-beam,
One star-beam of some high predominant star.
R. Why, little trifler, whither hast thou been
That thou return'st so fair fantastical?
F. Down by the fountain, where the dark cool alley
Yields into sudden light of cooler spray.
It is a noble evening — one to shame thee —
For the least hue of that all-colored heaven
Bears a more full and rich divinity
Than the best touch thy pencil ever gave, —
Thou smilest at me.
R. Rather should I sigh

To think that while I learn to love thee better,
And better prize all that belongs to thee,
In the fair company I live with always,
The tempting faces, and warm loving shapes
That make my little room a paradise,
Thou wandering about, from lighted fountains,
From groves at twilight full of changing magic,
Or yon great gallery picture hung with stars,
Gatherest contempt for that poor, mimic thing,
An artist.

F. Thou believest not thy words,
Else could I call a thousand witnesses
To swear me into innocence again.

R. Where are they?

F. Out alas! I had forgot—
I have them not—I know not where they dwell;
They roam in a dim field I may not come to,
Nor ever see them more; yet were they once
Familiar beings, inward to my soul
As is the lifeblood to the life.

R. The answer—
We have the riddle. Who are these unkind ones
Who knew the thing it is to be beside thee.
Looked on thy face, yet had the hearts to leave thee?

F. Oh there you are mistaken—you are too quick—
They had no eyes and could not see my face—

They had no power to stay—they must have left
me—
Each in his turn stood on the downcleft edge
Of a most mighty river, stood and fell,
Borne to the silent things that are no more.

R. Are they then dead?

F. Ay, dead; entombed within
A glorious sepulchre, to whose broad space
The world of present things is but an atom.
There they lie dead, and here I'd weep for them,
But that I have a fairy mirror by me
Shows me their spirits, pale and beautiful
With a sweet mournful beauty.

R. Thou art mocking me;
These are but fancies thou art speaking of,
The incorporeal children of the brain.

F. Aha, brave Œdipus! my lady Sphinx
Had stood in danger with thee. Hast thou guessed
it?
These friends once harbored with me, now departed,
These witnesses to my clear faith and fondness,
They are all thoughts, all glorious thoughts of thee,
Infinite in their number, bright as rainbows,
And in pervading presence visitant
Whenever I am forced to be alone,
And losing thee to talk with stars and streams.

R. And, by our Lady, 'tis a good exchange.

The stars and streams are silent — cannot chide
thee —
Will let a foolish woman talk by the hour
Her gentle nonsense, and reprove her never,
Nor with one frown dim their ambrosial smiles;
Thou find'st not me so easy.
F. Still suspicious!
What, must I tell thee all this day's employment;
Tell how I read the heavens with curious glances,
And by a sort of wild astrology
Taught me by a young god, whose name is Love,
But who before all things resembles thee,
I tried to shape in those high starry eyes
The very looks of thine?
R. Nay, own Fiammetta,
If we must needs have such usurping spirits,
And turn the bright heavens from the things they
are
Into poor semblances of earthly creatures,
They shall be all thine own — take them and wear
them;
Be thou the moon, the sunset, what thou wilt
So I behold thee.
F. I will be the sky!
No narrower bound than its far unknown limit
Shall keep me prisoner. Thou hast called me fair —
Often and often on my lips thou hast sworn it —

What wilt thou say when thou shalt see me come
To press thee in those blue celestial folds,
To gaze upon thee with a million eyes,
Each eye like these, and each a fire of love?

R. I would not have thee other than thou art,
Even in the least complexion of a dimple,
For all the pictures Pietro Perugin,
My master, ever painted. And pardon me
I would not have the heavens anything
But what they are and were and still shall be,
Despite thy wish, Fiammetta. 'Tis not well
To make the eternal Beauty ministrant
To our frail lives and frailer human loves.
Three thousand years perhaps before we lived,
Some Eastern maiden framed thy very wish,
And loved and died, and in the passionless void
Vanished forever. Yet this glorious Nature
Took not a thought of her, but shone above
The blank she left, as on the place she filled.
So will it be with us — a dark night waits us —
Another moment, we must plunge within it —
Let us not mar the glimpses of pure Beauty,
Now streaming in like moonlight, with the fears,
The joys, the hurried thoughts, that rise and fall
To the hot pulses of a mortal heart.

F. How now? Thy voice was wont to speak of love:

I shall not know it, if its language change:
The clear, low utterance, and angelic tone
Will lose their music, if they praise not love.
R. And when I praise it not, or cease to fold thee
Thus in my arms, Fiammetta, may I die
Unwept, unhonored, barred without the gate
Of that high temple, where I minister
With daily ritual of colored lights
For candelabras, and pure saintly forms
To image forth the loveliness I serve.
I did but chide thee that thou minglest ever
Beauty with beauty, as with perfume perfume:
Thou canst not love a rosebud for itself,
But thinkest straight who gave that rose to thee;
The leaping fountain minds thee of the music
We heard together; and the very heaven,
The illimitable firmament of God,
Must steal a likeness to a Roman studio
Ere it can please thee.
F. I am a poor woman, sir;
A woman, poor in all things but her heart,
And when I cease to love I cease to live.
You will not cure me of this heresy;
Flames would not burn it out, nor sharp rocks tear it.

R. I am a merciful Inquisitor;
I shall enjoin thee but a gentle penance.

F. The culprit trusts the judge, and feels no fear
In his immediate presence; a rare thing
In Italy! Proceed.

R. There was a thing
Thou askedst me this morning.

F. I remember —
To see the picture thou hast kept from me.
I prithee, let me.

R. It shall be thy penance
To find it full of faults, and not one beauty.

F. Where stands it?

R. There, behind the canopy.
A great Venetian nobleman, esteemed
For a good judge, they say, by Lionardo,
Paid me a princely sum but yesterday
For this poor portrait.

F. Portrait? and of whom?
Is it a lady?

R. Yes — a Roman lady —
About your stature; and her hair is bound
With a pearl fillet, even as your own.
Her eyes are just Fiammetta's; they are turned
On a fair youth, who sits beside her, gazing
As he would drink up all their light in his.

Upon her arm a bracelet: and thereon
Is graven——
F. Name it!
R. Raphael Urbinensis.
F. This kiss — and this — reward thee. Let me see it.

1832.

ON SYMPATHY.

Is it necessary to consider sympathy as an ultimate principle, or are there grounds for supposing it to be generated by association out of primary pleasures and pains?

IT was my first intention to have given you an Essay on a much more copious subject. I wished to detail the successive formations of the virtuous affections from simple feelings of sympathy, and to examine the true nature of the moral sentiments. This is much more interesting to my mind than the actual subject of the following Essay, but I began with it, and I had not time to get beyond it. The admission of sympathy as an ultimate principle would not invalidate any subsequent conclusions respecting the virtues that arise out of it; but the contrary opinion will perhaps give so clear an impression of the great powers of association, as to help very considerably the future investigation. And in itself I think the question a very curious and pleasing one. Before I begin to discuss it, I must premise that the word sympathy, which like most others in moral science has a fluctuating import, is used in this Essay to denote the simple affection of the soul, by which it is pleased with another's pleasure and pained with another's pain, immediately and for their own sakes.

Let us take the soul at that precise moment in which she becomes assured that another soul exists. From tones, gestures, and other objects of sensation she has inferred that existence, according to the simplest rules of association. Some philosophers indeed conceive an original instinct by which we infer design, and therefore mental existence, from the phenomena of animal motion, and the expressions of voice and countenance. I have no fondness, I confess, for these easy limitations of inquiry, these instincts, so fashionable in certain schools, and I know not why any new principle should be invented to account for one of these plainest of all the associative processes. Be this as it may, the soul, then, has become aware of another individual subject, capable of thoughts and feelings like her own. How does this discovery affect her? It is possible she may feel pleasure in the mere knowledge of mere existence in this other subject; since it is probable that pleasure is inherent in the exercise of all the soul's capacities as such, and, therefore, the idea of a new similar set of capacities may irresistibly call up the idea, and the reality of pleasure. For association, I need hardly observe, does not only produce ideas of what in the past is similar to the present, but revives in many cases the feelings themselves. But as these probabilities are rather of a shadowy complexion, let us move a step further. The person thus recognized by the soul will probably have been occupied in acts of kindness towards it, by which indeed its attention was first attracted and the recognition rendered possible. Before that recognition, therefore, pleasure has been associated with that person as a mere object. The infant cannot separate the sensations of nourishment from the form of his nurse or mother. But the expressions of voice and countenance in the person conferring this or any other pleasure were themselves agreeable, and such as indicate internal pleasure in that person. So soon, therefore, as the infant makes the recognition we spoke of, that is, assumes a conscious subject of those expressions, he is competent to make a second assumption, to wit, that the looks and tones in the other being, which accompany his own pleasure, are accompanied at the same time by pleasure in that other. Hence, whereever he perceives the indications of another's joy, he is prepared to rejoice, and, by parity of reasoning, wherever he perceives indications of pain, he is grieved; because those painful appearances have been connected by him with the absence of pleasurable sensations to himself, or even the positive presence of painful ones. A great step is thus gained in the soul's progress. She is immediately pleased by another's pleasure, and pained by another's pain. Close upon the experience of pleasure follows desire. As the soul in its first development, within the sphere of itself, desired the recurrence of that object which had gratified it, so now, having connected its pleasure with that of another, she connects her desire with his desire. So also from the correspondence of pains will arise a correspondence of *aversions*, by which I mean *active dislikes*, the opposites of desire. Thus the machinery of sympathy, it might seem, would be complete; and since I have exhibited a legitimate process, by which the soul might arrive at a state precisely answering to the definition with which I set out, you may expect perhaps that the argument of this Essay is already terminated. Indeed some philosophers appear to consider this a complete account of the matter. But when I reflect on the peculiar force of sympathy itself, and the equivalent strength of those reflex sentiments regarding it, which I shall come presently to examine, I cannot but think something more is wanted. It seems to me that several processes of association operate simultaneously in the same direction, and that the united power of all imparts a character to this portion of our nature, which each taken singly would not be able to produce. Let us again consider the soul at the starting-point, where it recognizes a kindred being. The discovery is made, and the soul dwells upon it fondly, wishing to justify its own inference, and anxiously seeking for means of verification. Every new expression of feeling in the other being, the object of its contemplation, becomes an additional evidence. The more it can discern of pleasure, the more it becomes confirmed in its belief. I have alluded to the probability that every new exercise of a new function, every change of state, is to the soul an enjoyment. Pain may supervene, but in the nature of the thing, to feel, to live, is to enjoy. Pleasure, therefore, will be the surest sign of life to the soul. Hence there is the strongest possible inducement to be pleased with those marks of pleasure in another, which justify, as it were, the assumed similarity of that other to its own nature. Marks of pain, in a less degree, will also be proofs. How then, I may be asked, does it happen we are not pleased with the pain of our fellow-being? Because another result of association here intervenes. The sudden interruption of any train of feeling in which the mind acquiesces, has a uniform tendency to displease and shock us. When the perception of suffering in another interferes with our satisfaction in contemplating him, and in pursuing our process of verification, if I may so call it, this contrast produces pain. Besides, as the image of his enjoyment recalled images, and thereby awoke realities of pleasure in ourselves, so the perception of suffering makes us recollect our own suffering, and causes us to suffer. Thus by a second chain of associated feelings, the soul arrives at the same result, at union of joys and sorrows, in other words, at sympathy. I should remark, however, that compassion is not unmixed pain, and the pleasure mingling with it may still be legitimately referred to that assurance of life, which the marks of suffering afford. I shall now proceed to a third principle, from which the same result may be deduced. This is the principle of imitation. All animals are imitative. To repeat desires, volitions, actions, is the unquestionable tendency of conscious beings. It was a profound remark of Bishop Butler, one of those anticipations of philosophic minds which are pregnant with theories, that perhaps the same simple power in the mind which disposes our actions to habitual courses, may be sufficient to account for the phenomena of memory. This is a very deep subject; and when we remember that the sphere of imitation is not confined to human, or even animal exertions, but appears to be coextensive with organic life, we have reason to be cautious in dealing with this principle. So far, however, as it applies to our desires, there seems ground for supposing that the soul may desire another's gratification from the same impulse that leads a monkey to mimic the gestures of a man. Novelty is in itself an evident source of pleasure. To become something new, to add a mode of being to those we have experienced, is a temptation alike to the lisping infant in the cradle and the old man on the verge of the grave. This may partly arise from that essential inherence of pleasure in every state to which I have alluded, partly from a pleasure of contrast and surprise felt by the soul on gaining a new position. Now nothing can be more new than such a foreign capacity of enjoyment as the soul has here discovered. To become this new thing, to imitate, in a word, the discovered agent, no less in the internal than the outward elements of action, will naturally be the endeavor of faculties already accustomed in their own development to numberless courses of imitation. For we imitate our previous acts in order to establish our very earliest knowledge. Through the medium of imitation alone, automatic notions become voluntary. It is then possible that through the desire to feel as another feels, we may come to feel so.

I know not whether I have succeeded in stating with tolerable clearness these three processes by which I conceive the association principle to operate in the production of sympathy. The number, however, is not yet exhausted, and those that remain to be described are perhaps more important, and will carry us more to the bottom of the matter, although for this very reason it will be difficult to avoid some obscurity in speaking of them. Some of you, perhaps, may be disposed to set me down as a mystic, for what I am about to say; just as some of you may have despised me as a mechanist, or a materialist, on account of what I have said already. In one and the other, however, I proceed upon tangible facts, or upon probabilities directly issuing out of such facts. It is an ultimate fact of consciousness, that the soul exists as one subject in various successive states. Our belief in this is the foundation of all reasoning. Far back as memory can carry us, or far forward as anticipation can travel unrestrained, the remembered state in the one case, and the imagined one in the other, are forms of self. With the first dawn of feeling began the conception of existence, distinct from that of the moment in which the conception arose: hope, desire, apprehension, aversion, soon made the soul live entirely in reference to things non-existent. But what were these things? Possible conditions of the soul, — the same undivided soul which existed in the conception and desire of them. Wide, therefore, as that universe might be, which comprehended for the imagination all varieties of untried consciousness, it was no wider than that self which imagined it. Material objects were indeed perceived as external. But how? As unknown limits of the soul's activity, they were not a part of subjective consciousness, they defined, restrained, and regulated it. Still the soul attributed itself to every consciousness, past or future. At length the discovery of another being is made. Another being, another subject, conscious, having a world of feelings like the soul's own world! How, how can the soul imagine feeling which is not its own? I repeat, she realizes this conception only by considering the other being as a separate part of self, a state of her own consciousness existing apart from the present, just as imagined states exist in the future. Thus absorbing, if I may speak so, this other being into her universal nature, the soul transfers at once her own feelings and adopts those of the new-comer. It is very possible there may be nothing in this notion of mine, which I doubt not many of you will think too refined. But it seems to deserve attentive consideration. The force of it lies in a supposed difficulty attending the structure of our consciousness; a difficulty of conceiving any existence, except in the way of matter, external to the conceiving mind. It may be objected, however, that this conjectural explanation is after all no explanation, since it can only account for an interest taken in the other being, but not for a coalition of pleasures or pains. The supposed identification is not assuredly closer than that which exists between the past and the present in ourselves, yet how often does our actual self desire different objects from those which allured us in a previous condition! The objection is weighty, but let us see what may be said against it. The soul, we have seen, exists as one permanent subject of innumerable successive states. But not only is there unity of subject, there is likewise a tendency to unity of form. The order of nature is uniform under the sway of invariable laws, the same phenomena perpetually recur.

And there is a preëstablished harmony in mind by which it anticipates this uniformity. I do not imagine any original principle distinct from association is necessary to account for this fact. But a fact it is, and the foundation of all inductive judgments. The soul naturally takes a great pleasure in this expectation of sameness, so perpetually answered, and affording scope for the development of all faculties, and all dominion over surrounding things. Thus a wish for complete uniformity will arise wherever a similarity of any kind is observed. But a still deeper feeling is caused by that immediate knowledge of the past which is supplied by memory. To know a thing as past, and to know it as similar to something present, is a source of mingled emotions. There is pleasure, in so far as it is a revelation of self; but there is pain, in so far that it is a divided self, a being at once our own and not our own, a portion cut away from what we feel, nevertheless, to be single and indivisible. I fear these expressions will be thought to border on mysticism. Yet I must believe that if any one, in the least accustomed to analyze his feelings, will take the pains to reflect on it, he may remember moments in which the burden of this mystery has lain heavy on him; in which he has felt it miserable to exist, as it were, piece-meal, and in the continual flux of a stream; in which he has wondered, as at a new thing, how we can be, and have been, and not be that which we have been. But the yearnings of the human soul for the irrecoverable past are checked by a stern knowledge of impossibility. So also in its eager rushings towards the future, its desire of that mysterious something which now is not, but which in another minute we shall be, the soul is checked by a lesson of experience, which teaches her that she cannot carry into that future the actual mode of her existence. But were these impossibilities removed, were it conceivable that the soul in one state should coexist with the soul in another, how impetuous would be that desire of reunion, which even the awful laws of time cannot entirely forbid! The cause you will say is inconceivable. Not so; it is the very case before us. The soul, we have seen, contemplates a separate being as a separate state of itself, the only being it can conceive. But the two exist simultaneously. Therefore that impetuous desire arises. Therefore, in her anxiety to break down all obstacles, and to amalgamate two portions of her divided substance, she will hasten to blend emotions and desires with those apparent in the kindred spirit. I request it may be considered whether these two circumstances, to wit, the anticipation of uniformity natural to the soul, and the melancholy pleasure occasioned by the idea of time, are not sufficient to remove the objection started above, and finally, whether this notion of the soul's identifying the perceived being with herself may not be thought to have some weight, especially when such identification is relied upon as a concurrent cause with the others first spoken of.

Before I proceed to examine what consequences such a passion as sympathy might be expected to have in the mind, and how far those consequences, as predicted from a general knowledge of the workings of association, are in conformity with the actual constitution of our minds, it may be well to make one remark as to the character of the system I have been explaining. That system asserts the absolute disinterestedness of sympathy. It is, as I understand it, no modification of the selfish theory. It has, however, been so represented, and I must allow there is a strong primâ facie appearance of its being so, owing to the fallacies of language. The selfish theory denies the disinterested nature of affection on grounds which prove, if anything, the absolute impossibility of disinterestedness, at least in any shape conceivable by a human intellect. What would be the correct inference from such a proof? Simply this, that the theorists are using words in a different sense from the common, and applying them to a distinction which never came in question, not to that real and broad distinction which those words designate for common understandings. But is this the inference really drawn by these philosophers? No, so it would make no theory. Either with a strange inconsistency they make use of their principle to *depreciate mankind*, thus recognizing in fact the possibility and naturalness of what they pronounce impossible and unnatural, or they employ it to narrow the interval between vice and virtue and to weaken the authority of the moral sentiments. Neither of these defects is fairly chargeable on the system I have recommended. What is the true distinction, according to common language and common feeling, between selfish and unselfish?

Certainly this: that the object of the first is one's own gratification, the object of the second is the gratification of another. The difference of names arises from the difference of objects recognized by the understanding. It relates entirely to a single act of the soul, taken in and by itself, limited by its object, and not at all considered in reference to its origin or its consequence. To require that pleasure should not have preceded this act so as to render it possible, or that pleasure should not inhere in the subjective part of this act so as to cause a subsequent reflex sentiment, is to require what the understanding assuredly never required, when it separated the class of selfish from that of unselfish sentiments. But I may be told that the view I have taken of sympathy, as originating in an adoption of the other being into self, is quite incompatible with the disinterested character. If a conscious agent can only be imagined as a separate and coexistent part of self, is it not obvious all love not only springs from, but is in itself a modification of, self-love? For here the object is the same as the subject: and though the logical distinction mentioned may be a good justification of the com-

excited by the idea of another's gratification. The distinction is in the nature of what the exciting idea represents, not in the mode of its rising, or the reasons of its efficiency. Now, although I have supposed it possible that the conception of a distinct conscious agent must pass through a process of imagination and feeling before it can be sufficiently realized to have any hold upon us, I must not be so misunderstood as to be thought to deny the intellectual conception itself. It is because the intellect apprehends another agent, that this process may take place, not because it is incapable of such apprehension. I hold therefore that the notions here laid down concerning the composition of sympathy are not liable to the fatal accusation of being incompatible with the disinterested character of the affections, in any sense at least which can have a bearing upon practice. But I think it still a curious speculative question, whether there is not a species of self-love of a very primary formation, anterior indeed to everything in the soul (considered as the subject of feeling) except the susceptibility of pleasure and pain. And I have my doubts whether the vast concourse of writers who speak of some such principle are fairly open, otherwise than through the imperfections and entanglements of language, to the impeachment of those modern reformers, who choose to restrain the words on which the debate turns to a different, a limited, though I admit an important, part of our nature.

It was my intention to have continued this Essay so as to exhibit the rise and progress of those pains and pleasures, aversions and desires, which arise in the soul in consequence of sympathy, and whose peculiar force I should have shown to depend on the peculiar powers of the several feelings composing sympathy. These may be comprised under the terms remorse and moral satisfaction, or any equivalent, there being no single word. I should then have detailed the gradual generation of the virtues from the primary feelings of sympathy, taking for my guide the principle of association. I should have shown gratitude, resentment, justice, veracity, inevitably resulting from combinations of the primary pleasures and pains with their offspring, sympathy, and with those reflex sentiments which regard it. I should have shown these sentiments overshadowing the generated affections as they had protected the parent one, and acquiring at every step additional force and authority. I should have attempted to prove that moral approbation and blame are not applied to agents and actions unconnected with ourselves in virtue of any faculty of approving or any *realist* ideas of Right and Wrong, but by a simple extension of sympathy, strengthened as that passion has become by the reaction of all the secondary affections, according to the obvious nature of association. I should have spoken of the self-regarding virtues, temperance, fortitude, prudence, and explained how far they come under the jurisdiction of the reflex sentiments. Finally, I should have endeavored to express how sympathy receives its final consummation, and the moral sentiments their strongest sanction, from the aid of religion, the power which binds over again (religare, according to some, is the etymology of the word) what the bond of nature was unable adequately to secure. But these considerations I must leave to some other and more favorable opportunity.

ORATION

ON

THE INFLUENCE OF ITALIAN WORKS OF IMAGINATION ON THE SAME CLASS OF COMPOSITIONS IN ENGLAND.

DELIVERED IN TRINITY COLLEGE CHAPEL,

December 16, 1831.

THERE is in the human mind a remarkable habit, which leads it to prefer in most cases the simple to the composite, and to despise a power acquired by combination in comparison with one original, and produced from unmixed elements. Doubtless some good motives have had a share in forming this habit, but I suspect pride is answerable for nine tenths of the formation; especially when anything immediately belonging to ourselves is the circumstance for which our curiosity requires an origin. Wherever we trace a continued series of ascending causes, we can hardly escape the conviction of our insignificance and entire dependence: but if by any accident the chain is broken, if we see darkness beyond a particular link, we find it easy, and think it fine, to flatter ourselves into a belief of having found a beginning, and the nearer we bring it down to ourselves the better satisfied we remain. Traces of this prejudice may be observed in every walk of intellect: philosophy, as might be expected, has been the greatest sufferer; but criticism, history, and the whole province of Belles Lettres, have been visited in their turn. One of its most amusing forms is to be found in those writers, less honest than patriotic, who are ready to invent a world of lies, for the pragmatical purpose of showing the aboriginal distinctness of their national literature, and its complete independence of the provision of any other languages. They seem to imagine, that if they once prove the nations of the earth to have grown, like a set of larches, each in its unbending perpendicular, and never encroaching on the measured interval that separates it from its neighbor, they have erected "monumentum ære perennius" to the character of human society. But widely different from their fancy is the method of nature. Far more sublime is that process by which the few original elements of society are dashed and mingled with one another, serving forever and coalescing within a crucible of incessant operation, and producing at each successive point new combinations, which again, as simple substances, are made subservient to the prospective direction of the Great observant Mind. Is it wonderful that, for the collection of comforts and luxuries, the spirit of commercial enterprise has levelled the barriers of countries, and triumphed over the immensity of ocean? And have we no admiration in reserve for that commerce of mind, which has continued as it commenced, without the forethought or intention of man, silently working, but unerringly, abating distances, uniting periods, harmonizing the most opposed thoughts, bringing the fervid meditations of the East to bear upon the rapid reason of the West, the stormy Northern temper to give and receive alteration from voluptuous languors of the Meridian? Surely the consideration of this universal and always progressive movement should make us examine the component parts of any national literature with no exclusive and limited feeling (for the literature of a people is the expression of its character), and to ascertain, by correct analysis, the number and relative proportion of its elements; to decide, by the application of history, from what juncture in social progress each particular complexion of sentiment has its origin, what is this but to become a spectator of new scenes in the Providential drama: and with what feelings but those of reverence and a sense of beauty should their harmonious variety be contemplated? Nor is this pleasure the peculiar portion of the speculative and secluded; it may be relished by all who have the advantage of a liberal education; it may be freshly drawn from the most obvious books, and even the common parlance of conversation; for we need only look to the different aspects of language to be perpetually reminded of those divers influences by which the national character has been modified. I open at hazard a volume of Shakspeare, and I take for an instance the first passage that occurs: —

> "That man that sits within a monarch's heart
> And ripens in the sunshine of his favor,
> Would he abuse the countenance of the king,
> Alack, what mischiefs might be set abroach
> In shadow of such greatness! With you, Lord Bishop,
> It is even so; who hath not heard it spoken,
> How deep you were within the books of God,

To us the Speaker in his Parliament,
To us the imagined voice of God himself?
The very opener and intelligencer
Between the grace, the sanctities of heaven,
And our dull workings; oh who shall believe
But you misuse the reverence of your place,
Employ the countenance and grace of heaven,
As a false favorite doth his prince's name,
In deeds dishonorable?"

Henry IV., P. II., A. iv., S. 2.

In these lines (sixteen in number) we shall find twenty-two words of Roman formation, and but twenty-one (excluding connective words) of Teutonic. Of the former, again, five are proper to French; the rest having probably passed through the medium of that language, but derived from a classical source. Among the last, one only is Greek; the others bear the imperial stamp of Rome. The whole is a beautiful specimen of pure English, and falls with complete, easy, uniform effect on the ear and mind. In this instance, and probably in any other we should select from the great master, the equipoise of southern and northern phraseology creates a natural harmony, a setting of full bass to keen treble, to destroy which altogether would be one inevitable consequence of altering the proportion of these two elements. And is it not a noble thing, that the English tongue is, as it were, the common focus and point of union to which opposite beauties converge? Is it a trifle that we temper energy with softness, strength with flexibility, capaciousness of sound with pliancy of idiom? Some, I know, insensible to these virtues, and ambitious of I know not what unattainable decomposition, prefer to utter funeral praises over the grave of departed Anglo-Saxon, or, starting with convulsive shudder, are ready to leap from surrounding Latinisms into the kindred, sympathetic arms of modern German. For myself, I neither share their regret nor their terror. Willing at all times to pay filial homage to the shades of Hengist and Horsa, and to admit they have laid the base of our compound language; or, if you will, have prepared the soil from which the chief nutriment of the goodly tree, our British oak, must be derived; I am yet proud to confess that I look with sentiments more exulting and more reverential to the bonds by which the law of the universe has fastened me to my distant brethren of the same Caucasian race; to the privileges which I, an inhabitant of the gloomy North, share in common with climates imparadised in perpetual summer, to the universality and efficacy resulting from blended intelligence, which, while it endears in our eyes the land of our fathers as a seat of peculiar blessing, tends to elevate and expand our thoughts into communion with humanity at large; and, in the "sublimer spirit" of the poet, to make us feel

> "That God is everywhere — the God who framed
> Mankind to be one mighty family,
> Himself our Father, and the world our home."

However surely the intercourse of words may indicate a corresponding mixture of sentiment, yet these variations of expression are far from being a complete measure of the interior changes. Man is a great talker, but how small the proportion of what he says to the ever-shifting condition of his mental existence! It is necessary to look abroad, and gather in evidence from events, if we would form a reasonable conjecture how much we stand indebted to any one country for our literary glories, and for that spirit which not only produced them, but in some measure, since we are Englishmen, circulates through ourselves. I propose, therefore, to make a few observations on that peculiar combination of thought, which resulted from the intercourse of Italian writers with our own: first, about the time the House of Lancaster began to reign, the period of Chaucer; and, secondly, at that magnificent era of genius, when the names of Hooker, Shakspeare, and Bacon attest how much, under the auspices of the Protestant Queen, was effected for the sacred ideas of the good, the beautiful, and the true. The first point to be considered is the real character of Italian literature; for we cannot measure its effect until we know its capacity. That language then, I may observe, a chosen vessel of some of the most glorious thoughts with which our frail nature has been inspired, was the last and most complete among the several tongues that arose out of the confusion of northern barbarians with their captives of the conquered empire. For a long time after that signal revolution, the municipal spirit, which kept the inhabitants of one town distinct from those of another, as regards marriages, social intercourse, and the whole train of ordinary life, prevented the various *patois*, included under the general name of Romane, from coalescing into regular languages. The mandates of government, the decisions of law, the declarations of religion, whatever was in its nature more important, and was intended to coerce a larger aggregate: these were by general custom reserved to Latin,—barbarous indeed, and as inelegant as impure, but still Latin in the main, and distinguishable by a broad line from the dialects that swarmed in the villages. The few wretched attempts at poetry that occasionally occur in this period of utter darkness, are always in a Latin form; and the fact that this is true even of soldiers' ballads, is decisive as to the extreme infantine weakness of those forms of speech, which were so soon to arise from their illiterate and base condition, to express in voices of thunder and music the wants and tendencies of a new civilization, and to animate with everlasting vigor the intellect of mankind. At length, however, after five centuries of preparatory ignorance, the flame burst from beneath the ashes, never again to be overcome. About the same time, in different parts of France, a distinct, serviceable, and capacious form was assumed by the Provençal and Roman Wallon, or, as they are usually called, the Langue d'Oc and Langue d'Oil. The former especially began to offer the phenomenon of a new literature, dependent for nothing on monastic erudition, but fresh from the workings of untaught nature, impressed with the stamp of existing manners, and reacting upon them by exciting the imagination, and directing the feelings of the people. A thousand poets sprang up, as at an enchanter's call; the distinctions of rank and wealth were levelled by this more honorable ambition; many were the proud feudal barons, who struck the minstrel lyre with emulative, often with triumphant, touch; nor few were the gallant princes, who sought in "lou gai saber" the solace of their cares, and the refinement of their martial tempers. Frederic Barbarossa! Richard of England! These at the head of the list, who could think it a disgrace to follow? After these, it is almost idle to reckon up other royal poets,—Alfonso and Pedro of Arragon, Frederic of Sicily, the King of Thessalonica, the Marquis de Montferrat, the Dauphin of Auvergne, the Prince of Orange,—all were anxious "de trouver gentiment en vers," and some, we are assured, showed their preëminence of merit. In proportion to the development of Romane literature, the characteristics of the romantic spirit became more distinct. These may be arranged under four classes, constituting the four great elements of modern civilization: Christianity, as preserved in Catholicism; the Teutonic principle, animating the Northern countries immediately, the Southern less directly, and less forcibly through the invasion of the barbarians; the Roman, of which we must say exactly the reverse, that it was indigenous to the Southern nations, and diffused only by military occupation over some Teutonic tribes; lastly, the Oriental, derived from the Arabians, and circulating especially through those provinces of Europe least remote from the extensive territories of their splendid domination.* Separate as these sources appear, it is certain the streams that issued from them had a common tendency, so that each seems only to strengthen what without it might equally have existed. The four moving principles consolidated their energies in two great results: enthusiasm for individual prowess, and enthusiasm for the female character. Imagination clothed these with form, and that form was chivalry. The Knight of La Mancha, who

* I have here taken no notice of the Celtic character, because I confess I cannot perceive any palpable results of it in the new literature. I am aware, however, that there is a party amongst our literati, which professes to support the claims of the Celts to a larger portion of influence than is commonly ascribed to them.

sought heroes in peasants, and giants in windmills, was not more deplorably mistaken than some modern adventurers, who endeavored to fix an historical period, at which the feats of knight-errantry may have actually occurred. In truth, feudality and chivalry correspond as real and ideal. The wild energetic virtues of baronial chieftains were purified from their heavy alloy, and sublimated into models of courteous valor, by those pious frauds of imagination, which ameliorate the future while they disguise the past. In the midst of a general dissolution of manners (the greater part being alike ignorant of a comprehensive morality, and neglectful of religious injunctions, which the enjoiners were the first to disobey), the orient light of Poetry threw a full radiance on the natural heart of woman, and, as in the other sex, created the high sense of honor it pretended to find. I have said that all the four agencies I have mentioned had their share in impressing this direction on the resurgent genius of Europe. Can it be doubted that the spirit of revealed religion, however little understood, wrought in the heart of man a reverence for the weaker sex, both as teaching him to consider their equality with him in the sight of God, and the privileges of Christian life, and as encouraging in himself those mild and tender qualities, which are the especial glory of womanhood? Can it be doubted, that if this were the tendency of Christianity, yet more emphatically it was the tendency of Catholicism? The inordinate esteem for chastity; the solemnity attached to conventual vows; the interest taken in those fair saints, on whom the Church has conferred beatitude, that after conquering the temptations of earth they might be able to succor the tempted; above all the worship of the Virgin, the Queen of Heaven, supposed more lenient to sinners for the lenity of her sex; and more powerful in their redemption by her claim of maternal authority over her Almighty Son — these articles of a most unscriptural, but very beautiful mythology, could not be established in general belief without investing the feminine character with ideal splendor and loveliness. But, as an Englishman, I should feel myself guilty of ingratitude towards the Goths, my ancestors, if I did not recall to mind that they were always honorably distinguished from their neighbors by a more noble view of the domestic relation; and it is not perhaps a chimerical belief that the terms of humble homage, with which cavaliers of the middle ages addressed the objects of their admiration, may have found a precedent in the language of those ancient warriors, who defied the colossal sovereignty of Rome, but bent with generous humility before the beings who owed to them their safety, whom they considered as the favorites of heaven, the tenements of frequent inspiration. The love, however, which animated the Troubadours was not only humble and devotional, but passionate and energetic. While they exalt their object to the rank of an angel, they would not have her cease to be a woman. Here other influences become perceptible, the warm temperaments of Italy and Spain, and the wild impetuosity of Eastern passion. To Islam, indeed, the Christian civilization of Europe owes more than might on first thoughts be imagined.* In the forms of Arabic

* I do not wish to be understood as adopting in its full extent the theory of Warburton and Warton, that all marks of Orientalism occurring in romantic literature came by direct transmission through the Saracens. It has been amply shown by many writers, since the days of Warton, that much will still remain unaccounted for, which can only be referred to the essential Asiatic character of the whole race, now in possession

imagination appeared most probably the first pattern of that amorous mysticism I have been describing, since the immemorial customs of their race supplied them with many of those reverential habits, to which, in the West, I have assigned different causes. Slavery, and that to our ideas most revolting, is the general condition of the sex in all Asiatic countries; yet within this coercive circle is another in which the relation is almost reversed; and the seraglio, which seems a prison without the walls, within might present the appearance of a temple. The cares, the sufferings, the dangers of common life, approach not the sacred precinct in which the Mussulman preserves the idol of his affections from vulgar gaze. Art and luxury are made to minister perpetually to her enjoyment. Slaves must become more servile in her presence; flattery must be pitched in a higher key, if offered to her acceptance. Customs like these, however pernicious to society, are certainly not incapable of

of Europe. But on the present occasion I shall not be expected to enter into so abstruse a question as that of the community of fiction: It is sufficient for my purpose that the Saracen influence is an undoubted fact, although some have injudiciously extended this fact to circumstances which are beyond its legitimate reach.

charming the imagination, and of giving it that peculiar turn which we find in the Gazeles of Persian poetry, the Cassides of Arabian, and the forms of which were early adopted by the congenial spirits of Provence and Castille. Still more evident is the influence of Mahommedanism on the delicate refinements of warfare, which formed the other element of chivalry, and the consequent heroic style of composition. From the time that, with the reign of the Abbassides, began the splendid period of Arabian literature and science, what more familiar to Christian ears than the illustrious notions of courtesy, and honor, which adorned the narratives of those itinerant Eastern reciters, seldom absent from European courts, and welcome alike to the festive hall, or the retirements of listening beauty? Nor were opportunities long wanting of personal encounter with those lordly children of the Crescent, who were so presumptuous as to outshine in virtue the devoted servants of Rome. The close of the eleventh century is memorable for the great contest in Spain, which terminated in the capture of Toledo, and the reduction of all New Castille under the sway of Alfonso the Sixth. This was indeed a noble struggle, and even at this distance of time may well make us glow with exultation. From all parts of Europe flocked the bravest knights to the standard of the Cid: to their undoubting imaginations the religion of the world was at issue, the kingdoms of God and Satan were met in visible collision: yet the mutual admiration of heroic spirits was too strong to be repressed, and neither party scrupled to emulate the virtues which they condemned as the varnish of perdition. The Christian population of Castille and Arragon had long been exposed to the humanizing influences of Moorish cultivation: not for nothing had the dynasty of the Ommiades been established, or the kingdom of Grenada flourished: nor if the successors of Abderaman were unable to withstand the flower of Castillian chivalry, should we in justice forget, that they had tempered the weapons by which they were overcome; and had they done less for humanity, they might have prospered better for themselves. The issue of this war, favorable as it was to the cause of Christendom, served to increase and diffuse this refined valor, and the literary culture which had fostered it. The conqueror of Toledo gave the noble example of an entire toleration; a numerous Moorish population continued to live with the Christian occupants; and, while they mingled in their pursuits, imparted largely the spirit of their own. The schools and learned institutions retained their dignities: the Mozarabs took rank in the court and the army; and when the French cavaliers returned to their native land, when Raymond of Barcelona obtained the crown of Provence, the good effects of their expedition soon became visible in softened prejudices, enlarged imaginations, and a more ardent love of letters.* The influence of the East was not, however, confined to the secret moulding of mind; it displayed itself in the outward forms of literary composition, few of which are not borrowed from Arabia. The

* In a very few years this intimacy with Eastern customs was renewed. The Crusades were preached, and again the Christian cause was set to the peril of the sword. It is needless to remark what a wonderful effect they must have produced in bringing the European nations into close contact with one another, and with that common enemy, who was in fact their best friend. The Crusades form, as might be expected, the most common topic of Provençal poetry, during the 12th and 13th centuries. The subjects of Trouveur fiction also experienced a sudden change. The achievements of Arthur and Charlemagne were forgotten: the quest of the S. Greal was abandoned; and in the words of Warton, "Trebisond took place of Roncesvalles."

tale, or novel, that most delightful vehicle of amusing instruction, affording such a range to inventive fancy, and pliable to such a variety of style, was undoubtedly rendered fashionable by the reciters I have already mentioned. All the light and graceful machinery of enchantment, the name and attributes of faerie (certainly the most charming expedient ever thought of to satisfy the human propensity to polytheism without incurring the sin of idolatry), are owed to these ingenious travellers, who little thought, when they received their dole of recompense from some imperious lord, whose care they had contributed to relax, what a bounty, beyond all recompense, they were involuntarily bestowing on the generations about to succeed to this Western inheritance. There was a yet more important transmission from the Levant, which decided the whole bent of modern poetry, I mean the use, at least the extensive and varied use, of rhyme.* This appears to be the crea-

* Rhyme has been said to contain in itself a constant appeal to memory and hope. This is true of all verse, of all harmonized sound; but it is certainly made more palpable by the recurrence of termination. The dullest senses can perceive an identity in that, and be pleased with it; but the partial identity, latent in more diffused resemblances, requires, in order to

tion of Southern climates: for the Southern languages abound in vowels, and rhyme is the resonance of vowels, while the Northern overflow with consonants and naturally fall into alliteration. Thus, although it is a great mistake which some writers have fallen into, the considering rhyme as almost unknown to the poetry of the Gothic races, we may fairly consider it as transported with them in their original migration from their Asiatic birthplace, while the alliteration, so common among them, appears a natural product of their new locality. No poetry, however, in the world was so founded on rhyme as the Arabian; and some of its most complicated were transferred without alteration to the Langue d'Oc, previous to their obtaining immortality in the hands of Dante and Petrarca. Those ingenious turns of fancy, so remarkable in the Eastern style, were also eagerly adopted by our Western imitators. But they imitated

be appreciated, a soul susceptible of musical impression. The ancients disdained a mode of pleasure, in appearance so little elevated, so ill adapted for effects of art; but they knew not, and with their metrical harmonies, perfectly suited, as these were, to their habitual moods of feeling, they were not likely to know the real capacities of this apparently simple and vulgar combination.

with a noble freedom and gracefulness: it seemed the natural mould of their minds. The subtlety of perception, and, at the same time, the sportiveness, that were requisite for the management of these compositions, is not the less curious and admirable in itself, that it was employed on classes of resemblance, which our more enlarged knowledge considers as unsubstantial and minute. The interval that separates the *concetti* of that era from the frigid sparkles of some modern wits, is generally commensurate with the eternal division of truth from falsehood, strength from weakness, beauty from deformity. Where the intellect waxes vigorous, without any large support from what has been termed "bookmindedness," it cannot but spend its vivacity on repeated and fantastic modifications of its small capital of ideas. There may be poverty of thought, in so far as there are few objects of thought, but the character of the thinking faculty is not poor; and hence there is a freshness about the far-fetched combinations of these poets, which makes them true to nature, even when to prosaic eye they seem most unnatural.

I have thus endeavored to trace the elements

of romantic literature, in their first state of composition under the auspices of merry Jonglerie: in describing them I have, in fact, been analyzing the Italian, for all the wealth of Provence accrued to the more fortunate writers of the Peninsula, who, while they lost nothing on that side, were at liberty to add immensely from another. The thirteenth century witnessed a downfall to Provençal glory yet more sudden and surprising than its rise. The barbarous war against the Albigenses laid desolate the seats of this literature; and the extinction of the houses of Provence and Toulouse reduced the Langue d'Oc, which for the space of three centuries had sat at the right hand of kings, with nations for her worshippers, and had said, like the daughter of the Chaldeans, "I shall be a lady forever," to the condition of a dependant menial in the courts of her haughty rival. Meanwhile the "lingua cortigiana," gradually extricating itself from those peculiarities of idiom which rendered the inhabitants of one Italian district unintelligible to those of another, assumed the rank of a written language, and began with better omens to carry on that war against the insolent Langue d'Oil, which the successors of Sordel and Arnaud de Marveil had ceased to maintain. If I were asked to name the reasons which gave this language so immeasurable an ascendency over its forerunner, I should say there are two, both arising from its geographical position. Italy had been the seat of the ancient Empire; it was that of Catholic religion. Not only would the recovery of those lost treasures of heathen civilization, the poets, historians, and philosophers of Greece and Rome, naturally take place in the country where most of them were buried; but there is ever a latent sympathy in the mind of a posterity, which recognizes with an instinctive gladness the feelings of their ancestors, when disclosed to them in books or other monuments. Who can doubt that the minds of Italians would spring up to meet the utterance of Cicero, Livy, and Virgil, with a far deeper and stronger sense of community, than any other nation could have done! * Therefore they not only acquired new objects of thought

* What a beautiful symbol of this truth is contained in that canto of the "Purgatorio" which relates the meeting between Sordel and Virgil. Centuries, and the mutations of centuries lapse into nothing before that strong feeling of homogeneity which bursts forth in the "O Mantovano!"

at the revival of literature, but they felt their own thought expanded and miraculously strengthened. This, then, I assign as the first reason of the superiority we perceive in Italian that it had a capacity of taking into itself, into its own young and creative vigor, the whole height, breadth, and depth of human knowledge, as it then stood. My second reason is that Italy was the centre and home of the Catholic Faith. An Italian, whatever might be his moral disposition, felt his dignity bound up in some sort with the name and cause of Christianity. Was not the Pope the Bishop of Rome? and in that word *Rome* there was a spell of sufficient strength to secure his imagination against all heresies and schisms. Again, the splendors and pomps of the daily worship; the music and the incense, and the beautiful saints and the tombs of martyrs — what strong hold must they have taken on the feelings of every Italian! It is true the profligacies of the Papal court, and many other circumstances, had gone to weaken the undoubting faith of Europe before the thirteenth century; but at that period, by the institution of Mendicant Orders, a fresh impulse was given to the human heart, ever parched and dying of thirst when religion is made a mockery. St. Francis has a claim upon our literary gratitude, rather more substantial, though less precise in form, than his reported invention of the *versi sciolti.* It seems clear, that the spirit awakened in Italy, through his means and those of St. Dominic, prepared the Italian mind for that vigorous assertion of Christianity, as the head and front of modern civilization, the perpetually presiding genius of our poetry, our art, and our philosophy. These, then, I consider the two directive principles of their literature: the first a full and joyous reception of former knowledge into their own very different habits of knowing; the second a deep and intimate impression of forms of Christianity. The combined operation of the two is seen in their love-poetry, which dwells "like a star apart," separated by broad spaces of distinction from every expression of that sentiment in other languages. Its base is undoubtedly the Troubadour poetry, of which I have already spoken, but upon this they have reared a splendid edifice of Platonism, and surmounted it with the banner of the cross. In his treatise "De Vulgari Eloquentia," Dante asserts of the Lingua di Si, that even before the date of his own writings, "qui dulcius, subtiliusque poetati sunt, ii familiares et domestici sui sunt." I think we cannot read the poems of Cino da Pistoia, or either Guido, without perceiving this early superiority and more masculine turn of thought. But it was not in scattered sonnets that the whole magnificence of that idea could be manifested, which represents love as at once the base and pyramidal point of the entire universe, and teaches us to regard the earthly union of souls, not as a thing accidental, transitory, and dependent on the condition of human society, but with far higher import, as the best and the appointed symbol of our relations with God, and through them of his own ineffable essence. In the "Divine Comedy," this idea received its full completeness of form ; that wonderful work of which, to speak adequately, we must borrow the utterance of its conceiving mind.

> "La gloria di colui, che tutto muove,
> Per l'universo penetra, e risplende,
> In una parte più, e meno altrove." *

* D C. Paradiso, c. i., v. 1.

This is not the occasion for entering into a criticism, or detailed encomium of Dante; I only wish to point him out as an entire and plenary representation of the Italian mind, a summary in his individual self of all the elements I have been describing, which never before had coexisted in unity of action, a signal-point in the stream of time, showing at once how much power was at that exact season aggregated to the human intellect, and what direction was about to be impressed upon it by the "rushing mighty wind," the spirit of Christianity, under whose conditions alone a new literature was become possible. Petrarch appears to me a corollary from Dante; the same spirit in a different mould of individual character, and that a weaker mould; yet better adapted, by the circumstances of its position, to diffuse the great thought which possessed them both, and to call into existence so great a number of inferior recipients of it, as might affect insensibly, but surely, the course of general feeling. Petrarch was far from apprehending either his own situation, or that of mankind, with anything like the clear vision of Dante whom he affected to undervalue, idly striving against that destiny which ordained their coöperation. His life was restless and perplexed; that continual craving for sympathy, taking in its lighter moods the form and name of vanity, which drove him, as he tells us himself, "from town to town, from country to country," would have rendered him incapable of assuming the decisive, initiatory position which was not difficult to be maintained by the proud Ghibelline spirit, who depended so little on others, so much on his own undaunted energies. On that ominous morning, when the recluse of Arqua expired, his laurelled brow reposing on the volume he was reading, the vital powers of Italian poetry seemed suspended with his own. The form indeed remained unaltered; so perfect was the state of polished cultivation in which he left it, that, even when the informing genius was departed, we may say of it as his own phrase, "Death appeared lovely in that lovely face." When, after a long interval, inspiration returned under the auspices of Lorenzo the Magnificent, the lineaments of that countenance had undergone a change, and their divinity was much abated. Much indeed had been going on in Europe, that could not but withdraw men from that state of feeling, which produced the creators of

Tuscan poetry. The lays of the Troubadours were now forgotten; the very shade of what once was Arabian greatness was passing away; ancient literature had become familiar and almost trite; the republican spirit of Italy was on the decline; the courtly idiom of Paris reigned in undisputed supremacy: its ease and gayety, its exuberance and inventive narration, its treasures of old chivalrous lore, its rude but fascinating attempts at dramatic composition, its perfect pliancy to that worldly temper which would pass life off as a jest; all this good and evil together began to give it an ascendency over the mind of Europe, already far advanced on the road of civilization. The poetry of Pulci, Boiardo, Ariosto, and Tasso, seems to me expressive of this change in men's ways of thinking and feeling. I do not mean that they are not thoroughly and genuinely Italian; that their poems, especially the immortal works of Ariosto and his rival, are not rich in manifold beauties; but that there is a laxity, a weakness of tone, in the deeper portion of their poetic nature; that their efforts are more scattered, and seem to obey less one mighty governing impulse, than was the case with the earlier masters; that, in a word, there was far less genial power, although perhaps far more brilliancy of execution. I would borrow the phrase of Brutus, and say, "I do not love these less, but Dante and Petrarch more." I feel, in passing from one to the other, exactly the same difference of impression, with which I should turn to a picture of Guido, Domenichino, or any other Bolognese painter, after contemplating the pure glories of old Tuscan or German art. I know nothing more difficult to define than the quality and limits of this difference; to consider it indeed would lead into higher questions than may be agitated on this occasion. This much, however, seems certain. There is in man a natural life, and there is also a spiritual: art, which holds the mirror up to nature, is then most perfect, when it gives back the image of both.

Having thus endeavored to ascertain the true character of Italian literature, I come now to consider this character in conjunction with the writings of Englishmen, confining the inquiry, as I have hitherto done, to the products of imagination, because in these alone such influences as extend beyond palpable imitation become perceptible, and because I do not find that any historical or philosophical Italians have materially affected, in any way, the literature of other countries. First, then, as in liege duty bound, let us look upwards to that serene region, "pure of cloud," wherein is revealed the form of Chaucer, our beautiful morning star, whose beams earliest breaking through the dense darkness of our northern Parnassus, did so pierce and dissipate its clouds, adorning their abrupt edges with golden lining of dawn,

"That all the orient laughed at the sight."

He indeed delighted to attend "the nods and becks and wreathed smiles," with which the Gallic Muse invited young imaginations to follow her to those coasts of old Romance, where sometimes were seen the tourneys and courtly pomp of Arthur or Charlemagne, sometimes the mystic forms of Allegory, clothing in persuasive shape the incorporeal loveliness of Truth. The Langue d'Oil, full of a wild freshness that proclaimed its origin in the triumphant settlement of the Northmen, abounded in rich and fanciful fables, which found a congenial response on this side of the Channel. The conquest of Poitou and Guienne during Chaucer's lifetime, by the warriors of Crecy and Poictiers, threw open those other stores, of which I have already spoken so largely: many Provençal poets followed the Black Prince to his father's court to enjoy their royal patronage and general favor. We need only cast a hasty glance over the pages of Chaucer to perceive how readily he drank at both these sources, especially the first, which indeed ever since the Conquest had been a spring of refreshment to English minds.* But we shall perceive also a vein of stronger thought and chaster expression than were common in Cisalpine countries: we shall recognize the subduing, yet at the same time elevating power, which passed into his soul from their spirits, who just before the season of his greatness had "enlumined

* Mr. Wordsworth, on being asked where the French poetry was to be sought for, is said to have replied, "In the old Chronicles." I believe that a more assiduous study of early French literature than is common at present would be repaid by the discovery of much poetic beauty, not merely in prosaic forms, but alluring us by varied graces of metrical arrangement. I hope my readers will bear in mind that I have been speaking on this occasion of two separate Frances: the one, the country of William de Lorris and Froissart, justly venerated by our Chaucers, our Gowers, our Lydgates, and the other racy thinkers of Norman England; the other, a much later invention, retaining few features, except such as were negative, of the Langue d'Oil, the country of Boileau and Voltaire, essentially hostile to the higher imagination, although possessed of advantages for discursive writings which I have mentioned further on.

Italie of poetrie." We know that he travelled to that land:

> "Quin et in has olim prevenit Tityrus oras." *

We have on record his admiration of "Francis Petrarke, the laureate Poet," and of that other wise poet of Florence, "hight Dantes." From Boccaccio he imitated, as masters alone imitate, that incomparable composition, "The Knighte's Tale," also the beautiful story of "Griseldis," and probably the "Troilus and Cresseide." In the latter he has inserted a sonnet of Petrarch; but it is not so much to his direct adoptions that I refer, as to the general modulation of thought, that clear softness of his images, that energetic self-possession of his conceptions, and that melodious repose in which are held together all the emotions he delineates. The distinct influence of the Italian character is more evident with respect to the father of our poetry, than afterwards with respect to Spenser and his contemporaries, precisely because it was in the first period more pure in itself, and had admitted little of the Northern romance. The second development of the Italian poetry was, as we have

* Milton ad Mansum, v. 34, as well as Spenser, gives Chaucer the name of Tityrus.

seen, formed out of the old chivalrous stories, and may be considered as formed on the Norman French, just as the first had been on the Provençal. It came, therefore, bearing its own recommendation, to our Norman land: exactly the same part of our national temper now caught with eagerness at Ariosto and Tasso, which, in less civilized times, had delighted in the Brut d'Angleterre, or the Roman de la Rose. No sooner had the mighty spirit of the Protestant Reformation awakened all dormant energies and justified all lofty aspirations, than literature of all sorts, but especially poetry, began to arise in England; and one of its first results, or steps of progress, was to bring us into close communication with this second school of Transalpine poets. Ascham, in his "Scholemaster," informs us, that about this time an infinite number of Italian books were translated into English. Amongst these were many novels which are well known to form the groundwork of, perhaps, the larger part of our early drama, including Shakspeare. It should seem too that our metrical language acquired many improvements from this study. Warton assures us, that "the poets in the age of Elizabeth introduced a great variety of measures from the Italian; particularly in the lyrical pieces of that time, in their canzonets, madrigals, devises, and epithalamiums." It is needless to multiply instances of so palpable a fact as is the Italian tone of sentiment in those great writers to whom we owe almost everything. What soothed the solitary hours of Surrey with a more powerful magic than Agrippa could have shown him?* What comforted the noble Sidney when he sought refuge in flight from the dangerous kindness of his too beautiful Stella? What potent charm could lure that genius, whose ambitious grasp an Eldorado had hardly sufficed, to utter his melodious plaint over "the grave where Laura lay?" From what source of perpetual freshness did Fletcher nourish his tenderness of soul, his rich pictorial powers, his deep and varied melodies? And what shall not be said of him, whose song was moralized by "fierce wars and faithful loves," that "sage, serious Spenser" of whom Milton speaks, and whom he "dares be known to think a better teacher than Scotus or

* The merciless blows levelled by editorial scepticism at the romantic story of Surrey have finished, it seems, by destroying the real Geraldine, as they began by dissipating her illusive semblance. See the last edition of Lord Surrey's poems, in Pickering's "Aldine Poets."

Aquinas?" It is worthy of remark that Spenser, attached as he was to the wilder strains of the chivalrous epic, has not, like most of his time, neglected the higher mood of the early Florentines. The "Hymns to Heavenly Love and Beauty," and many parts of the "Fairy Queen," especially the sixth canto of the Third Book, attest how thoroughly he felt the spirit of Petrarch, whom the generality of those writers seem to have known only through the Petrarchisti, so little do they comprehend what they profess to copy. It would have been strange, however, if, in the most universal mind that ever existed, there had been no express recognition of that mode of sentiment, which had first asserted the character, and designated the direction, of modern literature. I cannot help considering the sonnets of Shakspeare as a sort of homage to the Genius of Christian Europe, necessarily exacted, although voluntarily paid, before he was allowed to take in hand the sceptre of his endless dominion. I would observe, too, that the structure of these sonnets is perfectly Tuscan, except in the particular of the rhymes, — a deviation perhaps allowable to the different form of our language, although the examples of Milton and Wordsworth have sufficiently shown that it is far from indispensable. It is not easy to assign just limits to that glorious era, which, with rightful pride, we denominate the Elizabethan: but perhaps we may consider that strange tribe of poems inappropriately styled by Johnson the Metaphysical, as a prolongation of its inferior characteristics little calculated to form a fabric of themselves, although admirably adapted for ornament and relief. In some of these, however, there is a fervor and loyalty of feeling which show that the impression of the better Italian spirit was not effaced, although in constant danger of yielding to cumbrous subtleties of the understanding. I would in particular name Habington's "Castara," as one of those works which make us proud of living in the same land, and inheriting the same associations, with its true-hearted and simple-minded author. The restoration of Charles II. was the trumpet of a great woe to the poetry of England: from this time we may date the extinction of the Italian influence, as a national feeling, however it may occasionally be visible in the writings of scattered individuals.* But before the guardian angel of our land resigned for a season his flaming sword, unable to prevent the entrance of that evil snake, who ever watches round the enclosure of this island paradise, and seeks, by variation of shape, sometimes elevating a crest of treacherous lily whiteness, sometimes smoothing a polished coat of three magical hues, to introduce, as best he may, his malign presence into the abode of liberty and obedience,—before, I say, the higher literature of England became subject to Paris, its fainting energies were gathered up into one gigantic effort. Milton, it has

* Dryden, who led up the death-dance of Parisian foppery and wickedness, could not escape from his better nature, his strong conservative remnant of good old English feeling: but I see scarce any direct influence of the Italians in his writings. Of Pope, Thomson, Young, Goldsmith, Akenside, nothing can be said. The tesselated mind of Gray is partly made up of Italian reading: but there is too little vitality in his elegant appropriations to be communicative of life to that surrounding literature, which he had sense enough in some things to despise, but not strength enough to amend. In the present century we have seen a very successful attempt to transfer the light and graceful sportiveness of the Bernesque style into the weightier framework of our own language. I allude to Mr. Frere's "Whistlecraft," and the more celebrated productions of a late eminent genius, never perhaps so thoroughly master of himself as when indulging a vein of bitter mockery and sarcasm on subjects naturally calculated to awaken very different feelings.

been well said, constitutes an era by himself: no category of a class can rightly include him: we see at once in reading him, that he lives not in a genial age, and, unlike his predecessors, in whom knowledge as well as feeling has an air of spontaneity, he seems obliged to keep his will in a state of constant undivided activity, in order to hold in subservience the reluctantly ministering spirits of the outward and inward world. But in so far as this perpetually exerted energy has chosen for itself the place whereon it will act, it certainly brings him into close sympathy with his immediate forerunners, the Elizabethans, and through them with their Tuscan masters. Well, indeed, did it befit the Christian poet, who was raised up to assert the great fundamental truth of modern civilization, that manners and letters have a law of progression, parallel, though not coincident, with the expansion of spiritual religion, — to assert this, not indeed with the universality and depth with which the same truth had been asserted by Dante, yet with some relative advantages over him, which were necessarily obtained from a Protestant and English position; — well, I say, did it befit our venerable Milton to draw weapons for his glorious war from the inexhaustible armory of the "Divina Commedia," and acknowledge his honorable robberies in terms like these: "Ut enim est apud eos ingenio quis forte floridior, aut moribus amœnis et elegantibus, linguam Etruscam in deliciis habet præcipuis, quin et in solidâ etiam parte eruditionis esse sibi ponendam ducit, præsertim si Græca aut Latina, vel nullo, vel modico tinctu imbiberit. Ego certe istis utrisque linguis non extremis tantummodo labris madidus; sed, siquis alius, quantùm per annos licuit, poculis majoribus prolutus, possum tamen nonnunquam ad illum Dantem, et Petrarcham aliosque vestros complusculos, libenter et cupide comessatum ire: nec me tam ipsæ Athenæ Atticæ cum illo suo pellucido Ilisso, neque illa vetus Roma suâ Tiberis ripâ retinere valuerunt; quin sæpe Arnum vestrum, et Fæsulanos illos colles invisere amem."* What then shall we say of these things? The glories of the Elizabethan literature have passed away, and cannot return: we are removed from them by the whole collective space of two distinct literary manifestations. Is it certain, then, that we can do nothing but

* Epist. Benedicto Bonmatthæo Florentino, Milt. Pr. Op. p. 571, 40.

admire what they have been, and lament that they cannot be: or can it perhaps be shown, that although that Italian effluence has gone away into the past, and has been followed by others not more permanent than itself, it has yet a more immediate hold on our actual condition, than either of its successors? Let us for a moment consider these. I would not be understood, in what I have spoken concerning the influence of France, as believing that influence productive of unmixed evil. England, it should never be forgotten, had in the last century a great political part to perform. It was necessary perhaps that her language should receive some considerable inflexion, corresponding to the active tendency of the public mind, and expressive rather of the direct, palpable uses of life than of sentiments that overleap the present. For such a purpose the spirit of French literature, and the laws of French composition, were peculiarly fitted: nor is it a reasonable cause for regret that our language has taken into itself some of that wonderful idiomatic force, that clearness and conciseness of arrangement, that correct pointing of expression towards the level of general understanding, which distinguish the French tongue above all others with which we are acquainted, and render allowable a comparison between it and the Latin, which occupied nearly the same post in the old civilization as the organ, not of genial and original thinking, but of thoughts accumulated, set in order, smoothed down, and ready for diffusion. The close however of the last age, and the first quarter of the present, have witnessed a powerful reaction, as well in England as on the Continent, against the exclusive dominion of prosaic, and what are termed utilitarian tendencies in literature. It will not be disputed that the form at least of this reaction comes to us from Germany. Not until the offerings of Schiller and Goethe had been accepted, did Coleridge or Wordsworth kindle their sacrificial flame on the altar of the muses. Not until a whole generation of Germans had elaborated the laws of a lofty criticism, were its principles effective on our own writers. From them we received our good, and from them our evil. They taught us that the worship of Beauty is a vocation of high and mysterious import, not to be relegated into the round of daily amusements, or confined by the superstitious canons of temporary opinion. They held up to our merited derision that meagre spirit of systematized imbecility, which would proscribe the most important part of our human being, as guilty of impertinent interference with evident interest. But the sagacious remark of Bishop Lowth, that "the Germans are better at pulling down than at setting up," is not merely applicable to their historical criticism. It is a good and honorable thing to throw down a form of triumphant wrong, but unless we substitute the right, it had been well, perhaps, had we never stirred. The last state is often worse than the first. I do not hesitate to express my conviction, that the spirit of the critical philosophy, as seen by its fruits in all the ramifications of art, literature, and morality, is as much more dangerous than the spirit of mechanical philosophy, as it is fairer in appearance, and more capable of alliance with our natural feelings of enthusiasm and delight. Its dangerous tendency is this, that it perverts those very minds, whose office it was to resist the perverse impulses of society, and to proclaim truth under the dominion of falsehood. However precipitate may be at any time the current of public opinion, bearing along the mass of men to the grosser agitations of life, and to such schemes of belief as make these the prominent object, there will always be in reserve a force of antagonist opinion, strengthened by opposition, and attesting the sanctity of those higher principles, which are despised or forgotten by the majority. These men are secured by natural temperament, and peculiar circumstances, from participating in the common delusion: but if some other and deeper fallacy be invented; if some more subtle beast of the field should speak to them in wicked flattery; if a digest of intellectual aphorisms can be substituted in their minds for a code of living truths, and the lovely semblances of beauty, truth, affection can be made first to obscure the presence, and then to conceal the loss of that religious humility, without which, as their central life, all these are but dreadful shadows; if so fatal a stratagem can be successfully practised, I see not what hope remains for a people against whom the gates of hell have so prevailed. When the light of the body is darkness, how great is that darkness! Be this as it may; whether the Germans and their followers have or have not betrayed their trust, it seems at least that their influence is on the decline. The effects of what they have done are by no means extinct; the present generation is too much moulded by their agency to forget or escape it with ease: but the original causes have ceased to work, and the master-workers are departing from the earth. I believe the Revolution of 1830 has closed up the German era, just as the Revolution of 1789 closed up the French era. Looking then to the lurid presages of the times that are coming; believing that amidst the awful commotions of society, which few of us do not expect, — the disruption, it may be, of those common bands which hold together our social existence, necessarily followed by an occurrence on a larger scale of the same things that were witnessed in France forty years ago; the dispersion of those decencies and charities which custom produces and preserves, that mass of little motives, brought into unity and constancy of action by the mechanism of daily life, and far more efficacious in restraining civilized man from much headlong misery and crime than his pride is apt readily to acknowledge, — that, in such a desolation, nothing possibly can be found to support men but a true spiritual Christianity, I am not entirely without hope, that round such an element of vital light, constrained once more to put forth its illuminating energies for protection and deliverance to its children, may gather once again the scattered rays of human knowledge. In those obscured times, that followed the subversion of Rome, the muses clung not in vain for safety to the inviolate altars of the Catholic church. I have endeavored to point out some of the wonderful and beautiful consequences of this marriage of religion with literature; and I have been the more anxious to do this, as it has appeared to me by no means impossible, that the recurrence of analogous circumstances may produce, at no vast distance of time, a recurrence of similar effects. It is not wholly without the bounds of probability, that a purer spirit than the Roman Catholicism may animate hereafter a loftier form of European civilization. But should this be an idle dream (and indeed my own anticipations seldom incline to so favorable an aspect) it will not be the less useful or important, in times of unchristian ascendency, to fix our thoughts habitually on that first development of modern literature, which shows us the direct, and, as it were, natural influence of our religion on our conditions of society, and the expression of this in our inquiring thoughts and stirring emotions. An English mind that has drank deep at the sources of southern inspiration, and especially that is imbued with the spirit of the mighty Florentine, will be conscious of a perpetual freshness and quiet beauty, resting on his imaginations and spreading gently over his affections, until, by the blessing of heaven, it may be absorbed without loss, in the pure inner light, of which that voice has spoken, as no other can:

> "Light intellectual, yet full of love,
> Love of true beauty, therefore full of joy,
> Joy, every other sweetness far above." *

---

* "Luce intellettual, piena d'amore,
Amor di vero ben, pien di letizia,
Letizia, che transcende ogni dolzore."
D. C. Paradiso, c. 30.

ESSAY

ON

THE PHILOSOPHICAL WRITINGS OF CICERO.

"Ille, decus Latii, magnæ spes altera Romæ,
Ore effundit opes fandi certissimus auctor;
Tantum omnes superans præclaro munere linguæ,
Quantum iit ante alias Romana potentia gentes." —VIDA.

TO write worthily concerning the character of Cicero, would be an undertaking, than which few are more difficult, or more extensive. For, first, it is impossible not to be touched with reverence, and a kind of religious awe, when we look towards the figure of any great and noble mind, belonging, as regards his natural course, to times long departed, but living among us all, by his thoughts perpetuated in writing, which, actively circulating through numberless minds, and present without difficulty to several points of place and time, give us a far greater impression of efficiency than any act whatever (though voluntary, which these are not) of the same man, when conscious and alive. In fact, it is hardly to be thought surprising, that many should care for no immortality so much as this; for although there will be no sense, or pleasure of enjoyment in it, when it comes, they can relish it, at least, by anticipation, which has often a better taste than fruition, and they may have full assurance of its nature by observing the celebrity of other men. Some of these immortals, however, do not puzzle us much when, putting aside the first sentiments of wonder and respect, we step nearer to examine with precision their lineaments and true demeanor. But when we have to do with a mind of various powers, whose solicitous activity neither public business nor private study can exhaust, and which can steal time from the engrossing occupations of state policy for the pursuit of liberal knowledge, and the communication of it to mankind, we find ourselves involved in much perplexity, and feel that, even after some labor has been expended, it will be little better than guesswork that finally strikes the balance, and ascertains by relative estimation of unlike qualities his true station in the temple of fame. The jocular anathema, pronounced by Sir Robert Walpole on history in general, hits with peculiar force the judgments we form of motives and intellectual qualities, things so curiously complicated in the reality of nature, that our little knowledge has nothing to ground itself upon but a few loose rules collected by a very confined induction from external appearances. How little, in fact, does one creature know of another, even if he lives with him, sees him constantly, and, in popular language, knows all about him! Of that immense chain of mental successions, which extends from the cradle to the death-bed, how few links, comparatively speaking, are visible to any other person! Yet from these fragments of being (if the expression may be pardoned) you shall hear one decide as confidently about the unseen and unimagined whole, as a geologist from his chip of stone will explain the structure of the mass to which it belonged, and even the changes of fortune which it has received at the hand of time. Experience, however, the final judge, treats these two speculators in a very different manner. And what is the reason? Unfortunately, human beings are not lapidary formations: they are not even animals of pure understanding, which might come near it: their microcosm is as infinite in its forms as the world without us, and in one, as in the other, we must obey the laws by observation and experiment, before we can venture to command the elements by arbitrary combination. A question may be raised, whether, if the veil that obscures other existence from view were altogether removed, and that mode of immediate vision became usual, which Rousseau* fancied was more conceivable than the communication of motion by impact, we should, after all, derive much benefit from the change. But there can be no doubt it would wonderfully alter for the better our histories and biographical memoirs, and would effect a prodigious shifting of place among many worthies who are set high, or low, without much warrant, according to our present system of knowledge.

This Essay, however, has no such ambitious aim, as to include the whole character of Cicero within the scope of its observations. It is intended only to take a brief survey of one element in his diversified genius, the philosophical;

* See *Nouvelle Héloïse.*

but it will be difficult to mark the limits of this without an occasional glance at those other qualities, by which it is bounded, and which sometimes curiously intersect it. This will be evident if we consider that a question concerning the merits of Ciceronian philosophy naturally resolves itself into two parts. In what temper of mind, it should first be asked, did Cicero come to form and deliver his opinions? And, secondly, what those opinions were? Now the first of these is, beyond comparison, the most interesting and important. A man, it has been well said, "is always other and more than his opinions." To understand something of the predispositions in any mind, is to occupy a height of vantage, from which we may more clearly perceive the true bearings of his thoughts, than was possible for a spectator on the level. By knowing how much a man loves truth, we learn how far he is likely to teach it us: by ascertaining the special bent of his passions and habits, we are on our guard against giving that credit to conclusions in favor of them, which our notion of his discernment might otherwise incline us to give. But there is more than this. The inward life of a great man, the sum total of his impressions, customs, sentiments, gradual processes of thought, rapid suggestions, and the like, contains a far greater truth, both in extent and in magnitude, than all the fixed and positive forms of belief that occupy the front-row in his understanding. It is more our interest to know the first, for we know more in knowing it, and are brought by it into closer contact with real greatness. Opinion is often the product of an exhausted, not an energetic condition of mind: a few thoughts are sufficient to make up many opinions, and though these are always in some proportion to the degree of elevation allotted to their parent-mind, they are seldom, perhaps, its certain measure.

In the instance we have now to consider, many such predisposing influences will occur to the most careless observer. Cicero was a Roman, and we must view him with reference to the circumstances of Roman life, and the peculiar tendencies of its national feeling. He was a Roman statesman, and we must not forget the absorbing interest of politics in his time, and country, while we estimate the value he set on the calmer studies of his retirement. He was also a Roman gentleman, fond of social life, and capable of guiding and adorning its movements: he had elevated his family and name, by his own indefatigable exertions, from the ranks of provincial society; and was naturally ambitious of that life of literary brilliance which had already superseded in public estimation the honors of patrician birth, and was beginning to vie with the more substantial reverence paid to high dignities and large possessions. Above all, he was, by long habit and peculiar genius, a Roman orator, accustomed alike to the grave deliberations of the senate and the impassioned pleadings of the forum. All these influences (and some of them were not a little feverish and disturbing) he carried with him into the quiet fields and lucid atmosphere of philosophy. Whether he agitated that region by what he brought, more than he benefited himself, and through himself the world, by what he found, is an inquiry which may prove entertaining and useful, and which we shall be better able to bring to a satisfactory conclusion when we have considered rather more at length the relation of these previous tendencies to the investigation and discovery of truth.

It has been a favorite notion with those modern writers, who are fond of considering the unity of mood, produced by a constant action of similar circumstances on the mind of a nation, in rather an abstract point of view, that the Romans represent the *political*, as the Greeks did the *individual* development of human intelligence and energy. Whatever objections may lie against forms of expression, which, when habitually applied by speculators on history, are apt to mislead by a frequently recurring appearance of system, always seductive to the imagination, but proportionably dangerous to the observing intellect, it seems impossible to deny that much truth is contained in this remark. It is not of course meant, that the institutions of social convention did not attain a singular degree of perfection among the Grecian states, or that their complexion was not generally favorable to the cultivation of individual genius; but simply that no strong national spirit impelled the Greeks to national aggrandizement as the paramount object of their activity, which was the case with the conquering people who succeeded them in the career of civilization. A country of small republics, perpetually at strife with each other, had little unity of aim, except when menaced by barbarian inroads. Patriotism, indeed, was raised high in the scale of duties, and on the same plea that "omnes omnium caritates patria complectitur," the same energy was exerted for the public good, which afterwards, on a larger theatre, enforced the admiring submission of mankind. But the public sympathies of the Athenian were opposed to those of the Lacedemonian, and no single city threatened to absorb the world into the greatness of its name. The fascination of that name was wanting, and the sense of favoring destiny, which in the thought of every Roman blended his proud recollections of past triumph with the confident hope of an equally subservient future. Nor do we find that, where the bonds of Grecian polity were strongest, the vigor of literary genius was most conspicuous or effective. The severer, as well as the lighter Muses, fled from the walls of Sparta; for the patronage, extended by Lycurgus to the shade of Homer, failed to kindle the finer sentiments among the subjects of his legislation. On the other side (if we except the dramatic poets, whose local attachments were naturally strengthened by the necessities of their art), no strong sympathy with national advance or decline seems, under climates more congenial to art and knowledge, to have inspired the eminent leaders of human thought. Pindar attended on a court; Plato could exchange the liberal air of Athens for the atmosphere of Syracusan tyranny: Aristotle,* "the soul of the academy," was attached to it only by the life of its founder, and turned contentedly, after his death, to the court of Hermeas, and the counsels of Macedonian oppression. This comparative laxity of civil ties, owing perhaps in some measure to the capricious nature of those "fierce democraties" which made political eminence less desirable, because less secure, was conducive to that depth of meditation and comprehensiveness of views, which carried the Grecian spirit to heights of excellence, that will exercise the wondering gaze of our latest posterity. The sculptors and poets were left free to enjoy the unlimited inspiration of natural beauties, which are not of this age, or of that empire, but everlasting, and complete in themselves as the ideas they produce in the

* "'Ο *νους της διατριβης*," was the appellation given by Plato to his future rival.

meditative artist, who has a higher standard of perfection within him than the most glorious of recollected names — a Fabricius, a Brutus, or a Numa. Whatever elevation the contemplative and creative parts of our nature were fitted to attain, when left to the free exercise of their own functions, neither restrained, and, as it were, *overlaid* by a bond of national feeling intent on national glory, nor deriving an auxiliar, yet heterogeneous force from the diffusion of a spiritual faith ; such elevation, we may safely say, was attained by the Greeks. The fair inventions of their art, the pure deductions of their science, all the curious and splendid combinations of thought, which arise from the habit of viewing the circumstances of man in the single light of poetic beauty, or according to distinct forms of intellectual congruity, remain to us in their precious literature, and attest how clear, how serene, how majestically independent of merely local and temporary views, was the genius of ancient Greece, who laid the honey on the lips of Plato, and raised the temple of the graces within the bosom of Sophocles.

Everything in the Roman character was the

reverse of this, and announced to attentive reflection a different destiny, and a new evolution of mental nature. Sprung from the embrace of Mars, this people of determined warriors rose by slow degrees to an universal dominion, and every separate will, that came into action under the auspices of their patron god, seemed to bend itself by spontaneous impulse to fulfil his overruling intention and redeem his early promise. The infancy of Rome was nourished by a martial and religious poetry, which became extinct when the season of extended action arrived. Then the lessons taught and matured in probationary struggles with the brave Italian populations were applied to a tremendous battle against the several supremacies of Europe ; and, the scabbard being thrown away, that sword was displayed in irresistible splendor, which for a space of centuries was to tame the haughty and proudly spare the suppliant. Such was, throughout, the consistency of their progress, that all their institutions and customs bore the impress of one ruling idea ; and insensate things seemed to unite with human volitions in a glad furtherance of the glorious race. The paths of scientific discovery and secluded imagination were naturally unheeded by minds so strongly possessed with notions of "pride, pomp, and circumstance." Their ordinary pursuits were practical, and their highest aims political. They had no original literature, and they did not feel the want. There was much vigorous conception, but it all went into the outward world, the empire of their triumphant will.* When, at length, conquest brought luxury in its train, and artificial appetites sprang from the excess of social stimulus, the graces of a foreign lan-

* "The austere frugality of the ancient republicans, their carelessness about the possessions and the pleasures of wealth, the strict regard for law among the people, its universal and steadfast loyalty during the happy centuries when the constitution, after the pretensions of the aristocracy had been curbed, were flourishing in its full perfection, the sound feeling which never, amid internal discord, allowed of an appeal to foreign interference, the absolute empire of the laws and customs, and the steadiness with which, nevertheless, whatever in them was no longer expedient, was amended, the wisdom of the constitution, the ideal perfection of fortitude, realized in the citizens and in the state; all these qualities unquestionably excite a feeling of reverence which cannot equally be awakened by the contemplation of any other people." This summary of Roman virtues is extracted from the work of a philosophic historian, who proceeds to fill the opposite scale, and to mark out their vices with a wise impartiality. — See NIEBUHR. *Lecture prefixed to second edition of Translation, Hare and Thirlwall*, p. 26.

guage were first sought to supply a fashionable gratification, and soon produced their emollient effects of taste and refined pleasure; but they never touched the ground of character,* which was far too solidly fixed to admit of change from superinduction. Systems of philosophy were imported for the amusement and use of a highly civilized population; but amidst much ingenious discussion and collision of opinions, no sparks of strong philosophic thought were elicited; and those chasms in knowledge, which were left obscure by the burning lights of elder science, received no new illumination from the masters of the earth. If the obstacles to the rise of an original philosophy, grounded on the intrinsic character of the Romans, may fairly seem insuperable, they must doubtless be considered as deriving an immense accession of force from the peculiar condition of the republic in the age of Cicero. Corruption had reached the heart of the state; the few, in whom the lifeblood of patriotism still circulated, felt the indispensable importance and aw-

* Lucretius and Catullus are the confirming exceptions. That must indeed be a barren and fetid soil, in which poetry cannot strike a single root.

ful interest attached to an active life: the larger number, with whom a superficial acquaintance with theories, nicknamed philosophical knowledge, served as an excuse for indolence, or a varnish for vice, were constitutionally disqualified for the keen intuition of truth, and the generous mood of enthusiasm, in which suggestion strikes the mind like inspiration. The Greek teachers, from whom their little learning was immediately derived, were very unlike that former race, the θεοι παλαιοι of philosophy. There were exceptions, perhaps, at all events there were degrees of merit: a Posidonius,* or a Panætius, is not to be classed with the vulgar herd of sophists. But the general difference was too manifest to be mistaken: what in the hands of Plato had been an art, in those of Aristotle a science, was now become an easy trade. A minute fastidious casuistry supplied the place of that reasoning, and that "κρειττον τι λογου," which sought to elevate mankind to the level of true wisdom by an assiduous cultivation of sentiments possessed by

* Was it not a fine acknowledgment of the inherent supremacy of wisdom, when the imperatorial fasces were lowered by command of Pompey, before the person of Posidonius?

all, at least in the germ; sentiments, by whose action on a plastic imagination the most beautiful phenomena of mental combination are elicited, and a mass of desires and hopes receive their form and constitution, whose luminous nature repels the darkness of the grave. Wiser in their own generation than the children of light, these new instructors readily yielded to the prevalent temper of their age; and while they flattered the reigning profligacy of manners, by relegating morality into the arid regions of rules, maxims, and verbal distinctions, they effectually secured the profits and reputation of their own vagabond profession. The general tendency of men's minds at this momentous era, was unquestionably towards a sceptical indifference; such must ever be the effect of degenerate institutions and corrupted manners, accompanied with great operative energy in the machine of the state, and an habitual reliance of almost every individual mind on external and transitory things, the vicissitudes of fortune, and the obligations of palpable interest. It was an unbelieving age, and none who lived within its term escaped altogether the contagion. In periods of this description, the aphelia of national existence, some will generally be found who withstand to a certain extent the predominant tendency, and attest to a future generation the inherent dignity of our nature. Their efforts are limited, and their self-elevation is not constant; yet they are green places in the moral wilderness on which our thoughts should delight to linger.

If there be any truth in these observations, we should expect, *à priori*, what the examination of his writings will abundantly demonstrate, that the expressed mind of Cicero would exhibit signatures of both these impressions; the general impression, I mean, of national predilections, and active, external tendencies of thought; and that particular impression, originating in the character of the times, and leading to disputation about prevailing opinions, rather than independent research, to pulling down in the spirit of incredulity, without attempting to reconstruct in a temper of faith. But we could not have told beforehand, that he would be included in that small class of partial exceptions I have mentioned, and that the scepticism he shared with many was tinged and modified by a genial warmth, which was peculiarly his own.

Sometimes a disciple of Carneades, sometimes of Plato, he varies the tone of his language according to the alternate moods that possess him. In a memorable passage he owns, that to preserve the fair proportions of his moral edifice, it was necessary to keep out of thought and mention, "harum perturbatricem omnium academiam." *

I shall now consider a characteristic of Cicero's disposition, which was more dependent on himself, and the traces of which are everywhere perceptible in his life and writings. Whatever he thought, whatever he experienced, assumed with him an oratorical form. Truth had few

* "Exoremus ut sileat," he continues, "nam si invaserit in hæc quæ satis scite instructa et composita videantur, *nimis edet ruinas*, quam quidem ego PLACARE cupio, SUBMOVERE NON AUDEO." — De Legibus, i. 13. The principles of the Academic sect, "hæc ab Arcesilâ et Carneade recens," are unfolded in the books of Academic Questions, and those De Naturâ Deorum. In the Offices, l. ii. c. 2, he thus briefly expresses them: "Non sumus ii quorum vagetur mens errore, nec habeat unquam, quod sequatur: quæ enim esset ista mens, vel quæ vita potius, non solum disputandi, sed etiam vivendi ratione sublatâ? Nos autem, ut ceteri, qui alia certa, alia incerta esse dicunt, sic ab his dissentientes alia probabilia, contra alia improbabilia esse dicimus." Aulus Gellius, in a jesting manner, explains the difference between the Pyrrhonians and these Academics. "The latter," he says, were certain they could know nothing; the former were not more certain of that than anything else!"

charms for him, unadorned and αὐτη καθ' αὐτην; he delighted, indeed, in the analogies which reason presents; but it was because they are susceptible of brilliant coloring and emphatic display. Once, when undergoing the misery of exile, and disgusted for a time with the bold game he had been playing with the passions and habits that had made him what he was, he besought his friends "ut non oratorem se, sed philosophum appellarent, nam se philosophiam, ut rem sibi proposuisse, arte oratoriâ, tanquam instrumento, in rebus publicis tractandis uti." * Other times brought another language; and, in direct contradiction to the above, he has declared, in more than one passage,† what the internal evidence of his life and writings was amply sufficient to establish, that he learned philosophy "eloquentiæ gratiâ."

Much as has been said, since the idols were first stricken in the temple by the commissioned hand of Bacon, about the mischief of substituting poetical illustration for real cohesion of truth to truth, it may perhaps be found, on examination, that a rhetorical spirit is a more dangerous

* See Brucker, *Hist. Philosoph.*, vol. ii. p. 39, and his reference to Plutarch.

† See *Proem. Paradox.*, *Orator.* sub. init., Tusc. Quæst., 2, 3.

intruder. Poetry, indeed, is seductive by exciting in us that mood of feeling, which conjoins all mental states, that pass in review before it, according to congruity of sentiment, not agreement of conceptions: and it is with justice, therefore, that the Muses are condemned by the genius of a profound philosophy. But though poetry encourages a wrong condition of feeling with respect to the discovery of truth, its enchantments tend to keep the mind within that circle of contemplative enjoyment, which is not less indispensably necessary to the exertions of a philosophic spirit. We may be led wrong by the sorcery; but that wrong is contiguous to the right. Now it is part of our idea and description of oratory, that it appeals to the active functions of our nature. It is the bringing of one man's mind to bear upon another man's will. We call up our scattered knowledge, we arrange our various powers of feeling, we select and marshal the objects of our observation, and then we combine them under the command of one strong impulse, and concentre their operations upon one point. That point is in every instance some change in the views, and some corresponding assent in the will of the person, or persons, whom we address. Thus we are transported entirely out of the sphere of contemplation, and are submitted to the guidance of a new set of passions, far more vehement, confused, and perplexing, than those pure desires that elevate the soul towards the "οντως οντα," because they have far more immediate control over individual futurity, and are much more concerned with the representations of the senses. I do not mean to deny that the vivid impression of truth is naturally accompanied by its eloquent utterance. Wherever there is strong emotion, there will be always a corresponding vigor of expression, unless the channel between thought and language happens to be obstructed by peculiar causes. But eloquence is spread abroad among mankind, while oratory is the portion of a few. The one is the immediate voice of nature, and derives its charm from momentary impulse; the other is an art, circumscribed by definite laws which have their origin in the creative power of genius. Excited in the first instance by our social instincts, the faculty of speech has become to civilized man a source of independent pleasure, which mingles with, or rather constitutes, the delight of his solitary reveries and intellectual meditations. In proportion to the refinement of his feeling, the liveliness of his mental images, and the varieties of knowledge treasured up in memory, will be the graceful forms and multiplied combinations of his internal language. But as regards himself, if he has in any degree the power of searching out the relations of things by intellectual application, he will not suffer his trains of active thought to be trenched upon by those arrangements of diction, whose place is posterior to thought in natural order, and which appear to confer on the mind that forms them a kind of recompense for its keener labors of introspection. When again his eloquence is directed to others, a man of this description is too sensible of that truth, or belief, of which it is the spontaneous overflow, to have any reflex action of thought on his own relative position, and the power which he may exert to mould the determinations of those whom he addresses. He seeks to persuade, but it is because he is persuaded, and requires the concurrence of sympathy. He may lead his fellow-creatures from the truth; but this chance is unavoidable, so long as words are our only signs of notions and media of reasoning. Still everything has occupied its right place: the faculties have had free play, and each has kept clear of the other. But in a mind, whose conformation is oratorical, the whole process is in danger of being inverted and confused. The orator mistakes the suggestion of his art for the analogies of solid reason. He begins by arguing where he ought to infer, and thus deceives himself. Then he pleads when he ought to state, and thus deceives others. There is little danger, indeed, that an orator of the highest order, — a man, who not only feels the dignity of the mission which he fulfils, but who, from the clearness and multiplicity and uniform direction of his rapid ideas, acquires that intuitive and comprehensive intelligence, which by condensing, and, as it were, fusing his powers, almost seems to communicate to his soul a larger portion of existence, — there is little danger that such a man will relinquish his art, will leave this high mode of vision and power, will descend, as into plains and valleys, to the methods of ordinary knowledge, or (which is least probable) will transfer his attention to a new province of the higher intellect, the character of which is dissimilar, and requires capacities not moulded like his own. Let a man but enter deep into his favorite art, and he is not likely to make use of it to subvert the laws, or tarnish the qualities, of any other mental pursuit. Every art is the application of knowledge to some definite end; but the ends are many, and the methods are distinct. The fine or imaginative arts — painting, sculpture, music, and poetry — have for their end the production of a mood of delightful contemplation with the sense of beauty. A vivid impression of some mental state, as beautiful, tends to bring in a train of associated states, which will all be under the same mood of lively emotion, as the first in the train. If we change the character of the mood, the continuity of association will be broken, and there is nothing so disagreeable to the mind as any such interruption. Hence, if, while the mind is delineating its own previous states under the influence of some particular mood, any object is presented by casual association, the tendency of which is to excite feelings not congenial to that which has taken possession of the mind, there arises a perception of unfitness, and the object is rejected. This is the subtle law of Taste, that exists in the creative artist as a sort of conscience, against which his will may trespass, but his judgment cannot rebel. The same law is absolute for the orator:

but the difference in his case results from the difference of his aim, and, consequently, of his materials. He, too, resigns himself to one luminous mood, which extends its radiance over successive states, and is unwilling to admit any form of mental existence, besides itself. But his aim is the commotion of will, not the production of beauty. This, therefore, is the bearing of the emotion that casts an awakening light over his mind: by their analogy to this leading sentiment, the hosts of Suggestion are judged; and from a variety, thus harmonized, results the distinctive unity of his art. But the number of pure artists is small: few souls are so finely tempered as to preserve the delicacy of meditative feeling, untainted by the allurements of accidental suggestion. The voice of the critical conscience is still and small, like that of the moral: it cannot entirely be stifled where it has been heard, but it may be disobeyed. Temptations are never wanting: some immediate and temporary effect can be produced at less expense of inward exertion than the high and more ideal effect which art demands: it is much easier to pander to the ordinary, and often recurring wish for excitement, than to promote the rare and difficult intuition of beauty. To raise the many to his own real point of view, the artist must employ his energies, and create energy in others: to descend to their position is less noble, but practicable with ease. If I may be allowed the metaphor, one partakes of the nature of redemptive power; the other, of that self-abased and degenerate will, which "flung from his splendors" the fairest star in heaven. They who debase, in this manner, the persuasive art, are commonly called rhetoricians, not orators. They speak for immediate effect, careless how it is produced. They never measure existing circumstances by the relations of the πιθανον, internally perceived. In the mind of the true orator, all accidents of place and time seem to be attracted to the magnetic force of his conceptions, which have an order of their own, not wholly dependent on the observation of the moment. But the rhetorician makes himself the servant of circumstances, and yet, after all, cannot penetrate their meaning. His examination is close and coarse, and he sees little, in his hurry to see better; the orator stands upon a height, and commands the whole prospect, and can modify his view by the lens of genius. Between the pure orator and the mere rhetorician many shades of mixture intervene. To degrade that powerful mind, which in its maturity of vigor uttered "tonitrua magis quam verba" against the desperate Catiline, and whose later age produced the "divina Philippica," to the lowest of these ranks, would be to pass sentence on my own judgment: but I must hesitate, even against the opinion of many wise men, before I consent to elevate him to the highest. The loftier powers of imagination were altogether wanting. There was none of the vivid painting and instinctive sublimity, which make Demosthenes the model of ages. His happiest efforts are efforts still; the process of intellectual construction is always palpable; and though the ingenuity may be wonderful, and command our high approbation, our minds have in reserve something higher than approbation, and ingenuity will not call it forth. Cicero won, and ruled his audience, not by flashes of inspiration, but by industrious thought. The thoughts were not wonderful in themselves, were not born one out of another by a generation so rapid as to seem mysterious; but were accumulated by separate exertions of will, and produced their effect by the gross amount of numberless deliberations. Where understanding is more active in production than feeling, the predominance of rhetoric (to use the word "in malam partem") over true oratory is the certain result. But when this happens to any mind, it will be no easy matter to restrain this predominant tendency within the limits of its own pursuit. The delicate sense of fitness, which grows with the growth of the contemplative feelings, becomes weak when they are neglected; and the busy intellect, unembarrassed by its inconvenient monitions, begins to meddle with all the range of practical and speculative knowledge in a temper of incessant argumentation.

From these considerations it is evident that Cicero labored under strong previous disadvantages in his approach to the sanctuary of Wisdom. The "φυγα μονου προς μονον," preached by the latter Platonists, was not possible for him. He did not come *alone;* he brought with him a thousand worldly prepossessions, which were to him as the veil of the temple at Sais, hiding impenetrably, "that which was, and had been, and was to be." He adventured, nevertheless; and if he wanted altogether the originality and freshness of the Grecian thinkers, we owe to his industry, patience, and acuteness, the general diffusion and reduction to popular language of much that had been finely thought, and without him might never have obtained free currency among mankind. I shall proceed to notice briefly the opinions maintained by him on some of the most important subjects of human speculation.

It is doubtless in the character of a moral instructor, that Cicero challenges the largest share of our admiration. The simplicity and distinctness of his precepts render them intelligible to all, while the gravity and persuasive energy, the richness and graceful elegance of his manner, tend to fix them in memory, and interest the imagination in their behalf. Seldom or never does he rise to the occasional elevation of Seneca, but he is free also from that writer's exaggeration and causeless refinements. All that department of morality, which contains the duties of justice, and from which public and private legislation immediately emanate, was treated by him with the greatest copiousness and accuracy. This the view I have taken of his ruling habits would lead us to expect; and it is certain that this branch of philosophical knowledge could not but borrow additional vigor from his political pursuits. After the example of Plato, he composed six books "De Republicâ," (the newly-recovered treasure of our fortunate age!) on which he evidently rested much of his reputation, because he had applied to their composition the utmost maturity of his thoughts. His notions of government were large and republican; yet they differ perhaps as much from the popular schemes of the eighteenth and nineteenth centuries, as from Filmer's patriarchal theory or the profligate slavishness of Hobbism. They are the principles by which Rome sprang up and flourished; the corruption of which changed her vigorous prosperity into splendid misery of decay. They contain the idea of a balanced constitution, with a preponderating influence of the higher ranks, as the best means offered by the experience of ages for approximating to that ideal condition of a state, which the ancients never lost sight of, the ἀριστοκρατια or government by the wisest and best. We meet no traces in what Cicero has written of his considering a nation as a mere aggregate of individuals on a particular point of geographical position, the majority of whom have an inalienable right to bind the minority by their will and pleasure. That venerable name, the Nation, implied for him a body of men, actuated by one spirit; by a community, that is, of habits, feelings, and impressions from circumstances, tending to some especial development of human nature, which without that especial combination would never have existed, and fulfilling therefore some part of the great Providential design. That other word, the State, was not less sacred; for it denoted the natural form of action assumed by the nation; the mass of well-cemented institutions by which the particular character of its condition of feeling was best expressed in habitual conduct, so as to enable it to be continually, but gravely progressive. His attachment, however, to the interests of stability and order never for a moment induced Cicero to forget his Roman abhorrence of the kingly office and title. In everything he spoke for law and counsel, proscribing arbitrary will, I have said that he carried his politics too far into philosophy; it is time to say the converse, that his politics were uniformly philosophical.

That important division of Ethics, which enforces the moral necessity of self-restraint, and prescribes its most salutary methods, furnished our author with a wide field for his rhetorical powers. This subject may, indeed, be considered as exhausted by the ancients: the wit of man will probably say nothing finer, or more calculated to set this duty in the clearest light of reason, than has already been put on record by the heathen moralists. Many of them have surpassed Cicero in the energy of their conceptions: but it would be difficult to point out any of their arguments for the power of man over himself, which are not touched upon in the books "De Officiis," the "Tusculan Questions," and others of a like description. It is true we find little that appears entirely his own; he used with no niggard hand the stores of his predecessors, and hardly seemed to have much confidence in what he said, unless he could get somebody else to vouch for it. The Stoic, Panætius, supplied him with the whole scheme, and most of the details in his Offices. From the Epicureans, whose general doctrine he regarded with aversion, he seems to have borrowed those views concerning friendship,* which diffuse a gentle light over the

* I mean their conviction of its importance, and earnest recommendation of it by counsel and by practice, not their theory of "*φιλια δια χρειας*," against which Cicero justly inveighs. The friendships of the Epicureans were famous all over the world.

sterner aspect of his other opinions. The inflexible followers of Zeno and Chrysippus were entirely devoted to the heroic attributes of human will: * they often mistook pride for virtue; the selfish feeling that leads men to persevere in a particular course of thought and conduct, in order to prove to themselves their power of determination, for the humble and self-sacrificing spirit, which desires only to know itself as the servant of conscience and of God. Their κατορθωμα, or ideal life of rectitude, was entirely devoid of passion, and incapable (had they known it!) of virtue, as of vice. The later Stoics, indeed, were made of better stuff: a new light had then begun to shine in the darkness of the world, and the warmth of its beams made them unconsciously relax the folds of their "Stoic fur." "Αμα ἀπαθεστατον εἶναι, ἅμα δε φιλοστοργοτατον," is the milder form in which the imperial sage contemplated his idea of moral perfection. Before the time of Cicero, the meek and passive

Gassendi is so impressed with the amiable picture of concord, and pleasant intercourse, that he is ready to believe "talem Societatem cælestis concordiæ sinu genitam, nutritam, ac finitam." — *De vita et moribus Epicuri* l. ii. c. 6.

* "Την προαιρεσιν," says Epictetus, in the spirit of the founder, "ουδε ὁ Ζευς νικησαι δυναται."

affections were held by these scholastics unworthy of the loftiness of virtue. Fortunately, however, he was not, like them, a philosopher by profession; he was a Roman gentleman, and would not consent to give up feelings that adorned society, and constituted domestic life. His dialogues "De Amicitiâ" and "De Senectute" have a fine mellow tone of coloring, which sets them perhaps above all his other works in point of originality and beauty.* They come more from the man himself: spontaneous pleasure from his heart seems, like a delicate ether, to surround the recollections he detains, and the anticipation he indulges. How grand and distinct is the person of Cato! What a beautiful blending of the individual patriot, as we know him from history, with the ideal character of age!

When we pass from the eloquent moralities of Cicero to examine the foundations of his ethical system, we find a sudden blank and deficiency. His praises of friendship, as one of the duties as well as ornaments of life, never seem to have

* I learn, with pleasure, that this is also the opinion of one of the greatest of our great men now alive, — the Reformer of English Poetry, the author of the "Lyrical Ballads," and the "Excursion."

suggested to his thoughts any resemblance of that solemn idea which alone solves the enigma of our feelings, and while it supplies a meaning to conscience, explains the destination of man. That he had read Plato with delight, we see abundant tokens, and his expressions of admiration and gratitude to that great man remain as indications of a noble temper: but that he had read him with right discernment can hardly be supposed, since he prefers the sanctions of morality provided by the latter Grecian schools to the sublime principle of love, as taught by the founder of the Academy. My meaning perhaps requires to be explained more in detail.

Love, in its simplest ethical sense, as a word of the same import with sympathy, is the desire which one sentient being feels for another's gratification, and consequent aversion to another's pain. This is the broad and deep foundation of our moral nature. The gradations of superstructure are somewhat less obvious, because they involve the hitherto obscure process by which there arises a particular class of emotions,* affecting us with pleasure or with pain, according as the condition of our affections is

* I refer to Sir J. Mackintosh's "Dissertation on Ethical Philosophy," (prefixed to the Supplement of the "Encyclopædia Britan-

sympathetic, or the reverse. These emotions are, in one sense, the strongest we possess, because they are independent of our senses, and of external circumstances, and are only conversant with the sources of action: yet, for this very reason, they too often succumb to other passions, less intimately connected with the permanent parts of our constitution, as active beings, but nourished by the changing accidents of sensation; and, in this view, we may lament, with Butler, that "conscience has not power, as she has authority."

The accession of this new mode of consciousness introduces a new kind of affection to other beings, compounded of the original sympathy, and of what has been termed moral complacency.* A notion of similar susceptibility gave occasion to that primary sentiment; and now a community of moral disposition is required for the exercise of this secondary sentiment. We do not cease to be moved by the first: but we have superinduced another, more restricted

nica,") the most important contribution, in my very humble judgment, which, for many years, has enlarged the inductive philosophy of mind.

* See "A Dissertation on the Nature of Virtue," by Jonathan Edwards, — clarum et venerabile nomen, of which America may be justly proud!

in its choice of objects, but attaching us more powerfully, because derived from a more developed nature. Other developments of our faculties will successively produce other similarities; and determine, in different directions, our sensibility; but since our whole frame of thought and feeling is affected by our moral condition, and "an operation of conscience precedes every action deliberate enough to be called in the highest sense voluntary," * this great principle of *moral community* will be found to pervade and tinge every sort of resemblance, sufficient to give rise to attachment.

To inspire men with this virtuous passion, which however dispersed over particular affections, and perceptible in them, has, like conscience, from which it springs, too little hold on sensation to act often from its own unaided resources, was the great aim of the Platonic philosophy. Its mighty master, who "πτηνῳ διφρῳ ἐφεζομενος" discerned far more of the cardinal points of our human position than numbers, whose more accurate perception of details has given them an inclination,† but no right, to sneer at his immor-

* Mackintosh, *Dissert.*, p. 181.

† We need not wonder at the flippant Bolingbroke for jesting at

tal compositions — Plato saw very early, that to communicate to our nature this noblest kind of love, the love of a worthy object, would have the effect of a regeneration to the soul, and would establish conscience in nearly the same intimacy with the world of the senses, which she already maintains with our interior existence. Hence his constant presentation of morality under the aspect of beauty, a practice favored by the language of his country, where from an early period the same *το καλον* had comprehended them both. Hence that frequent commendation of a more lively sentiment than has existed in other times between man and man, the misunderstanding of which has repelled several from the deep tenderness and splendid imaginations of the Phædrus and the Symposium, but which was evidently resorted to by Plato, on account of the social prejudices which at that time depressed woman below her

Plato (see Fragments and Minutes of Essays, passim): the lofty intellect of Verulam may well be permitted to occupy its view with the abundant future, even to the detriment of his judgments on antiquity; but what excuse shall be made for Montesquieu, when he coolly pronounces the Platonic dialogues unworthy of modern perusal, and is half inclined to wonder what the ancients could find to like in them? — See *Lettres Persannes.*

natural station, and which, even had the philosopher himself entirely surmounted them, would have rendered it perhaps impossible to persuade an Athenian audience that a female mind, especially if restrained within the limits of chastity and modest obedience, could ever possess attractions at all worthy to fix the regard, much less exhaust the capacities of this highest and purest manly love. There was also another reason. The soul of man was considered the best object of ἐρως, because it partook most of the presumed nature of Divinity.* There are not wanting in the Platonic writings clear traces of his having perceived the ulterior destiny of this passion, and the grandeur of that object, which alone can absorb its rays for time and for eternity. The doctrine of a personal God, himself essentially love, and requiring the love of the creature as the completion of his

* When a general admiration for Plato revived with the revival of arts and learning, the difference of social manners, which had been the gradual effect of Christianity, led men naturally to fix the reverential and ideal affection on the female character. The expressions of Petrarch and Dante have been accused as frigid and unnatural, because they flow from a state of feeling which belonged to very peculiar circumstances of knowledge and social position, and which are not easily comprehended by us who live at a different period.

being, often seems to tremble on the lips of the master, but it was too strange for him, too like a fiction of wayward fancy, too liable to metaphysical objections. "It is difficult," he says, "to find, and more difficult to reveal, the Father of the Universe." * There he left it, and there it remained, until the message of universal baptism was given to the twelve. Few or none of the immediate successors to Plato were impressed with the religious character of his philosophy; or if their hearts were conscious of a new and stirring influence, while they perused those sacred writings, their understanding took no note of its real tendency, but ascribed it to the effect of eloquence, or the Socratic method. The Alexandrian school indeed read with open eyes,†

* In Timæo.

† Many tenets, however, of the New Platonists were perversions from the original doctrine to serve an especial purpose. These factious recluses hated Christianity even more than they reverenced its precursor; and for the erotic character, impressed on the new religion, they would have gladly substituted visions of intellectual union with the Absolute, and complete abstraction from the inlets of sensation. The old Platonic language, out of which they manufactured their systems, was made use of probably by its author, as the best means he could devise for elevating the minds of his hearers above low and vulgar motives. I have no faith in those who fancy a scheme of his real opinions may be constructed

but Christianity had given them the hint: and it is beyond contradiction, that, before the Christian era, the only part of the earth's surface in which the First and Great Commandment was recognized, hardly occupied a larger extent than the principality of Wales, and was inhabited by a set of stiff-necked people, whom the polite and wise of this world esteemed below their contempt. Upon this insulated nation how wonderful had been the effect produced! In their singular literature a strong light was thrown upon recesses of the human heart, unknown to Grecian or Roman genius. Their thoughts pursued a separate track, and their habits of life, consonant to those thoughts, were unlike the customs of nations. In them we see a new phase of the human character, the same that has since been expanded by the Christian dispensation, and the loftiest we can conceive to

from his works, or that it was any part of his design to improve mankind by the communication of psychological knowledge. When he relates a legendary tale, like that of Atlantis in the Timæus, we do not suppose it necessary to suppose his credence of the story, but are content to take it for a beautiful piece of mythology, illustrating and serving the main purpose of the dialogue. Why should we not believe the same of his purely metaphysical dissertations?

exist in any body of men. It proceeds from the recognition of God, as a living and proximate agent, constituting the course of nature and suspending it at will, raising up and overthrowing nations by particular providence, and carrying on a perpetual war for the salvation of each individual soul. The spirit of holy love flows naturally from this faith, and fulfils the obligations of conscience. But it seems impossible that the unrevealed Divinity, however credited by natural reason, should inspire such transports as glowed in the bosoms of Hebrew prophets, or dulled the torture of those flames and racks on which Christian martyrs were eager to expire. Revelation is a voluntary approximation of the Infinite Being to the ways and thoughts of finite humanity. But until this step has been taken by Almighty Grace, how should man have a warrant for loving with all his heart and mind and strength? How may his contracted and localized individuality not be lost in the unfathomable depths of the Eternal and Immense? Can he love what he does not know? Can he know what is essentially incomprehensible? The exercise of his reasoning faculties may have convinced him that a Supreme Mind exists, but the same faculties should have taught that its nature is perfectly dissimilar from the only mind with which he is acquainted, and that when he gives it the same name, it is with reference to the similarity of the respective effects. If regardless of the limits within which he is bound to philosophize, he admits a little Anthropomorphism into his system of belief, yet he will hardly venture to consider a passion, resembling human love, enough to deserve the same appellation, as in any degree compatible with that independent felicity, which he ascribes to the Being of beings. How then can he love a Spirit, to whose happiness he bears no relation, and whose perfections, since they are vast, must be vague, embodied in no action, concentrated upon no point of time? The thing is impossible, and has never been. Without the Gospel, nature exhibits a want of harmony between our intrinsic constitution, and the system in which it is placed. But Christianity has made up the difference. It is possible and natural to love the Father, who has made us his children by the spirit of adoption: it is possible and natural to love the Elder Brother, who was, in all things, like as we are, except sin, and can succor those in temptation, having been himself tempted. Thus the Christian faith is the necessary complement of a sound ethical system.

Ignorant by his position of this fact, untaught by imagination and meditative feeling, the attendant δαιμονες of Plato, to discern the tendencies of man towards this future consummation, the author of Roman philosophy sought a foundation for his moral system in the opposite hemisphere of mind. He turned from the groves of Academus, and the refreshing source "μαλα ψυχρου ὑδατος," * to embrace the stately doctrine of Stoicism, or that of the Peripatetics, which he considered as differing rather in words than matter. He left the heart for the head, sentiment for reason ; and placed himself boldly in the ranks of those, who, reversing the order of nature, have endeavored to confound the character of our reflection on feeling, with the character of feeling itself, and seek to account for the moral obligation of beings whose activity derives from emotion, by theories only respective of a subsequent congruity in perception. The great and palpable distinctions between the Epicurean and Stoical systems are exposed on the

* See the exquisite passage in the *Phædrus*, sub init.

surface of history, and it would be idle to repeat an enumeration, so often made, and so familiar to the most hasty reader. But they may be considered in a more universal relation, than perhaps they yet have been, as illustrating the different positions of human intelligence, with respect to religion on one hand, and philosophical truth on the other. Some justice perhaps remains to be done to Epicurus, if it can be shown, as I think it can, that his inspection of human nature elicited results of great importance to the science of mind, and conformable to the discoveries of modern analysis, although he did not perceive the real connection and place of these facts, and suffered himself to cover their meaning by a paralogism of specious simplicity, because his mental sight was more quick and keen than it was steady, his imagination not sufficiently delicate to inspire such pure wishes as might have kept up attentive research in the right quarter.

It is important to keep in mind, while we investigate the progress of ancient philosophy, that the province of metaphysical analysis was not (and before the Christian era, could not safely be) disjoined from that of moral instruction. A school of philosophy stood in the place, and answered the purpose, as far as it was able, of a national church. To trace the origin of emotions, and the connection of motives in the mind, was an object, which, however interesting to the lover of truth, yet was justly considered subordinate to the enforcement of moral duties, and the exhibition of the beauty of virtue to the heart. It is a circumstance of the utmost moment in the history of our race, and one which seems an admirable sign of superintending wisdom, that while problems relating to the original formation and secret laws of conscience continue to allure and baffle our speculation, its main results have never admitted of sufficient doubt to perplex those simple reasonings upon them, which from the earliest ages, and in the darkest times, have made the plainest form of address from man to man, for the encouragement of good, and the depression of evil. But it is clear, also, that the obviousness of these materials for moral argument, and the necessity, felt by every good man, and felt in proportion to his intensity of meditation on these subjects, of using his mental energies to inculcate the lessons deduced from them, must have operated in no slight degree to prevent or confuse a calm, strict, intellectual examination of these all-important parts of our constitution, as objects of inductive science. Truth is a jealous, as well as a lovely mistress; and she will never brook in her adorers a divided attention. On the other hand, such is the awful solemnity that invests the shrine of virtue, that we cannot wonder if they who perceived the signatures of divinity upon it, were reluctant to examine its structure, and determine its proportions. From these premises, I think, we should be led to expect a more rigorous prosecution of the metaphysics of Ethics among those sects of philosophy, which have least claim on our moral approbation and reverence. We should not look for careful distinction, or close deduction, where we discover the ardor of a noble enthusiasm, and admire an exalted conviction of the purposes, for which our nature was framed, and the dignity to which it may arrive. We should seek them rather among colder temperaments, devoid of imaginative faith, and susceptible of no emotion so strongly, as of the delight in dispelling illusion, and clearly comprehending the fundamental relations of our ideas. In laying down this position, I hope I shall not be understood to assert a real superiority in this latter class of thinkers. The previous part of this Essay will sufficiently testify my opinion, that the man who is deficient in susceptibility of emotion will make a sorry survey of mental phenomena, precisely because he will leave out of his account the most extensive and efficient portion of the facts. On the other hand, one who contemplates nature through the medium of imagination and feeling, perceives innumerable combinations of subtle emotion, which are entirely out of the other's sight, and does infinitely more to increase the gross amount of human knowledge than the mere logical observer. We must distinguish, however, between the principles of mental growth, and their products. We are more concerned to know the latter, because it is the infinite variety of these which constitutes our existence. To this knowledge more is ministered by passion than by all the forms of dispassionate perception. But for the particular purpose of searching out the simple principles, on which these manifold results are dependent, the requisite habits of thought are entirely different. The mind must, as much as possible, abstract itself from the influence which all associated modes exert on the will, and permit no feeling, except the desire of truth, to come in contact with the conceptions of the understanding. Of course this will be especially necessary, when the object of research happens to be the character and origin of our moral sentiments: for as none carry such authority with them, so none are more likely to act as a disturbing force. This view receives abundant illustration from the history of every period in the progress of philosophy; but, as has been already intimated, the facts it embraces are most palpable among the ancients, because Christianity has materially altered our situation with respect to ethical studies. That mighty revolution which brought the poor and unlearned into the possession of a pure code of moral opinion, that before had existed only for the wise, and crowned this great benefit by another, of which we have spoken above, which is still more incalculably valuable, the insertion of a new life-giving motive into the rude mass of human desires, could not fail to add freedom and vigor to intellectual inquiry, by the satisfaction it afforded to moral aspiration, and the certainty, or even triteness, imparted by it to many topics, which in former days had occupied much of the time and thought of philosophers. A little reflection, indeed, will serve to show us that the causes of hindrance are not removed, but only weakened by the change, and that during some periods in the growth of Christian civilization, they will operate with a force, nourished by the circumstances, and fulfilling the purpose of those peculiar epochs. But into these considerations I have not now to enter: I wish to apply the rules of judgment I have endeavored to establish to the origin of these rival factions of the Porch and the Garden.

The first philosopher who fairly handled the question of Final Good * (a question which once

* Theories, which made pleasure the chief good, were not indeed unknown before his time, since the school of Cyrene had expressly taught this opinion, and we learn from Aristotle that Eudoxus had similar views. But Aristippus was a coarse sensualist, like our own Mandeville, and the influence of Eudoxus does not appear to have been extensive, or his theory anything better than a formula for selfish habits. In the best schools of antiquity this question is little dwelt upon, and never started in the precise, scholastic shape which it assumed when dialectics became fashionable. Even Aristotle, the great representative of the analytic and theorizing tendencies of human intellect, evades the real metaphysical question concerning the nature of virtue, while his delineations of the habits it produces, are most of them excellent, and his collection of facts of mental experience invaluable, both as a specimen of induction, and an integral part of our sum of knowledge.

set in agitation has continued to excite the most contentious discussion, and has not yet been consigned to a satisfactory repose) was the first also who uplifted a daring voice against the solemn articles of universal belief. Epicurus, who had laid his sacrilegious hand upon the altars of mankind, was not deterred from his pursuit of first principles by any superstitious reverence for the unapproachable sanctity of virtue. Instead of assuming certain impressions as causes, before he had ascertained them not to be effects, he thought it best to begin at the beginning, to discover first by experience some ultimate element in the mind, and then, returning by the way of cautious induction, to trace the extent of its operations, before he ventured to petition Nature for another principle. In this return he committed some very important mistakes: but it has appeared to me that his beginning was correct, and his erroneous additions easily separable from the incumbered truths. When this eminent man commenced his reflections on human life, his attention seems to have been most forcibly arrested by one primary fact. He saw that man, besides the perceptions of his senses, has two distinct natures; two distinct classes, that is, of mental states, in which he successively, or simultaneously exists; the one "χωρις λογου," founded in his susceptibility of pleasure and pain, and comprehending all the wonderful combinations of these elements from the simplest forms of delight and grief to the most composite invólutions of passion: the other, which is made up of *conceptions* of what has previously existed either for the senses, or the emotions, or this very conceptive faculty, and which, while it brings us irresistible evidence of our connection with something *past*, inspires us with an equal certainty that we can govern something *future*. He perceived (few so clearly) that to the first of these natures alone is intrusted the high prerogative of directing those states of mind which immediately precede action. Pleasure he found in every desire, desire in every volition; spontaneousness in every act. Throughout the whole range of consciousness he could find no instance in which a conceptive state, a mere thought, stood in the same close relation to any voluntary process, which is occupied by the various conditions of feeling. Having made this discovery, that pleasure is the mainspring of action, he lost no time in communicating it to the world; but, unfortunately, in his haste to apply this principle, he coupled it with another, utterly unproved, and, as it soon appeared, not only incapable of proof, but productive of the most detrimental consequences to all who received it for truth. He asserted, that as Pleasure is a constituent part of every desire, so it must needs be the only object desired. The assertion has in all ages found an echo, and, while it cannot be matter of surprise that such doctrine should find supporters among the profligate, or the feeble, among republicans declining to luxurious ruin, or the courtly flatterers of a munificent tyranny; yet even an habitual observer of those metaphysical cycles, in which human opinions have their periodical seasons of fluctuation, might perhaps be inclined to deviate from his "nil admirari," when he sees a fallacy, liable to such easy detection, reproduced and defended in some more favored generations. We all in common conversation and common thought presume the *object* of a desire, that which it exclusively regards, and by which it is limited, to be the very thing which makes a difference between the *quality* of that desire, and the quality of any other. Now, desire can only be excited by a thought of the object;* and as we can certainly form a thought of our neighbor's pleasure, as well as of our own, it seems absurd to contend, that no such thought can be the exciting cause, and represent the external object of our desire.† The reality of benevolence is the

* Strictly speaking, nothing but *the thought* should be called the *object* of desire. For desire implies futurity, and nothing future can *actually* exist, although it may be represented. If we wish to give an exhaustive definition of that internal condition, which we experience when we desire, we must include not only the strong pleasurable impulse, together with the painful sense of privation, but an accompanying judgment that our thought is not fallacious, and will have a corresponding reality in the nature of things.

† The idea of our own previous pleasure may sometimes coexist with, or form part of such a thought, but when we feel generously it occupies a small place, and in point of fact *is never the part regarded.* The desire of happiness considered as *permanent well-being,* is still more repugnant to the presence of virtuous desire, which is always intensely occupied with some *proximate* point of futurity, beyond which it does not cast a glance. To excite the desire of happiness, or rational self-love, (*amour de soi,* as distinguished from *amour propre*) in order to produce a *return* to virtue, is laudable, and very effectual. In the imperfect condition of humanity this is the strongest impulse to those heights which the soul is "competent to gain," but not "to keep." Upon them, however, "purior æther Incubat, et largè diffuso lumine ridet." The act of loving another excludes self-love. An eternity, then, which should consist in love of God, would imply, by the terms of the definition, the impossibility, not of feeling felicity, nor even of reflecting upon it, but certainly of *desiring* its continuance for

corner-stone in the sanctuary; "those who fall upon it will be broken." However a right feeling may have made their conclusions better than their premises, when they come to touch upon this subject the inconsistency of their theories will appear. But those, "upon whom it shall fall"—who have been fatally led by their speculations into correspondent practice—"it will grind them to powder!" "C'est la manie," says Rousseau, "de tous les philosophes de nier ce qui est, et de prouver ce qui n'est pas." Epicurus, having commenced with a mistake of the latter kind, in assuming one thing as proved, because he had shown another to be true, proceeded to deny, or at least to pass over, the most important function of our nature. No one, he said, could live rightly without living pleasurably; and no one pleasurably, without living rightly. But he omitted to say, that the pleasure arising from virtuous action is a *peculiar* pleasure, *differing in kind from every other;* because it gratifies a peculiar desire, which is not excited by the conception of any external circumstance, but solely by the thought of pure,

its own sake. That one sublime love would embrace the whole range of desirous susceptibility in the mind.

disinterested affection, or qualities conducive to it. By this confusion of the pleasures and pains, dependent on moral desire, with others which result from extrinsic circumstances, and never therefore can affect the essentials of our emotive constitution, although they may accidentally be connected with its operations, the door was opened to those dangerous heresies, which set up external advantages, as the legitimate aims of virtue, and discourage not only the refined enjoyments that rest in contemplation, but that large proportion of a happy life, which is composed of subtle and minute pleasures, accompanying action and evanescent in it, leaving few distinct traces perhaps in our visible existence, but unspeakably valuable, because they communicate a healthful tone to our whole mental system. In spite of these grievous errors, whose consequences ran riot through many generations, there was this merit in the Epicurean theory, that it laid the basis of morality in the right quarter. Sentiment, not thought, was declared the motive power: the agent acted from feeling, and *was* by feeling: thoughts were but the ligatures that held together the delicate materials of emotion.

But the doctrine, which has conferred immortality on the name of Zeno of Cittium, contained no sound *psychological* principle. It was wrong in the beginning, wrong in the middle, wrong in the end. It was not less opposed to the Epicurean system in its fundamental principles, than in its practical results. Impressed with the grandeur of moral excellence, and the beauty of that universal harmony which it seems to subserve, the Stoics thought they could not recede too far from the maxims of their irreligious opponents.* They protested against the simple tenet, from which such fatal consequences were ostensibly derived. "Not the capacity of pleasure," they said, "but the desire of self-preservation, was the original cause of choice and rejection in the human mind." They did not perceive they were beginning a step lower than the Epicureans, without in the least affecting that axiom, which alone in fact could make this step possible. For how can we conceive a desire of which pleasure is not a component part? There can be no desire in the mind, until some object is

* Zeno came into the field before his rival: but there can be no question that the Stoical doctrines were much influenced, and kept in extremes, by the repelling force of the new opinions.

contemplated as delightful. Again, Self only exists to our consciousness as the common character of a series of momentary beings. The proposition, I desire my preservation, includes, if it is not defined by, this other; one of these momentary beings exists in the pleasurable thought of a possible successor. Now, what has made the thought pleasurable? Unquestionably, a previous experience of similar states to that which the thought represents. A majority of such states, then, must have been attended with pleasure; and any argument for the early origin and universal tenure of our appetite for existence, goes to establish on a firmer basis that priority and universality of the obnoxious Ηδονη, for which Epicurus contended, since it necessarily presumes that agreeable feeling is attached to the exercise of every faculty. The next great dogma of the Stoics was sadly destitute of metaphysical precision, however useful it might be in moral exhortation. Man ought to live agreeably to nature. The nature of man, they proceeded to explain, was rational, and the law of right reason therefore was the criterion of conduct, and the source of obligation. This law, they said, was imprinted on every mind: it was permanent, it was universal; it was absolute: there could be no appeal from a decision, which was the voice of unchangeable Divinity. By listening to this internal mandate we acquire a sense of moral obligation, which nothing else can confer: for we are irresistibly led to perceive our position, as parts of a system, and the consequent impropriety of all acts that tend to an individual purpose, instead of furthering the great plans of universal legislation. It does not seem very clear, whether the supporters of this theory added to it, as many since have done, the notion of an *immediate* perception of Right and Wrong by the intellect, or whether they derived the intellectual conviction simply from a reflective survey of the several bearings and relations of mental states, and a strong conviction from experience, that whatever holds good for one intelligent and sentient being, will hold good wherever these qualities obtain. These, however, are the two forms which the Intellectual theory has assumed, and in neither of these, I think, can its lofty pretensions be justified. To the first opinion, that of immediate perception, it may be sufficient to reply, that until it can be shown that our notion of Right expresses *essentially* * anything more than a relation and character of feeling, it would be highly unphilosophical to substitute for this simple, reflective notion, which we all understand, a phenomenon, perfectly dissimilar by the terms of its definition from every other mental state, and yet producing no effect in the mind, that might not as well be produced by those natural processes which prevail in every other instance. The second view is undoubtedly correct in itself, but the "budge doctors" have taken it out of place. It embraces the result of certain mental combinations, not their origin, or their law. We come to know that we are parts of a system, and to perceive that additional charm in virtue, which it derives from association with intellectual congruity, long after we have felt ourselves moral beings; and it may be questioned whether the addition makes much differ-

* I say "essentially," because it is undoubtedly true that many notions have been so joined with this by custom, as to coalesce with it in the eyes of ordinary reflection. That of a Supreme *Governor*, for instance, and our duty to him as living under his rule, which is clearly transferred from our observation of civil society. That of Utility, also, and of Beauty; and these are more readily *imagined* by the mind, as being more connected with visible forms, than a feeling which has no outward object, but is terminated by a spiritual disposition like itself.

ence in the conduct of any, except perhaps the few whose minds have been exclusively directed to the peculiar pleasures of scientific meditation. But the vice of this celebrated theory lies deeper — in the *motive* of its adoption; the wrong wish to obtain a greater certainty for the operations of feeling than its own nature affords, supported by the wrong supposition that this certainty would be found within the domain of intellect. "Man is, what he knows." The pregnant words of Bacon! but this is only true, because he knows what he feels. We are apt to be misled by the common use of language, which sets reason or reflection in one scale, and impulse or feeling in the other, and appropriates a right course of conduct to the former alone. The fact is, as may be evident to any who will take the pains to consider, that reflection has no more immediate influence on action in the one case than in the other. But here lies the difference: reflection may bring up conceptions of many feelings, good, bad, and indifferent, so that the mind may choose; but those who act from the impulse of one predominant passion without allowing the intervention of any conceptive state, debar themselves from their power of election, and voluntarily act as slaves.

We are now better enabled to consider the question, which of these two sects, Stoic or Epicurean, did most for the advance of psychological knowledge, and, if the foregoing observations be founded on truth, we cannot, I think, hesitate to pronounce, that it was not that sect which did most for the general increase of moral and religious cultivation. The ardor, with which the followers of Zeno contemplated the holiness of conscience, led them to subvert the fundamental distinctions of nature, in order to establish that adorable queen on what they considered a securer throne. On the other side, the sophists of the Garden, who unfortunately for themselves withstood the great instincts of humanity, and turned the legitimate war against superstition into an assault on the strongholds of religious faith, had no temptation to neglect or pervert those observations of experience, which at first sight seemed to favor their misguided predilections. They stopped too short, and they assumed too much; but they pointed to some primary truths, which, though simple, were, it seems, liable to neglect, and the nearest deductions from which it has taken many centuries to disentangle from error, the unavoidable consequence of greater laxity in investigation, prompted by the same anxiety to promote the cause of morals by confusing it with that of science, which in a different, and certainly less pardonable form, threw Galileo into his dungeon, and still raises a factious clamor against the discoveries of Geology, and any effectual application of criticism to the style and tenor of the Biblical writings. That in the eternal harmony of things, as it subsists in the creative idea of the Almighty, the two separate worlds of intellect and emotion conspire to the same end, the possible perfection of human nature; that in proportion as we "close up truth to truth," we discover a greater correspondence between the imaginative suggestions, on which the heart reposes, and the actual results of accumulated experience, so that we may enlarge and strengthen in ourselves the expectation of their perfect coincidence in some future condition of being; that the revelations of Christianity, while they approve themselves to our minds by their thorough conformity to the human character, appearing, as Coleridge expresses it, "ideally, morally, and historically true," afford a pledge of this ultimate union, and in many important respects a realization of it to our present selves;

these considerations should encourage every man, who makes them a part of his belief, not to refuse his assent to a truth of observation because it is impossible to prove from it a truth of feeling, and still less to flatter mankind into an agreeable delusion by suborning a fictitious origin to notions, which are not really less expressive of eternal truth, because they result from those simple elements and general laws, which the human intellect is invited, because it is enabled, to master, but beyond which "neque scit, neque potest."

In adopting the Stoical system, Cicero pledged himself to its errors, and became involved in its confusion. He was less dogmatical than his teachers; thanks to the Academic bias: but he was also less subtle, less strong-sighted, and never clearly understood the question in debate. Justly incensed at the indolence and spreading immorality which characterized the Epicureans of his time, he commenced a war of extermination against the doctrine of "Gargettius ille," to whose authority they appealed with almost filial reverence. But he neither did justice to his real merits, nor perceived where his fallacy lay. There is a singular perplexity in his arguments on this subject, and a feebleness even in his declamation. We learn from himself that his antagonists (not those who, created for the purpose of being refuted, figure in his dialogues, but the less easy gentlemen whom he met with in real life) complained loudly of his misapprehensions; and the fretful spirit, in which he alludes to the charge, betrays a consciousness that it was not wholly unfounded.*

* "Itaque hoc frequenter dici solet a vobis, nos non intelligere quam dicat Epicurus voluptatem. Quod quidem mihi siquando dictum est (*est autem dictum non parum sæpe*) etsi satis clemens sum in disputando, tamen interdum soleo subirasci." — *De Fin.* l. ii., c. 4. If we compare the elegant sketch of Epicurean philosophy in Diogenes Laertius, and the authentic writings there preserved of Epicurus himself, with this second book, we shall be at no loss for errors of omission and commission on the part of Cicero. For example, he puts the case of an extravagantly drunken fellow, who, he says, quoting the words of Lucilius, supped always "libenter," but never "bene." Therefore, he infers, the Supreme Good cannot consist in pleasure, since good and pleasure do not always coincide. As if it might not be true that all pleasures, *quoad pleasures*, are good, because akin to the "*αταραξια*," sought as the final good, and yet it might be necessary to reject certain pleasures, not because they were such, but because their result would be a preponderance of misery! Epicurus never confounded the subordinate and relative importance of ordinary pleasures with the indispensable importance of that pleasure, which consisted "vivendo bene." In the book De Senectute, we find "Quocirca nihil esse tam detestabile, tamque pestiferum, quam voluptatem; siquidum ea, cum major esset

However unsound may have been these first principles of Ciceronian philosophy, and however uncongenial to the elements of positive religion, they were far from exhibiting any repugnance to the fundamental articles of Natural Theology. A Supreme Lawgiver was the natural complement of an universal law; and they who extended so wide the rightful empire of reason upon earth, could not fail to rejoice when they saw her seated, without opposition, and without fear of change, on the throne of the universe. That Cicero gave a cordial, if not always an unhesitating adhesion to the first article of rational belief, may be fairly gathered from many passages in his works, in which he treats of this important subject. His intellect perceived its evidences, and his imagination exulted in its grandeur. It is not easy perhaps for us, who live in a Christian country, at an advanced period of Christian civilization, and have been familiarly acquainted with the great propositions of Theism from our earliest childhood, hearing them week-

atque longior, omne animi lumen extingueret." — *De Sen.*, c. 12. He is speaking of corporeal pleasure; but can anything be more absurd than to proscribe a thing altogether, because, if increased to an imaginary and extraordinary extent, it will tend to destroy another thing more valuable than itself?

ly from the pulpit, and meeting them daily in some shape or other, in literature or conversation; it is not easy, I say, for us to conceive the silent rapture, and the eloquent praise, with which the philosophers of former time approached that idea of a Supreme Mind, which had been the object, and seemed to contain the recompense of their solitary meditations. In addition to its natural beauties, there was this relative attraction, that it was unknown and supposed inaccessible to the multitude. The vast proportion of the race, who drew human breath, and felt human sensations, but on whose mental organization not much creative power had been expended, these poor ιδιωται must be abandoned to live and die under the influence of prone credulity, perhaps of superstitious depravation: but it was the privilege of superior intelligence to offer a pure and reasonable worship in the "Edita *doctrina sapientum* templa serena." Perhaps the Roman statesman was especially gratified, when he learned to contemplate the universe under the forms of order and administration. At least, this is the aspect he most delights to present to us. All created beings, according to him, form one immense commonwealth; and never has his eloquence so stately a march, or so sonorous a measure, as when, closely treading on the vestige of Plato, he announces the indelible sanctity of human law, and its foundations, not in blind concurrence, but in the universal analogies of an Eternal Mind.

His arguments are of the description usually called à posteriori, and are exactly adapted, by their clearness and their strength, to produce general impression, and to silence, even where they do not convince. He dwells on the natural relation which experience proves to exist between the supposition of Deity and the tendencies of human belief; on the general, if not universal, custom of nations, ancient and recent, barbarian and civilized; on the stability afforded by Theism to the conclusions of reason, the institutions of polity, and the natural expectation of a future state. Above all he directs attention to the harmony of the visible universe,* the

* "Esse præstantem aliquam, æternamque naturam, et eam suspiciendam admirandamque hominum generi, pulchritudo mundi, ordoque rerum cœlestium cogit confiteri." — *De Divin.*, l. ii., c. 72. "Quæ quanto consilio gerantur, nos nullo consilio assequi possumus." — *De Nat. De.*, l. ii., c. 38. "Cœlestem ergo admirabilem ordinem . . . qui vacare mente putat, is ipse mentis expers habendus est." — *De Nat. De.*, l. ii. See the whole of this book, especially the eloquent translation of a passage from Aristotle.

order and beauty of the celestial motions and the subserviency of material objects to the convenience of organic life. How should the innumerable and wonderful combinations, which our apprehension is tasked in vain to exhaust, be referred to an origin of inapprehensive fate, or void casualty? How may a world, where all is regular and mechanically progressive, arise from a declension of atoms, which would never be considered a possible cause of the far inferior mechanism resulting from human invention? It is the character of this argument to increase in cumulative force, as the dominion of man over surrounding nature becomes enlarged, and each new discovery of truth elicits a corresponding harmony of design. Beautiful as the fitness of things appeared in the eyes of Cicero, how insignificant was the spectacle when compared to the face of nature, as we behold it, illuminated on every side, and reflected in a thousand mirrors of science? What *then* was the study of the mortal frame? What the condition of experimental physics? What the knowledge of those two infinities which awaited invisibly the revealing powers of the microscope, and the "glass of Fiesole?" Long after the genius of whom I write had passed from his earthly sphere of agency, "the contemplation of an animal skeleton flashed conviction on the mind of Galen, and kindled his solitary meditation into a hymn of praise."* It was later yet by many ages, when the voice of one, to whom science is indebted for her new organization, and learning for her manifold advancement, proclaimed to a timid generation, "that much (physical) philosophy would bring back a man to religion." Still nearer our memory that patient thinker — who laid open to the eyes of his understanding the simple governing law, and the interminable procession of subject worlds — Newton found room for the Creator in the creation, and passed with ease from the interrogation of second causes to the exalted strain of piety, in which he penned the concluding chapter of his Principia.

But to whatever extent our choice of materials for this argument has been enlarged, and whatever additional beauty and interest have accrued to their application, the argument itself, resting upon simple notions of the understanding, and an induction, which, though large, was yet

* COLERIDGE. *Aids to Reflection.*

abundantly supplied by the earliest objects of sensation, may be considered as almost coeval with the intelligence of man, and had no less philosophical weight under the sway of Ptolemy than beneath the enlightened ascendency of Copernicus; no less dignity of reason in the mouth of Anaxagoras, when to his survey of the various phenomena presented by matter and motion, he added the solemn and necessary formula of completion, "Accessit Mens," as when adorned in later times by the graceful industry of Ray, or the lucid strength of Paley. Let us transport ourselves, in imagination, to the contemplative solitude and lofty conversations ot our Roman philosopher, when wearied with the business of the city, or despairing of the republic (then in danger of forgetting her hatred of single domination at the feet of the most accomplished of usurpers), he retired to shady Tusculum, or limpid Fibrenus, or the shores of that beautiful bay, which "nullus in orbe sinus prælucet." In those memorable periods of seclusion from a world, which was tempestuous and distressful then, and has not changed its character now, he had leisure to observe the wonders of natural operation, and to speculate on those final causes, which give them a higher meaning than the bare senses can perceive. He saw the earth covered with fruits from which man derived his sustenance: the procession of the seasons, the alternation of day with night, bespoke a providential care for those vital functions, whose tenure is so frail, while their empire is so extensive. If he directed his eyes to the Italian heaven, we can hardly perhaps assert that the same prospect would be disclosed to him, which appears to a modern observer: for knowledge will vary and tinge, not indeed the perceptions of sense, but the emotions arising out of them, with which they are closely intertwined, and which language, never rapid enough to go along with quick mental succession, comprehends under the general expression, significant of the sensitive act. Yet to the mere sight that prospect was the same. The stars rose and set in their appointed courses. The moon presented her various phases with a regularity that never deceived anticipation. The appearance of a wandering comet was too rare to dislodge the impression of design, while even learning, unable to explain that phenomenon, was content to lend its aid to superstition, and to consider the apparently lawless intruder as a commissioned herald of change, and "perplexer of monarchs." That which after all is the most important thing we can observe, and of which our perception and belief are necessarily more immediate than of anything else, *the Mind itself*, furnished abundant evidence of purpose by its minute and multiplied correspondencies. Could Cicero think of his own being, and not find it full of mysterious harmony? Fearfully and wonderfully he, like all of us, was made. Endless are the divers undulations of sentiment and idea, which pass through, if they do not compose, the sentient being: yet they fluctuate according to settled laws, and every faculty keeps its prescribed limits, without any variation, or the least disturbance.*

* It will be right also to remember, that while the exact similarity in the *kind* of mutual fitness, which in so many dissimilar instances one thing bears to another, prevents our considering the argument itself as acquiring any accession of intrinsic strength in proportion to the growth of knowledge, the most powerful among the sceptical objections to its validity have increased in that very ratio. Sextus Empiricus was a bold doubter, but he wanted the advantages of position possessed by David Hume. Until the analysis of mind had been rigorously pursued by inductive philosophers, so many states of mental existence appeared simple and ultimate, which have since been shown to be compounded, and the abuse of the words Faculty, Power, Reason, Imagination, and some others, had so flattered men into the impression that they possessed

But the "perturbatrix Academia" was not entirely silent. Cicero knew that, if he missed

a great deal of proper activity in the soul, independent of, and anterior to the actual states of which they were conscious, that the dependent, composite, and divisible character of the only thinking and feeling substance with which they were acquainted was apt to escape observation, or at least not to appear in its completeness and universality. When questioned concerning the origin of things, a modern Pantheist feels a repugnance to the usual answer, because it extends *causation* beyond the system, comprehending within itself the subjective form as well as the objective application of that mode, and because it makes an imaginary repetition of one part in a system (*i. e.* of an effect seemingly organized and therefore by the argument from Final Causes justifying an inference of design) to account for the existence of the whole system, and to be itself the self-existent and designing cause. Whatever may be the real strength of this shaft, it will always glance aside from those who have grounded their assurance on the testimonies of revealed religion. The supposed objector may by them be ranked in the innocuous company of Berosus, Ocellus Lucanus, and our good old friend in the novel, who was so apt a learner of their "*αναρχον και ἀτελευταιον το παν.*" They will probably be disposed to recognize the hand of Providence in this, that the most necessary article of belief was supported in times of inferior knowledge by an argument, which, from the constitution of the human understanding, is adapted to produce the strongest impression, and that philosophy was not ripe for the suggestion of anything even plausible on the other side, until a city of permanent refuge had been prepared for human weakness. But the self-satisfied Deist, who in his anxiety for the simple and the rational, has reduced to so small a number the positive articles of his belief, will do well to examine, whether the remainder have all that *absolute* impregnability, and *demonstrative* clearness, which he seems so persuaded of.

truth by the way of free inquiry, "he should not miss the reward of it." * In the person of the Academic Cotta he has displayed that principle of his own mind which always rebelled against too much appearance of certainty. The dialogues "De Naturâ Deorum," and the book "De Divinatione," are excellent specimens of Cicero's best rhetorical talents, his acuteness, his quick perception, and his legal sagacity. It would be much against my conscience to ascribe to him either wit or humor: yet there is sometimes an archness of remark, and a learned pleasantry, which have not unfrequently reminded me of Bayle.

The doctrine of human immortality is so excellent a theme for the energy of declamation, and the triumph of debate, that, were there no other and better reason, we might on this account have expected to find Cicero its eloquent defender. But his heart needed it, as well as his head. Struggling all his long and varied life with political and private tempests, banished by the intrigues of one, betrayed by the perfidy of another, slighted by those on whom he had conferred inestimable benefits, yet assured still by his own feelings of the sanctity of affection, and the intrinsic excellence of virtue, it was natural

* LOCKE.

indeed that a man, to whom life had been such a scene of trial, should find peculiar satisfaction in anticipating a state hereafter, in which the inward strength should be greater, and the outward conditions less severe. There is no topic, accordingly, to which Cicero applied himself with greater ardor, and none perhaps on which he had succeeded better in communicating his own view to the minds of succeeding generations. The mode of thought in which he apprehends the subject, the expressions he employs, the figures and allusions which illustrate and point his arguments, have long since become familiar commonplaces, and continue, I suppose, in more cases than we incline to imagine, to give habitual color to the uncertain notions of "that mob of gentlemen who think with ease."

In opposition to his general course of sentiment on this subject must be ranked a few sentences, scattered through his works, in which the other, the darker view, suggests itself, and is not for awhile authoritatively repelled. Some of these dubious expressions occur in letters to Epicurean friends, and may be considered as accommodations to their fixed opinion.* Others

* See *Epist. Famil.* 5, 16; *ib.* 21, 6, 3; *ib.* 4; *ib.* 21.

are the offspring of mental distress, and represent with painful fidelity that mood between contentment and despair, in which suffering appears so associated with existence that we would willingly give up one with the other, and look forward with a sort of hope to that silent void where, if there are no smiles, there are at least no tears, and since the heart cannot beat, it will not ever be broken. This is within the range of most men's feeling, and it were morose to blame Cicero for giving it expression. The truth is, however, that a cloud of doubt could not but obscure the land of promise from the eyes of Pagan moralists. The wise distrusted this doctrine, because it was favored by their passions. The good thought the possession of virtue might perhaps be its own reward. It must be allowed that the subtle, verbal arguments, by which Cicero, in common with most other ancients, sought to confer an appearance of logical proof on propositions which can never admit a higher evidence than probability, must have seemed, when they did not happen to be in a humor for dialectics, as frail and unsatisfactory as the pretended demonstrations of their opponents. What, for instance, can be more vague and sophistical than the curious piece of reasoning which Cicero inserts in his Republic, as a worthy and dignified conclusion to the most solemn part of that performance ?* Nay, lest any of the due effect should be wanting, he puts it into the mouth of an immortal being, who wishes by the communication of convincing truth to raise the inheritor of his earthly glory to a participation in his celestial repose. It was transferred from the Phædo of the divine Athenian, where it stands, I must confess, in rank and file with many others not more conclusive than itself. But I have already declared my belief, that they have done wrong to the memory of Plato, and have shown themselves incapable of the spirit of his philosophy, who suppose that in his Dialogues the main impression is intended to be produced by the direct statement of opinion, or any inculcation of complete notions by the way of argument. Admirable as the *method* is, with which the Socratic colloquists conduct their debates, the validity of the premises or of the conclusions was not equally an object of attention in the comprehensive mind that invented their discussions. Not that he was indifferent to truth; but he

* See *Somn. Scip.*, at the end of the "De Republicâ."

chose to convey it dramatically, and trusted more to the suggestions of his reader's heart than the convictions of his critical understanding.

Two things are especially worthy of notice in Cicero's exposition of his views concerning futurity. The first is, that contrary to the opinions of most ancient philosophers, he promises the highest rewards to those who cultivated an active life, and busied themselves in political pursuits for the advantage of the state.* In this we again recognize the leading idea of the Roman mind: hardly content with bringing this world into subservience to the four magic letters, which had more harmony for them than the Tetractys of Pythagoras, the "gens togata" would fain have extended the empire of convention over those shadowy regions, which are ever peopled with different inhabitants, according to the different dispositions of man's prolific imagination. The second is, his contemptuous disbelief of the doctrine, that for the wicked "Æternas pœnas in morte timendum." There seems, indeed, to be no natural connection, but the contrary, between this doctrine

* See *Somn. Scip.*, at the end of the "De Republicâ." When they get to heaven, however, they are to be busied "cognitione rerum et scientiâ."

and our inherent hope of immortality. Seldom do we find an instance of such a belief gaining ground, independently of positive religion, or analogous traditions. Accustomed to transfer our notions of earthly legislation to the idea of the Divine character, our thoughts readily ascribe remedial punishment to the moral regulation of the universe, but are by no means equally inclined to admit the infliction of absolute ruin as compatible with Supreme Benevolence. But it is not so easy as we imagine, to adjust the deep of creation by measurements of fancy, impelled by passion. "Omnia exeunt in mysterium," was the maxim of the schoolmen. That tremendous mystery, which involves the nature of evil, may include the irreversible doom of the sinful creature within some dreadful cycle of its ulterior operations. This view is indeed gloomy, and such as the imagination of man, for whom there are ills enough at hand without a gratuitous conjecture of more, will not naturally contemplate. Yet for this very reason perhaps it is a presumption in favor of any scheme, pretending to revelation, that it contains this awful doctrine.

It does not appear that Cicero ascribed any

proper immateriality to the immortal essence of thought. Distinct indeed from the concretions of earthly elements, but endued with extension, and apparently with palpability, it had no right from the character of its substance to infinity of duration.

"As to Physics," says Middleton, "Cicero seems to have had the same notion with Socrates, that a minute and particular attention to it, and the making it the sole end and object of our inquiries, was a study rather curious than profitable, and contributing but little to the improvement of human life. For though he was perfectly acquainted with the various systems of all the Philosophers of any name, from the earliest antiquity, and has explained them all in his works, yet he did not think it worth while either to form any distinct opinions of his own, or at least to declare them."

From the brief and imperfect survey we have now taken of these philosophical works, some general notion may be formed of the rank which Cicero is entitled to occupy among the benefactors of mankind, and the services he has rendered in that great controversy between light and darkness, the issues of which are deeply interesting to us all. We have observed that he writes under the influence of those national predilections, never absent from the literature of Rome, and compressing the individual genius of her children within limits required for her attaining and preserving a complete dominion over the manners of many generations. He obeyed this influence, and by obeying, became a principal instrument of its extension. We have found him averse to original investigation, but studious of comparison, and more careful to describe historically the thoughts that had hitherto agitated the minds of men, and to transmit them in connected formulas to posterity, than to throw off the weight of example, and try what results his individual intellect might arrive at by a fresh examination of particulars. It is as true perhaps as an epigrammatic expression well can be, that the Romans stand to their Grecian predecessors in the relation of actors to dramatic poets; and Cicero may be considered as the prompter, supplying them with those thoughts which it was their business to embody in representation. We have seen how his rhetorical habits gave a turn to every exertion of his mind, and while we admire the acute sagacity with which all varieties of opinion are subjected in turn to the elegance and freedom of liberal discussion, we perceive not a few traces of that injustice, often latent in designed impartiality, and that incapacity for the due appreciation of truth, which sometimes lurks in the apparent candor and good faith of an eclectic disposition. His honesty of intention, and extensive observation of the vicissitudes in human society, with the prominent causes on which they depend, have given to his ethical compositions a value and effect, which the reasons already enumerated will not permit us to ascribe to the greater portion of his abstract inquiries. But even these, although they abound with maxims of general use and importance for the regulation of the habits, and for the conservation of social order, were shown to be deficient in vitality, because pervaded with no principle of permanent enthusiasm, sufficient at once to sanction the moral law, and to supply the strongest of human motives to its fulfilment. Nothing but positive religion can properly furnish this principle, yet the defect at least was perceived, and the remedy sought with earnestness, by the great disciple of Socratic wisdom. In the absence of this requisite, Cicero endeavored to found his system of morality on certain metaphysical positions, which he collected from the works of others, but which not only were erroneous, or insufficient of themselves, but were by him often misunderstood and misrepresented. Those primary truths of Theology, which acquire a natural hold on a cultivated understanding, and suit the course of our common sentiments, without awakening those more complicated forces of emotion, which can only be set in action by a spiritual faith — the doctrines, for example, of Divine existence and attributes, and of a future state, were inculcated, we have seen, generally with warmth, and always with pleasure. But even here the Academy vindicated her rights; and the mind of our philosopher was of that sort which cannot be satisfied without some belief in several things, or with much belief in any.

Such then, it has appeared, was the philosophical temper of Cicero; such the opinions which arose from its direction, and have exercised so remarkable an authority over the lives of many men, and the literature of many periods.

Subject, like all human reputations, to a flux and reflux of public esteem, at some epochs he has been the chosen instructor of youth, and the favorite of studious age;* at others he has seemed either above or below the level of general feeling, and has encountered comparative neglect. But these fluctuations have never materially altered the surface, whether they came to elevate, or to depress. General knowledge, clearness of expression, a polished style, and that indefinable pliancy to the consent of numbers, which is sometimes called *tact*, sometimes common sense, according to the greater or less particularity of the occasion; these will always be passports to public approbation, because they are qualities which may be easily appreciated by the great mass of educated society. It is impossible to deny that these are possessed by Cicero in an eminent degree. In reading him we never lose sight of the orator,

* He was very popular with the early Fathers. Jerome's zeal, it is well known, brought him into suffering. Augustin, whose books of anathema against doubters and Academics amply secured his person from angelic visitation, speaks of Cicero in terms of reverence, even while he rejects his authority, and plainly signifies that this rejection was considered a philosophical heresy.

the statesman, the man of the world, and what diminishes his importance to lovers of higher truth, than he could teach, — truth absolute, single and severe, dwelling apart from worldly things and men, and requiring to be spiritually discerned, because it is spiritual, — is precisely that circumstance which secures his favor with the majority. But whenever there occurs any great shock of European opinion, any revulsion of ancient creeds and settled habits of assent, the consequence of long prevalent immorality and a general indifference to religion, an era of reaction is likely to follow, in which much intense feeling will quicken the lifeblood of society, and much will be counterfeited that never was felt. Without any purpose of imposture, men will deceive themselves and others, and while they fondly dream that they are elevated above the multitude by the loftiness of their views and the originality of their impulses, they are often only inhaling the dregs of an epidemic passion for excitement; and some perhaps may be lulled by self-love in this singularly illusive dream, until they are forcibly awakened by the pangs of a lacerated conscience, and the failings of an impaired understanding. Such an era, if I mistake not, is that in which we live; and it is not at epochs of this description, when men are least tolerant of labor, and most ambitious of the results to which labor conducts; when the imagination craves a constant stimulus with a morbid appetite, sometimes leading to delirium; when the prurient desire for novelties, arranged in system, is mistaken for the love of truth; and, because pleasure is the end of poetry, it is supposed indifferent what kind of pleasure a poem confers; it is not now, and in times like the present, that Cicero, the sedate, the patient, the practical, will retain his influence over the caprices of literary fashion.* Already he is superseded in our public schools, and I might add, were it not for the circumstances in which I am now writing, forgotten at our Universities. The language of literature no longer bespeaks the study of those golden periods, which charmed the solitude of Pe-

* A late writer, who aspired to the honor of reviving the Academic system among the moderns, as Gassendi revived the Epicurean, has left us an elegant, though partial estimate of Cicero's philosophical merits. — *Drummond's Academical Questions*, p. 318. Another exception will be found in an ingenious living author, who goes the strange length of setting Cicero above Bacon. — See *Landor's Imaginary Conversations*.

trarch, and enriched the conversation of Erasmus. Undoubtedly the classical Latin, indebted to the interest taken in Cicero's writings for some of the concern that preserved its existence in times of profound ignorance, returned in some degree the benefit at that brilliant period of supremacy, which it enjoyed between the revival of learning and the prevalence of modern tongues: these, however, having gained ground for some time by hardly sensible gradations, now openly threaten to occupy the most remote and sacred corners of critical erudition. When it was absolutely necessary to converse and write in the language of the dead, it was natural to turn over his pages "nocturnâ manu et diurnâ," that so the student might become imbued with his sentiments, and easily adhere to his expressions. How far the fame of Cicero is independent of these considerations will be easily ascertained by our posterity, but must be a perplexing question for ourselves. I do not think it probable that the generations to come, however different may be their ruling impulse from that which constitutes the characteristic virtues and vices of the present age, will restore either the philosophical works of Cicero, or that literature whose spirit they express, to the immense popularity they once enjoyed. Some books, like individuals and nations, have their appointed seasons of decline and extinction. It is not in the nature of things, that books consisting entirely of *relative opinion*, or which present society under a merely conventional aspect, should retain an ascendency over public opinion when the features of society are no longer in any respect similar. But in compositions, of which pure genius claims the largest share, these accidents of place and time are preserved, as the straws in amber; nor need we apprehend that any lapse of generations, or augmentation of knowledge, will consign works, like these we have been considering, to the shelf of the commonly learned, or the study of the inquisitive antiquarian.

REMARKS

ON

PROFESSOR ROSSETTI'S

"DISQUISIZIONI SULLO SPIRITO ANTIPAPALE."

THESE remarks were originally intended to appear in one of the periodical publications. Accidental circumstances having prevented their appearance, in the form at least and at the time desired by the author, he has been induced to publish them in a separate shape; partly by the wish he feels to contribute his mite towards bringing into notice a work which, if it had been written in English, would have made, probably, a great sensation; partly because he is desirous of entering his protest against those novel opinions of Professor Rossetti, which he believes to be alike contrary to sound philosophy and to the records of history. With regard to any sentiments of his own, contained in the following pages, which may be thought liable to a similar charge of paradox, he will be content to shelter himself under the language of Burke, confessing that they are not calculated "to abide the test of a captious controversy but of a sober and even forgiving examination; that they are not armed at all points for battle, but dressed to visit those who are willing to give a peaceful entrance to truth."

REMARKS

ON

PROFESSOR ROSSETTI'S "DISQUISIZIONI SULLO SPIRITO ANTI-PAPALE."

"Maximum et velut radicale discrimen est ingeniorum, quod alia ingenia sint fortiora ad notandas rerum differentias, alia ad notandas rerum similitudines. Ingenia enim constantia et acuta figere contemplationes et morari et hærere in omni subtilitate differentiarum possunt. Ingenia autem sublimia et discursiva etiam tenuissimas et catholicas rerum similitudines et cognoscunt et componunt. Utrumque autem ingenium facile labitur in excessum, prensando aut gradus rerum aut umbras." — BACON DE AUGM. SCI.

IN these words, not unworthy the calm wisdom of Bacon, we have the large map of human understanding unrolled before us, divided into two hemispheres, of which it would be difficult to name the most extensive, or the most important to general happiness. We could as ill spare the mighty poets, artists, and religious philosophers of the second division, as the patient thinkers, the accomplished dialecticians, and the great body of practical men, who must be classed under the former. If, on the one hand, we are by nature μεροπες ἀνθρωποι, dividers of words, and the thoughts that give rise to words, we are no less creatures dependent on the imagination, with all its wonderful powers of associating, blending, and regenerating, for the conduct of our daily life, and the maintenance of our most indispensable feelings. Between the two classes of individual character, distinguished by their larger respective shares of these opposite faculties, there must always be more or less of contest and misunderstanding, which, however, only serves, by sharpening the activity of both parties, to produce an ultimate equilibrium ; and trimming, so to speak, the vessel of human intellect, promotes the great cause of social progression. Few persons, perhaps, are indisposed to make this allowance, so far as regards the broader distinctions, such, for instance, as divide a Newton from a Shakspeare. The two peaks of Parnassus are so clearly separate, that we run little danger of confounding them. But there is a doubtful piece of ground where the cleft begins ; a region of intellectual exertion in which the two opposite qualities are both called into play, and where there is consequently the greatest risk of their being confused. Unfortunately, too, this debatable land is of the most direct importance to our welfare; for within it are comprised those inquiries which regard our moral and intellectual frame, and which aspire to arrange the chaos of motives and actions in some intelligible order of cause and effect. The history of philosophical criticism, both as applied to the annals of events, and as busied in abstract speculations, is for the most part a record of noble errors, arising from the abuse of that principle which leads us to combine things by resemblances. Yet it may be doubted, whether these errors have not done as much for the discovery of truth, as the more accurate inquiries of the philosophers who detected them. Enthusiastic feeling is the great spring of intellectual activity; but none are animated by this enthusiasm without some apparent light to their thoughts, some idea that possesses them, some theory, in short, or hypothesis, which interests their hopes, and stimulates their researches by a stronger allurement than the unaided loveliness of truth. These leading ideas are rarely accordant with reality; but in the pursuit of them lights are struck out, which fall happily on the minds of other men, and may ultimately prove of great service to the world. Even when, as in some fortunate examples, the idea, which is fearlessly followed through labor and trial, is found to correspond with the actual relations of nature, we know not how much is owing to what may be termed a *contagion* of genius from other minds, less favored in attainment, but not less ardent in pursuit.* Genius,

* This is less true, or at least less obvious in science, where more depends on pure intellect. When we consider Newton misunderstood and misrepresented by Hooke and Huyghens, who set their own unproved hypotheses, concerning the nature of light, on a level with his sublime observations of actual properties, we are disposed to think of his genius as moving in a different plane, and meeting theirs only where it intersects. Yet how various must have been the multiplicity of impressions, which made Newton a mathematician, a patient thinker, a discoverer! How many of these may have been owing to Hooke and Huyghens themselves! Had they, had Kepler, and Descartes, never worshipped idols with glorious devotion, the authors of the Principia and the Mécanique Céleste might never have led the way to the altars of true Science. The work of intellect is posterior to the work of feeling. The latter lies at the foundation of the Man; it is his proper self, the peculiar thing that characterizes him as an individual. No two men are alike in feeling, but conceptions of the understanding, when distinct, are precisely similar in all. The ascertained relations of truths are the common property of the race. This fact it is, which

indeed, is the child of Heaven, but a human child; and innumerable circumstantial causes are operative on its nature and development. It is the consciousness of intellectual power, not the possession of right opinions, which agitates beneficially the spirit of a nation, and prepares it for intellectual discovery. Feeling is the prime agent in this, as in other human operations; and feeling is more susceptible of being moulded by error than by truth, because the false appearances of things are numberless, while of the true we know little even at present, and that little continually diminishes as we go backward through the field of history. We would not be understood as encouraging a careless sentiment respecting truth, or as dissuading inquiries from the only sound method of philosophizing, which implies a constant distrust of hypothesis, and an incessant appeal to the records of experience. Hypothesis, we agree with a

gave rise to those systems of semi-platonic philosophy which represented Reason as impersonal, and existing only as a divine universal medium in and around our individual minds. Such was the doctrine of many of the Old Fathers, in particular of Justin Martyr, and Augustin; it was revived with considerable extensions by Malebranche; by his English disciple, Norris; and recently, in its original shape, by Mr. Coleridge.

late eminent writer, should be employed only as a reason for trying one experiment sooner than another. But although it would be worse than folly to recommend darkness in preference to light, it is not foolish to remind men that Nature may have made this darkness subservient to the better distribution of light itself. Man, indeed, must sternly turn from seductive fancies, when he seeks sincerely for truths. His sublime course is straightforward forever. But Nature coöperates with him in secret, and by a magical alchemy, which it is ours to reverence, not to imitate, can transform those very errors, against the intention of their unconscious victims, into new disclosures and enlargements of knowledge.

The author of the very ingenious and interesting work before us, stands in need of all the indulgence, as he deserves all the censure which we have just expressed towards the tribe of pertinacious theorists. He is one of the boldest and one of the cleverest among them. His style is lively, and often rises to eloquence, while the nature of his hypothesis lends to historical details all the wildness and novelty of romance. He has amassed considerable information on the limited range of subjects which regard his immediate pursuit; but he appears to want extensive reading,* and that philosophical discrimination

* We would recommend him to beware how he meddles with ancient history. Speaking of the philosophical doctrines of Pythagoras, he calls them "dottrina, onde nacque l'assurdo Panteismo." Whatever may be the absurdities of Pantheism, they can hardly exceed those contained in these few words. Pythagoras was not inclined to the Pantheistic system, but that system is as old as the world. It was articulated among the first stammering accents of Philosophy in the oriental birthplace of our race. When the Persians, somewhat later, began to indulge in high speculations, they invented a different scheme, that of emanation, to which the tenets of Pythagoras probably bore a close affinity. From him it may have passed into the hands of Plato. The Stoics adopted similar views. The later Platonists pursued the system of emanation into many fanciful, but coherent ramifications. The Eleatic school, contemporary with Pythagoras, but unconnected with him, seem to have been the first Pantheists of the west. This is disputed by some modern critics, but the arguments of Xenophanes concerning the homogeneity of substances appear as strictly Pantheistic as any proposition in the Ethics of Spinosa. All is necessarily one, he says; for the Infinite can produce nothing homogeneous, since two infinites are an absurdity: nor yet anything heterogeneous, because an effect can contain nothing which is not involved in its cause; therefore, whatever in the new substance differed from the old, could not be produced by it, but must come of nothing, which is impossible. Afterwards, by a more compressed argument, he contends that it is impossible, vi termini, for Infinity to set anything beyond itself. It is curious that the acute deductions of Xenophanes from a theory of Causation, generally received until the time of Hume, should never have suggested

which might be expected to arise from it. Never was a more characteristic specimen of the second class of thinkers, designated above in the words of Bacon. He cares for nothing but resemblances, finds them in every hole and corner,* and takes them on trust when he cannot

themselves to those subtle thinkers, among the Schoolmen and their successors, who strove to erect a demonstration of Theism on the idea of Cause. They could hardly, one would imagine, avoid perceiving the fragility of their distinction between a thing contained formally, and one contained eminently. Yet upon the presumed force of that distinction rest not only the Cartesian arguments, but the celebrated chapter of Locke, "on our demonstrative knowledge of the existence of God." The school of Pythagoras, if we may trust Mr. Coleridge's account, ("Aids to Reflection," p. 170 *in not.*) wished to guard against the errors of Pantheism by a strange application of mathematical phraseology, representing the Universe as a geometric line, not produced from a point contained in it, but generated by a Punctum invisibile et presuppositum, entirely independent of its product. It must be owned, however, in the words of M. de Gerando, (Biog. Univ. art. Pythagore,) "Il n'est pas dans l'histoire entière de la Philosophie un problême plus curieux, plus important, et en même temps plus difficile, que celui qui a pour objet de déterminer la véritable doctrine de Pythagore."

* He cannot even resist their charms, when they are of no possible service to his hypothesis, and indeed militate directly against it, by showing how little trust we should place in such sports of nature. The following is an amusing specimen: "It was not observed without wonder, that Landino, who was learned in astrology, wrote these words on the subject of the Veltro, (in the first Canto of the Inferno.) 'It is certain, that in the year 1484, on the 15th day

find them. The most heterogeneous elements are pressed into the service of his hypothesis with almost tyrannical eagerness. He has one way, and one alone, of accounting for everything strange or unintelligible, or doubtful, in the whole extent of history; nay, for many things hitherto thought clear enough, but not agreeing with his fancy. A man must be careful indeed, in whose words or actions Signor Rossetti would not discover something to help out his argument. If two persons at opposite ends of the world do but chance to light on the same mode of expres-

of November, at 13 hours and 41 minutes, will be the conjunction of Saturn with Jupiter in the Scorpion. This indicates a *change of religion:* and since Jove predominates, it will be a *favorable change.* I have, therefore, a firm confidence that the Christian Commonwealth will then be brought into an excellent condition of discipline and government.'" The first edition of Landino's Commentary has for its date, Florence, 1481, that is three years previous to the event prognosticated, or, as he says, calculated by him. Well, in the very year and month marked out, *Luther was born!* not, indeed, on the 25th, but on the 22d of November. The hours and minutes were not recollected by his mother. (See Bayle, *art.* Luther.) It is well known that Luther called himself the scourge of Babylon, sent to extirpate it from the world: which exactly corresponds with the character given by Dante to the Veltro, who is to prosecute the she-wolf. The passage, in old editions, is written thus: Il *Ueltro* verrá, &c. How would the astonishment of those who perceived this prophecy have been increased, had they also observed that *Ueltro* is the exact anagram of *Lutero.*

sion, our learned professor calls out, like honest Verges, "'Fore God, they are both of a tale!" For him there is mystery in the most trivial incident. He would think, with Sir Thomas Brown, "it was not for nothing David picked up *five* stones in the brook." It seems to us that Signor Rossetti would not be the worse for a few wholesome reflections, which seem never to have presented themselves to his mind, but which might be gained perhaps from a few months' study of that most unprofitable kind of production, the commentaries on the Apocalypse, or the divinity of the Cocceian school. He might learn among the embarrassing riches of interpretations, equally good in appearance, and equally erroneous in fact, that as all is not gold that glitters, so all is not art that seems so. The world is full of coincidences that mean nothing. To find design in everything, is as great madness as to find it not at all. There is a laughing spirit in Nature which seeks perpetual amusement in parodying her more serious works, and in throwing before such observers as Signor Rossetti forms of apparent regularity, but unsubstantial as momentary shapes of uncertain moonlight. Indeed the imitations of life, which in the material world often illude our senses, may be considered analogous to these chance-creations in the moral universe, which spring up on every side for those who care to examine them.

It must be acknowledged, however, the theory we are about to consider has its brilliant side. A secret society, we are told, whose original is lost in the mysterious twilight of oriental religions, has continued, from the earliest historical point at which its workings can be traced, to exercise an almost universal influence on the condition of the civilized world. These μυστηρια, and esoteric doctrines, which in Egypt, in Persia, and even in Greece and Italy, preserved the speculations of the wise from the ears and tongues of an illiterate multitude, passed, with slight but necessary modifications, into the possession of the early Christian heretics. The Gnostic schools of Syria and Egypt transmitted to their successors, the Manicheans, a scheme of discipline, which became more and more necessary, from the increased centralization of power in the orthodox prelates of Rome. As the usurpations of Popes and Councils over the free consciences of men became more glaring and intolerable, the spirit of resistance, which dared not show itself in open rebellion, sought and cherished a refuge, where hatred of the oppressors might be indulged without danger, and a pure doctrine might be orally and symbolically preserved, until happier times should return. The Pauliceans, whose opinions were for the most part Manichean, preceded the more illustrious and more unfortunate Albigenses, in this mode of warfare against spiritual as well as temporal tyranny. The celebrated order of Templars, so widely diffused throughout Europe, so considerable by the rank and influence of its members, did not differ from the Albigenses in the secret object of their endeavors, or the more important part of their mysterious rites. From the time of Frederick II., the Italian party of Ghibellines began to assume an equal rank among these secret opponents of Roman supremacy. Whatever might be the distinctive characters of these three denominations, their symbolical language was sufficiently in common to allow of uninterrupted intercourse and combination. The rise of a new literature in the eleventh and twelfth centuries afforded them a new weapon, far more terrible than any they had hitherto employed, and capable of being directed to a thousand purposes of attack and defence. Since that fortunate event, we are gravely assured, the destinies of Europe have been, in their hands; and the great revolutions which have agitated us are almost entirely due to their indefatigable operation. No track of literature has been untrodden by these masked assailants. In poetry, in romance, in history, in science; everywhere* we find traces of their presence. Their influence in some shape or another, has been exerted on all nations, and, it might almost be said, on every individual mind. The genius of Luther was no more than a puppet, infallibly directed by their invisible agency. In the Protestant reformation they attained one object only of their unwearied pursuit, the over-

* The Alchemists are claimed by our author. The philosopher's stone was not meant to be a stone; and if any were fools enough to seek it, they were but dupes of those, whom they thought their masters. Metaphysicians do not fare much better. The celebrated Raymond Lulli wrote all his works in gergo. The philosopher of Nola, Giordano Bruno, is ranked with Lulli, on whose logic he commented. We must crave leave to doubt whether any secrets exist in the writings of poor Bruno, except such as are made so by the obscurity of his metaphysical doctrines. Nor does his fate seem to require Rossetti's Deus in machinâ, the secret society. The author of "Spaccio della Bestia Trionfante" naturally perished at the stake.

throw of ecclesiastical domination. They relaxed not therefore in the prosecution of their ulterior aim; and in the revolution of 1789 came the thrilling announcement of a second, a more decisive victory. Still the earth is not entirely free: priests and despots still remain to enervate and to destroy: their labors, therefore, are not complete, and the Freemasons of this day, legitimate inheritors of the persecuted Templars, are still pressing forward* to the grand work of final regeneration.

But, averting for a time our eyes from these splendid consummations, let us examine in detail the several methods of assault by which a few

* It is remarkable how intrepidly the Professor passes over disputed points. To read him, one would imagine the connection of modern Freemasonry with the ancient societies was a fact universally admitted. Yet many learned persons have been of opinion that, in its present form, or any nearly resembling it, the Masonic institution can be traced no higher than the times of the Protectorate. The Templars, with their mysterious Baphomet, are covered with still greater obscurity. We know no historical grounds for considering the Albigenses as an organized society. Some Shibboleths they probably had; for the persecuted always stand in need of such protection; but the complicated proceedings and extensive correspondencies, ascribed to them by Rossetti, appear to exist only in his lively imagination. His assertions respecting the Ghibellines are even less supported by historical authorities.

daring politicians got possession of all avenues to the Western Parnassus. Here it is necessary to acquaint the inexperienced reader, who dreams of nothing less, that, about the commencement of the fourteenth century, occurred a great change in the constitution of these societies. Up to that period the symbolical language had been entirely of an amatory character. The love poems * and love courts of Provençe and

* Our author is perhaps not acquainted with the Provençal language, or he would hardly have failed to bring illustrations of his theory from that quarter. Indeed it seems so indispensable for one who seeks to explain the peculiar characteristics of Italian poetry, to examine diligently the early compositions from which those characteristics were unquestionably derived, that we cannot help feeling some surprise at the neglect of them by Signor Rossetti. He tells us, it is true, that the "Lives of the Trovatori" by Nostradamus are written in gergo, and cites, by way of example, the story of Pier Vidal, who was hunted by the wolves (i. e. according to the new lights, by the Romish party): but the poems themselves, although the originals of all the subsequent love poetry, and in particular of many things strange, and some admirable, in Dante and Petrarch, are never quoted. Yet in these he would have found at least as many phrases and idioms, which, by skilful adaptation, might have startled the reader into a momentary belief in his hypothesis. The Albate, a class of poems, in which the word "alba" recurs at the close of every stanza, would doubtless have suggested to him the name and fortunes of the Albigenses. We recommend to his notice the Albata of Guillaume d'Altopol, addressed to the Virgin, "Esperansa de totz ferms esperans," &c., and that very beautiful one of Giraud de Bornel, in which the

Toulouse, were vehicles of political discussion, of active conspiracy, of heretical opinion. An

burden runs, "E ades sera l'Alba." He may make a good speculation also in a singular kind of composition (said to have been invented by Rambaud d'Orange, who is mentioned by Petrarch in the Fourth Capitolo of the Trionfo d'Amore), which consists in verses overlaid with a running commentary in prose or verse, professing to explain, but often obscuring their text. It is probable that the Reggimenti delle Donne of Barberini, and the Tesoretto of Latini, are composed in imitation of these. The following specimen, in which the line is by one poet, and the paraphrase or interpretation by another, will please Signor Rossetti: and it must be owned they are obscure enough to be of service to his theory. "E poia i hom per catre gras mont les." In plain English, "And man ascends by four very slow steps." The comment, which is by Giraud Riquier, who lived towards the end of the thirteenth century, runs thus:

"Ver dis: segon que m'pes,
E que truep cossiran,
Li gra son benestan:
Lo premier es ONRARS,
E'l segons es SELARS,
E'l ters es GEN SERVIRS,
E'l quartz es BON SUFRIRS.
E cascus es mot lens,
Tal qu'el pueya greumens
Hon ses elenegar."

"He says truth; as I think, || and find, considering, || the steps are well suited. || The first is, To honor; || and the second, To conceal; || and the third, To do gentle service; || and the fourth, To suffer well. || And each is very slow, || so that scarcely mounts it || a man without panting." The quaint style in which the Tro-

ingenious chain of antitheses, so contrived as to suggest, in expressions apparently the most un-

vatori generally designate their mistresses, sometimes employing abstract terms instead of names, as Lov Bel Diport, Mon Plus Leial, Mon Cortes, sometimes professing to name them only by description, will appear to the Professor a strong argument for the unreality of those ladies. Take, for example, the poem of Arnaud de Marveil, of which the following is an inadequate imitation:

"Lady, whose eyes are like the stars of heaven,
Out of pure dark sending a glorious light:
Lady, whose cheek in dainty blushes bright
Vies with the roseate crown to angels given:
Lady, whose form more trances human sight,
Than all who erst for beauty's palm have striven:
Lady, whose mind would charm the unforgiven,
And make them worship in a brief delight:
I will not name thee; happy is my lot,
That, tho' I speak the simple truth of thee,
The curious world may read, and know thee not;
For now all foolish lovers' lays are such,
And thy due praise is every woman's fee:
Else were it naming thee to say so much."

We are, however, decidedly of opinion, that, although the antitheses and studied obscurities, which supply to Rossetti's theory its only color of plausibility, are more abundant in these poems than in the more chaste and classical school which succeeded them, he would find even greater difficulty to establish his hypothesis upon them with any tolerable security. The facts with which he would have to deal are too stubborn, too historical. The Cours d'Amour were no secret meetings, but assemblies "frequent and full," at which princely ladies presided, deliberated, and resolved. What secret treason was intended by the Countess de Champagne, meaning, secrets of profound signification, or denunciations of bitter animosity, served to unite men of genius, however remote from each other, in the one great cause of a veiled, but terrible Liberty. When poetry, after its decline in Southern France, began to revive under brighter auspices in Italy, the same system was for some time continued. Cino da Pistoia, Cecco Ascolan, both the Guidos, and other foster-fathers of the new language,* rhymed after the fashion of their

daughter of Louis le Jeune, when she made her memorable decision, "En amour tout est grace; en mariage tout est necessité: par conséquent l'Amour ne peut exister entre gens maries!" Here we have *infidelity* preached to be sure, but in rather a different sense from that which the Professor is hunting for, and one less likely to be offensive to the gay rulers of that time. At least we may judge so from the answer of the Queen, when the above decision was appealed against — "A Dieu ne plaise, que nous soyons assez osées pour contredire les arrets de la Contesse de Champagne?" History assures us, that the loves of the Troubadours were real and natural. They largely cultivated the practice as well as the theory of gallantry. We should like to have heard their hearty laughter at an erudite professor, who should have attempted, in their presence, to argue away the fair forms, which they wooed and often won, into shadows and types, and mere subjects of intellectual enjoyment.

* It is among these writers that the new theory finds its best portion of materials. Their infinite obscurity, perhaps in some measure owing to a corrupt text, gives ample scope for arbitrary constructions. The lover of poetry will not here lose by adopting Signor Rossetti's interpretations, as he does in the case of better

Provençal predecessors, and expounded their political theories in the deceitful form of sonnets and canzones. It seems, however, that old Death, as they piously denominated the Holy See, got notice of these amorous pasquinades, and would have speedily succeeded in exterminating the obnoxious lovers, had it not been for a master-stroke of policy on their part. What does the reader imagine? They threw away their love-tales, and took up missals; went duly to matins, instead of "brushing their hats o' mornings;" in short, exchanged the symbols hitherto in use for others of a similar antithetical character, but grounded on the venerable mysteries of Catholic religion. This change was effected by Dante. We have the announcement of it in the "Vita Nuova," the result in the "Divina Commedia," the commentary, for those

writers. Some meaning is preferable to none. It is curious that Ginguené has said, as if by anticipation of Rossetti, "l'on pourrait en quelque sorte les croire tous amoureux du même objet, puisqu' aucun d'eux ne dit le nom de sa maîtresse, aucun ne la peint sous des traits sensibles." That critic abandons in despair some passages of Cecco and Cino, which brighten up under the new lights sufficiently well. See the sonnets "Muoviti, Pietate, e va incarnata," &c. "Deh, com sarebbe dolce compagnìa," &c., and some others in the collection of Poeti Antichi, published by Allacci.

who have ears to hear, in the "Convito," the "De Vulgari Eloquentiâ," and others of his minor works. On this account, and not for a more obvious reason, he is styled "creator linguæ" by such of his admirers as were also of the sect. On this account he is represented under the designation of Adam,* both by himself in vari-

* The chapter "Dante figurato in Adamo," is one of the most singular in this singular book. In the "De Vulgari Eloquentiâ," Dante inquires what the first word was that Adam spoke, and supposes it to have been EL, the name of God. "Absurdum, atque rationi videtur horrificum, ante Deum ab homine quicquam nominatum fuisse, cum ab ipso et per ipsum factus fuisset homo." In the Paradiso occurs a parallel passage. Dante, in the 26th canto, represents himself as questioning Adam on the same subject, who answers, "Pria ch'io scendessi all' infernale ambascia, I si chiamava in terra il sommo Bene EL si chiamò di poi." Instead of leaving this among the many instances of recondite subtlety to be met with in times of darkness, Rossetti ingeniously brings, in illustration of it, an enigmatical epigram, usually ascribed to Dante, though perhaps on no very good authority.

"O tu che sprezzi la nona figura,
E sci di men che la sua antecedente,
Va e raddoppia la sua susseguente,
Per altro non t'ha fatto la Natura."

The "nona figura" is I, the ninth in the alphabet. "Not worth an H," is a common proverbial expression in Italy. The "double subsequent" makes the Greek word "Κακα." Now the common tradition has been, that some one of the Neri faction derided Dante for his smallness of stature, calling him an I, and that in revenge this epigram was written. This, however, is far too

ous parts of his works, and by contemporary (initiated) writers. On this account, too, his adventures form the subject of many artfully constructed romances, in which his name, and allusions to his poem, may be traced by many subtle indications. After his death, however, the old disguise of love poetry, never entirely abandoned by himself, appears to have been resumed by his successors; nor when from the pen of Petrarch this derived still more extensive celebrity and security, do we find that the other veil, that of Catholicism, was resorted to by any writers of eminence. In other countries, nevertheless, and later times, religion was found again convenient for the concealment of irreligious politics. Many modern societies, the first grades of which bear a Christian character, led up their

commonplace a solution for our Hierophant. The I, according to him, denotes Imperatore, and he supposes it to have been for some time the secret symbol used by the sect, until for some reason or other it was changed to E L, Enrico Lucemburghese, about the time that Dante commenced his poem "Pria ch'io scendessi all' infernale ambascia." The strange notice of Beatrice's character in the Vita Nuova, where she is declared to be the Number Nine, "because she was perfect, and because the Holy Trinity was the root of her being," seems to the Professor a corroboration of his view of the "nona figura." The same number, too, recurs frequently in masonic language.

neophytes by degrees to a very different termination. Nor is the practice unknown to recent literature. The writings of Swedenborg, according to Rossetti, afford an admirable illustration of Dante; and far from being worthy of rejection as the contemptible ravings of a fanatic, are in reality an interesting exposition of masonic ceremonies.*

But upon what foundation, the astonished reader will inquire, on what foundation does this strange fancy-castle repose? Where are the authentic documents which are to reverse the

* We are inclined to put some faith in Signor Rossetti's account of Swedenborg. It has always struck us, whenever we have dipped into his writings, that they are intended rather as parables and satires, than anything more serious. They are quite unlike the heated conceptions of an enthusiast. Swedenborg is methodical and heavy, equally destitute of imagination and of wit, but sometimes making clumsy attempts at the latter. We think it not improbable, that his angels and spiritual worlds among men may refer, as Rossetti supposes, to some society of which he was a member. Perhaps, however, the account the Seer has left us of his first vision may be thought to furnish so simple an explanation of his subsequent reveries, that nothing further can be required. "I had eaten a hearty supper," he tells us, "*perhaps too hearty:* and I was sitting alone in my chair, when a bright being suddenly appeared to me, and said, 'Swedenborg, why hast thou eaten too much?'" Instead of being bled, the simple Swede founded a sect, many thousand of which exist at this day, and in this country!

decisions of history? Where the credible witnesses, whom we must believe henceforward in contradiction to all our usual media of information? It is incumbent certainly on the learned Professor to answer these questions without delay, that we may at least have something to believe in compensation for what he has torn from us. If we are indeed to change the old scholastic maxim into "De apparentibus et de non existentibus eadem est ratio," let us at least be assured that these substitutions of Signor Rossetti are not illusory also. At present we feel the same sort of impression from his work which has sometimes been produced in us by certain wonderful effusions of philosophy in a neighboring country, where Reality and actual Existence are held cheap, and considered as uncertain shadows, in comparison with some mysterious essences of Possibility and Incomprehensibleness, which lie close bottled up, at the bottom* of all our thoughts and sensations!

* Hegel, who died last year of Cholera at Berlin, has been for some years undoubted occupant of the philosophic throne, at least in the North of Germany. The Southern states still revere the authority of Schelling, from whom Hegel, having been his disciple, thought proper to revolt. He occupied himself much in finding a solution to a problem of his own, "How to deduce the Universe

But here at all events we are on plain ground of human life. We demand that the consideration be shown us, for which we are to give up the inheritances of common belief, and to swear "in verba magistri," that nothing is as it seems in the whole course of history. We are far from denying that an undercurrent may be discovered of much greater magnitude and importance than has hitherto been imagined; but we require positive proof of its existence in the first place, and afterwards of every additional inch of ground assigned to its progress.

In such investigations as these, from their very nature ambiguous and perplexed, the greatest delicacy of discrimination, and the most cautious suspense of judgment, are absolutely neces-

from the Absolute Zero." We are not aware that he found one to his satisfaction; one of his followers, perhaps, was more successful, who published a pamphlet to prove that "the historical Jesus was a type of the non-existence of the Deity!" The Hegelites say, that the most important object of Philosophy is to trace the boundaries between Wesenheit or the Ground of Being, and Unwesenheit, or the Ground of Not Being. If they could succeed in this, they think they would carry all before them. We dare say they are right in so thinking; but the first step is rather expensive. Some of them enlarge upon a fundamental principle of Dunkelheit, or Darkness, which they seem inclined to deify, and indeed every syllable of their writings may be considered an appropriate homage to such a power.

sary, or we are lost at once in the wildest dreams. But the gentleman, with whom we have to do, never stops, never deliberates, never doubts. On he drives, in full conviction that all his past reading is in his favor, and full faith that all his further reading will confirm it. Indeed his trust in what Providence will do for him is highly edifying. If he has not yet discovered a single passage even in an obscure author, which by due wrenching of construction might be brought in evidence for some favorite notion, he considers that notion no less demonstrated, than if he had produced the concurrent testimony of all ancient and modern writers. The possible future is to him as secure as the actual past.

His great proposition, on the truth of which almost everything depends, that this * Setta

* "Before the time of Dante, the Gay Science had established its extensive fabric of illusory language on two words, Amore, Odio, from which branched out a long series of antitheses, Kingdom of Love, Kingdom of Hate; pleasure, pain; truth, error; light, darkness; sun, moon; life, death; right, left; fire, ice; garden, desert; courtesy, rusticity; nobleness, baseness; virtue, vice; intelligence, stupidity; lambs, wolves; hill, valley, &c. &c. Hence was derived the name Setta d'Amore. 'Sospiri,' signified verses in gergo. 'Cuore' indicated the great Secret. Dante added to the list of symbols those of God and Lucifer; Christ and Anti-

d'Amore did really exist, is not, he confesses it, established by proof in the present volume. For the present, he says, we must content ourselves with an hypothesis: abundant documents exist, enough to make a large book, by which the matter can be set beyond all doubt. Strange that he should not have thought it expedient to produce these documents, if they are in his possession, and not merely assured to him by the strong faith to which we have alluded! Strange, that he should labor through half this volume to establish the existence of this sect by laboriously collected parallelisms of different passages in unconnected poems, and not dispense with all this unnecessary trouble by the simple process of proving the fact in the first instance! Are his lips sealed perhaps by a masonic oath? This can hardly be, for he promises to communicate these secrets at no distant period; and in several parts of his book he gives us to understand that his information on the masonic rites is entirely derived from published works on the subject, or from such other means as are either lawful, or at

christ; Angels and Demons; Paradise and Hell; Jerusalem and Babylon; the Lady of Modesty and the Lady of Harlotry; with several others of the same kind." — ROSSETTI, cap. 13.

least do not subject him to penalties for indiscretion. But if he has not the fate of the unfortunate Bracciarone before his eye,* of what can he be afraid? Truly, we apprehend his reading on these matters has led him to form a greater partiality for the cunning of the *Fox*, than for the generous, breast-opening *Pelican*, or the simplicity of the superior *Dove.* If indeed, the coincidences he has hitherto offered to our notice are the only proofs he can adduce, we cannot consider them as decisive or substantial. We do not deny that they are very curious and interesting. We know not whether Signor Rossetti has employed more art in assembling them than we have been able to detect; † but, as they stand, they certainly justify a presumption, that something beyond what meets the ear was intended by some of the writers, whose works he examines. Still, we are a long way

* Bracciarone, according to our author, was subjected to persecution for betraying the Chiave, or Secret of the Sect.

† Occasionally we have found his quotations unfaithful. It is not fair to extract part of a sentence from "The Convito," in which Dante derives the word "Cortesi" from the word "Corte," without paying the slightest attention to the clause immediately following, in which he declares himself to mean the usage of ancient Courts, and not as such as then flourished.

from the "imaginations all compact," which he would force on our acceptance.

We are not entitled to assume identity of purpose, wherever we find identity of expression. Because certain societies, existing at different epochs, make use of similar metaphors in order to designate their secret proceedings, it will not follow that those proceedings are identical, or that any connection exists between them beyond that of mere exterior language. Similar circumstances are constantly producing similar results. Now all secret societies are, in respect of their secrecy, similarly situated; all have the same necessity of expressing, in their symbolical language, that relation of contrast to the uninitiated, on which their constitution depends. It is natural, therefore, that all should seek for metaphorical analogies to indicate this contrast; and those analogies will be sought in the contrasts of outward nature,—in the opposition, for instance, of light to darkness, warmth to cold, life to death, and all the others which Signor Rossetti considers as affording decisive proofs of affiliation, whenever they occur in the text-books of separate societies. Meanwhile, masonic lodges, even in the view of our ingenious author, do not occupy the whole of God's earth. The ordinary passions of our nature continue in operation, without much regard to them. But these ordinary passions require the occasional use of metaphors; and as the prominent objects in the material universe are always ready at hand, it will sometimes happen that the same comparisons may be employed by persons who never dreamed of secret conspiracies or initiatory rites. Still less, therefore, is the occurrence of phrases in a common book resembling those in some symbolic exposition, any evidence of necessary connection between things so widely distant. The novice, who has passed through his terrifying ordeal in the open grave or coffin, may be told that he rises to new life in the secluded privacies of his lodge; but it by no means follows that Dante must allude to this circumstance when he uses the same figure. It may happen that more than one Italian poet fixes some leading incident of his story at the first hour of the day, simply because that time of morning has a beautiful, and therefore a poetical character; but there seems no need of recurring for a further explanation of so intelligible a fact to some mystical question in a catechism of American masons. It may happen again that the solemnity and religious importance attached by Platonic lovers to all circumstances connected with their passion, may have led them to assign to the festivals of the Christian church* any prominent event in the lives of their ladies. Or accident and imitation may well be conceived to account for such resemblances; nor should it more surprise us to find some secret transactions of the Templars dated on the same days which this or that poet may have selected, than to find an English law

* When Signor Rossetti proceeds to examine the Romantic Poets, he will not forget to put in requisition that Canzone, in which Ariosto, in a delightful strain between banter and solemnity, tells us how he first met his mistress on "The summer festival of good St. John," and how amidst the dances and banquets, the music and processions, the streets and theatres crowded with lovely forms, yet, "in so fair a place, he gazed on nothing fairer than her face." Midsummer's day, the feast of St. John, is still a great time of rejoicing among the Freemasons. Signor Rossetti can hardly have failed to remark this *proof* of his theory. But we really expect his thanks for suggesting to him a passage in Rousseau's "Confessions," which, we doubt not, in his hands may prove a key to all that was inexplicable in the character of that unfortunate man, besides throwing much light on the stormy times of the Revolution. Just before the description of his adventure with Mademoiselles Galley and Graffenreid, a description on which are lavished all the charms of an inimitable style, occurs this important remark, more valuable for our Professor than all the eloquence and sentiment in the world: "*C'était la semaine après le St. Jean.*"

term dating from Easter, or English rents paid at Lady-day. We do not, however, mean to represent all Signor Rossetti's instances of coincidence as worth no more than these we have mentioned. His proof is of a cumulative character, and injustice is done to it by citing detached parts. We will proceed to examine rather more closely his theory respecting Dante, because this is the most important portion of his work, and will afford the best specimen of his mode of inductive reasoning.

In the "Comento Analitico," published by Rossetti in 1826–7, he broached a comparatively small number of paradoxes, to those contained in the present disquisition, yet amply sufficient to startle the public, and to provoke no very lenient criticism. Wincing under the attacks he has sustained, our bold adventurer does not, however, retreat from his post; on the contrary, he makes an advance, intending to carry the enemy's camp by a coup de main, or to terrify them at least to a dislodgement, by threats of still more intrepid assaults for the future. The "Comento" represented Dante as a politician, whose hatred to the Papal party induced him to devise a great political allegory, of which his principal poem consists; but that he was averse to Catholic doctrines was not there asserted. Rossetti's defence of himself for this excess of caution, since even then he allows he knew the whole complexion of the case, is rather amusing.* Now, however, the veil is thrown off. Dante is not only an Imperialist, but a Freemason; not only an opponent of the temporal power of Rome, but an uncompromising Reformer, whose views on religious subjects were anything but Catholic. Petrarch, Boccaccio, and a host of others less illustrious, were to the full as heretical; and in his capacity of a faithful son of the Church, the Professor makes some faint show of being scandalized at the impieties which his industry has discovered. This improved theory has, it cannot be denied, one important advantage over its own embryo condition. While political hostility was alleged as the only motive which could actuate Dante and Petrarch in assuming these strange disguises, it was not easy to answer the obvious question, "Why should these men have taken such infinite pains to say in secret what on numberless occasions they had said in public?" The poet who wrote that bitter line "Là dove Cristo

* See the last chapter.

tutto dì si merca," and many others not less plain spoken, could hardly have thought it necessary to mask his sentiments. All his writings amply confirm the energetic declaration he has left us concerning his own character,

> "Che s'io al Vero son *timido* amico,
> Temo di perder vita tra coloro,
> Che questo tempo chiameranno antico."

If, however, as we are now informed, the spiritual supremacy of Rome was no less abhorred than her usurped temporalities, some answer may be found to an objection otherwise so fatal. Some motive certainly in this case would appear, for resorting, in the terrible days of the Inquisition, to these wonderful shifts and subtleties. Still, we do not see how Signor Rossetti strengthens his cause by bringing together instances of strong language openly used against Rome, since the more he shows to have been uttered without disguise, the less shall we be inclined to admit its necessity. In the direct argument he altogether fails. We see no reason to suppose that the Ghibelline party, as a body, entertained infidel sentiments; and certainly none whatever that Dante, in particular, was not a submissive son ot the Church. Rossetti may make some converts, but there is one who will never come over to his opinion — the Muse of History.* She tells us that the Bianchi, of whom Dante was a leader, and with whom he suffered, were not originally Ghibellines. They were a division of the Guelf party. It is notorious that Dante fought in his youth against the Ghibelline Fuorusciti, and his use of "vostri," in the dialogue with Farinata, sufficiently indicates to what party he considered himself naturally to belong. When the force of circumstances drove the Bianchi into a closer connection with the Imperialists, there is no ground for supposing that they offered in sacrifice to Cæsar all the prejudices in which they had been educated. At all events, until the injustice of the Neri rulers had affected the alliance of their new with their ancient enemies,† it

* The Cancellieri Bianchi and Cancellieri Neri, were originally factions at Pistoia. Gradually these names migrated to the capital; and the partisans of the Cerchi began to be denominated White, while Corso's followers took pride in being Black.

† Let it be remembered, too, that Dante married a Donati, and that, when invested with authority as one of the Priori, he impartially exercised the restrictive powers of the law against the leaders of both factions. Posterity would have heard nothing of his Ghibellinism, had not the ill-omened presence of Charles de Valois given power and a desperate mind to the adherents of Donati. See the narrative of Dino Compagni, the best authority on these subjects.

is utterly improbable that Dante and those of his faction were versed in all the wild words and daring opinions, which might be current in the Emperor's court. Yet Rossetti would have us believe that before the events occurred which detached him finally from the Roman party, he was already as deep in heresy as the supposed author of "De tribus Impostoribus."

We should certainly feel grateful for any theory that should satisfactorily explain the Vita Nuova. No one can have read that singular work, without having found his progress perpetually checked, and his pleasure impaired, by the occurrence of passages apparently unintelligible, or presenting only an unimportant meaning, in phrases the most laborious and involved. These difficulties we have been in the habit of referring, partly to corruptions in the text, for of all the works of Dante * there is none in which the editions are so at variance, and the right readings so uncertain; partly to the scholastic forms of language with which all writers at the revival of literature — but none so much as Dante, a stu-

* Dr. Nott informed the writer of these remarks, that he had been enabled, by collating several Italian MSS. not generally known, to rectify many apparent obscurities in the Comedia itself.

dent in many universities, and famous among his countrymen and foreigners for the depth of his scientific acquirements — delighted to overload the simplicity of their subject. Certainly, until Signor Rossetti suggested the idea, we never dreamed of looking for Ghibelline enigmas in a narrative apparently so remote from politics. Nor did it occur to us to seek even for moral meanings, that might throw a forced and doubtful light on these obscurities. Whatever uncertain shape might, for a few moments, be assumed by the Beatrice of the Comedia, imparadised in overpowering effluences of light and music, and enjoying the immediate vision of the Most High, here at least, in the mild humility and modest nobleness of the living and loving creature, to whom the sonnets and canzones are addressed, we did believe we were safe from allegory. Something indeed there was of vagueness and unreality in the picture we beheld: but it never disturbed our faith; for we believed it to arise from the reverential feeling which seemed to possess the poet's imagination, and led him to concentrate all his loftiest sentiments and pure ideas of perfection in the object of his youthful passion, consecrated long since and idealized to his heart, by the sanctities of the overshadowing tomb. It was a noble thing, we thought, to see the stern politician, the embittered exile,* the man worn by the world's severest realities, who knew how sharp it was to mount another's stairs, and eat another's bread, in his old age; yet, amidst these sufferings and wounded feelings, recurring with undaunted memory to the days of his happy boyhood: not for purposes of vain regret; not for complaints of deceived expectation; not to color the past time with the sombre tints of the present: but to honor human nature; to glorify disinterested affection; to celebrate that solemn, primeval, indissoluble alliance between the imagination and the heart. It was this consideration, we confess, that imparted its principal charm to the character of Beatrice, both in the Vita Nuova, and the great poem,

* It is by no means certain that the Vita Nuova was composed after the stormy period of Dante's life had begun. Rossetti takes for granted that it was written after 1302, the date of his exile. He, of course, rejects entirely the apparent authority of Boccaccio in his Vita di Dante, where it is expressly stated that the poet wrote it in his twenty-seventh year, *i. e.* about 1292. It may, however, have been retouched afterwards. Certainly the conclusion seems to refer to the Comedia as a work already in hand; yet we have no reason to think any of this was written before 1300, the date assigned by Dante himself.

which seemed its natural prolongation. We liked to view these works in what appeared to be their obvious relation; nor could we ever read without emotion that passage in the conclusion of the former, in which the poet, feeling even then his lips touched by the inspiring cherubim, speaks loftily, but indistinctly, of that higher monument he was about to raise to her whom he had already celebrated with so ample a ritual of melodious eulogy. In the Paradise, and the latter part of the Purgatory, we have intimated already, that the reality of Beatrice Portinari seemed, for a time, to become absorbed into those celestial truths, of which she had always been a mirror to the imagination of her lover. Described throughout as most pure, most humble, most simple, most affectionate, and as the personal form in which Dante delighted to contemplate the ideal objects of his moral feelings, is it wonderful that she should become at last for him the representative of religion itself? We rise indeed a step higher by this bold personification, but that step is on the same ascent we have climbed with him from the beginning. Judged by the exact standard of calculated realities, it was no more true that Beatrice deserved the praises of those early sonnets, than that she is worthy to represent the Church, or Religion, in the solemn procession through terrestrial Paradise. Imagination gave her the first; imagination assigns the last: according as our tempers are disposed, we may blame the extravagance of the fiction, or sympathize with that truth of feeling, which raises round its delicate vitality this protecting veil; but we cannot, in fairness of reasoning, assume the absence of any real groundwork in the one representation of Beatrice, unless we are prepared to deny it also in the other. Signor Rossetti, indeed, is fully so prepared. He considers such a passion, as is usually thought to be depicted in the poems of that time, as utterly chimerical and absurd; and wonders at the stupidity of those learned men who have written volumes on the contrary supposition. On this point we shall have a word to say presently. Here we confine ourselves to maintaining that a character may be allegorical in part, without being so altogether. We are not inclined, therefore, to admit the force of Rossetti's argument, founded on the famous scene of the chariot; because, when we have cheerfully granted that the daughter of Folco

Portinari was never robbed of the Christian Church by a Babylonian harlot, we do not agree with him that we have conceded all that is of moment in the question. We are still, it seems to us, at liberty to contend, not merely that a Florentine lady, named Beatrice, did actually exist, and was beloved by Dante, but that she is the very Beatrice whose imaginary agency he exhibits to us in his poem, and whose real conduct he describes in his "Life." But while we are determined, by the force of what our author dismisses at once as foolish prejudice and second-hand sentimentality, not to yield a single inch of ground further than facts oblige us, we frankly confess his observations have made so much impression on us, that we *fear* (at the risk of the Professor's contempt, we must use that word) there may be more of allegory in the two last of the Cantiche of the Comedia, than we had hitherto imagined. He need not triumph in this concession. We are ready to die fighting in the cause, rather than go the whole lengths of a theory which would have us acknowledge nothing in the "dolce guida e cara," whose smile brightened the brightness of Paradise, but a mixture of a possible good Pope and a possible good Emperor!

Besides, the new interpretation of the Vita Nuova appears to us forced and desperate. It might not be difficult, we imagine, to find twenty other hidden meanings at least as plausible. We will, however, give it at length, that our readers may judge. The whole of that treatise, then, it appears, is a narration, in *gergo*, of one fact,— the change from Madonna Cortesia or Imperialism, to Madonna Pietà or Romanism. In proof of this, we have the second vision quoted: "Il dolcissimo Signore, il quale mi signoreggiava, per la virtù della gentilissima donna nella mia immaginazione, apparve come pellegrino leggiermente vestito e di vili drappi." This indicates, we are told, that Dante was about to undertake an allegorical pilgrimage, clothed in Guelfic garments. Love, who looked "as if his seignory had passed away," proceeds to tell the poet, "Io vengo da quella donna la quale e stata lunga tua difesa, e so che il suo venire non sarà: e però quel cuore ch'io ti faceva aver da lei io l'ho meco, e portolo a donna, la quale sarà tua difensione, come costei; e nominòllami, sicchè io la conobbi bene." Then Love disappears, and the poet remains "cambiato in vista," (that is, says Rossetti, in his outward appearance), and tells us, "Dico quello che amore ni disse, avvegnachè non compiutamente, per tema ch'io avea di non scoprire il mio segreto." This secret is the name of the new lady to whom he is to feign love. The evil rumors which began to gather against Dante, on the occasion of this "nuova difesa," for "troppa gente ne ragionava oltre ai termini della Cortesia" (that is, many persons not belonging to the Imperial party), occasioned some stern behavior in Beatrice, who denied her lover the accustomed salutation. In other words, the Imperial party began to suspect him of being a Papist: "which," the Professor adds, with some naïveté, "was natural enough, seeing that all the world has hitherto made the same mistake." Then follows a dream of Dante, in which Love appeared to him, and said, "Fili mi, tempus est ut prætermittantur simulacra nostra." After which he is commanded to make a Ballata, in which he should speak to his Beatitude, not immediately, but indirectly, and should place in the midst of it some words, adorned with sweetest harmony, that might declare his real intention to the lady herself. The Ballata follows, and the poet directs it to seek his Madonna, "Presso ch'avresti chiesta pietate."

According to the new interpretation, this Ballata is a symbol of the Divina Commedia, and the words "nel mezzo" refer to the description of terrestrial Paradise in the latter part of the Purgatory, concerning which we shall hear a good deal presently. The sonnet, which comes next in order, preceded by a prose paraphrase in Dante's usual fashion, does not certainly present a very intelligible sense, according to its literal acceptation.

Tutti li miei pensier parlan d'Amore,
  Ed hanno in lor sì gran varietate,
  Ch'altro mi fa voler sua potestate,
  Altro folle ragiona il suo valore,
Altro sperando m' apporta dolzore,
  Altro pianger mi fa spesse fiate,
  E sol s' accordano in chieder Pietate,
  Tremando di paura ch'è nel core!
Ond' io non so da qual materia prenda,
  E vorrei dire, e non so ch' io mi dica,
  Così mi trovo in amorosa erranza.
E se con tutti vo fare accordanza,
  Convienemi chiamar la mia nemica,
  Madonna la Pietâ, che mi difenda.*

* Whether "Pietâ" is in this instance adequately translated by "Pity," seems rather difficult to determine. On Rossetti's hypothesis, it signifies "Piety." There are, however, innumerable passages in Dante, which, without the most barefaced violence, could not be brought to bear such a construction of the word. In the Vocabolario della Crusca, only one instance is cited, (from

I have no thought that does not speak of love;
  They have in them so great variety,
  That one bids me desire his sovranty,
One with mad speech his goodness would approve;
Another, bringing hope, brings pleasantness,
  And yet another makes me often weep:
  In one thing only do they concord keep.
Calling for Pity, in timorous distress.
So know I not which thought to choose for song;
  Fain would I speak, but wild words come and go,
  And in an amorous maze I wander long.
No way but this, if Concord must be made,
  To call upon Madonna Pity's aid;
  And yet Madonna Pity is my foe.

"I say Madonna," Dante adds, "speaking, as it were, disdainfully." In the new theory this mysterious Madonna Pietà represents the Catholic religion; and the sonnet is an announcement of the new disguise found necessary for the sect. Dante then vindicates his frequent personifications of Love, quoting Ovid, who puts into the mouth of Love as of a human person, "Bella

Casa), in which Pietà is used in this sense: — "Buon animo, conforme alla perpetua Pietà e religione di Dio." Generally speaking, Pietà may either be rendered by compassion, or it has a wider signification, answering in some degree to that of Pietas in Latin, or *εὐσεβεια* in Greek, as e. g., in this passage from the Tesoretto of Latini: "Pietade non è passione, anzi una nobile disposizione d'animo, apparecchiata di ricevere amore, misericordia e altre caritative passioni."

mihi video, bella parantur, ait." "And by this my book may be rendered clear to any one that doubts respecting any part of it." Of course this quotation from Ovid is eagerly laid hold of by Signor Rossetti, who considers it a key of the whole treatise, and it must be owned it suits his purpose well. The death of poor Beatrice, although not the next incident mentioned by Dante, is the next he finds serviceable: and the mode of describing it affords room for much triumph on the part of our new interpreter. "Quomodo sola sedet civitas plena populo! Facta est quasi vidua domina gentium! Il Signore della Giustizia chiamò quella gentilissima," &c. Now it seems there is extant a Latin letter, written by Dante to the conclave of cardinals on the occasion of the death of Clement V., exhorting them to elect an Italian pontiff, and thus to bring back the chair of Peter from Avignon to Rome. This letter begins with the very words above mentioned, "Quomodo sola sedet," &c. By this step Dante declared himself a partisan of Romanism, anxious for the supremacy of the eternal city. It was, therefore, according to Rossetti, an act of deception, a bait thrown out to nibbling Guelfs, and exactly of a piece with his scheme of concealing heresy in an apparently orthodox poem. It is evident, the Professor thinks, that the death of Beatrice indicates the completion of the change to seeming Romanism, and that this extract of the Latin letter was introduced to show it. He expatiates on the indifferent, unimpassioned style in which the death is first mentioned: the strange passage in which Beatrice is declared to be the number nine, three times three, on account of her perfection, and because the Trinity was the root of her moral being, appears to him a decisive proof that no real person is here described, but a fictitious, allegorical creation, such as he has pointed out. This, however, is far from being the only signification which he attaches to the death of Beatrice. The important change of *gergo* occurred, once for all, under the auspices of Dante; but what then are we to make of Laura, Fiammetta, Selvaggia, and other objects of Platonic affection, equally indispensable to the Professor's theory?* His excursive fancy scorns to be con-

* To the list, which he already considers large enough to need his explanation, may be added the Caterina of Camoens, the Elisa in the Eclogues of Garcilaso, the "departed saint" of Milton, the Thyrza of Byron, the Lucy of Wordsworth, and half a hundred more, whom we should be weary of enumerating. Perhaps in some

fined to the limits of a single interpretation, even when it is the cherished fruit of his own labors. That all those ladies should die before their lovers, is too great a prodigy for his scepticism to digest. There must be a deep secret in it; and by dint of searching in masonic books, and studying Swedenborg, he thinks he has discovered it. These "donne gentili," it turns out, are only beautiful truths, relative to a future perfect government, which the initiated naturally fall in love with, and whose pretended deaths relate to a mysterious ritual function in the secret societies. Thus Beatrice is a part of Dante, and Laura of Petrarch. The grief of these faithful lovers for their departed mistresses, is grief only in the external man, beyond which the uninitiated can understand nothing. But the inner soul, which lives a true life in the possession of its great secret, rejoices all the while, and smiles at the hypocritical tears of its outward countenance. Reserving to ourselves the privilege of offering some objections to this strange account, when we come to speak of Petrarch, we will

future edition we may hope for an opposite list of poets, who have died before their mistresses; a fact equally curious, it seems to us, and equally worthy of masonic interpretation.

now lay before our readers two extracts from that portion of Signor Rossetti's work which treats of the "Divina Commedia."

This poem, he tells us, is a political allegory throughout. The Inferno represents Italy, the Abisso at the end being Rome, and the episodic scene in the ninth canto being intended to shadow forth the state of Florence, and the arrival of Henry of Luxemburg. Purgatory is the actual condition of the Setta d'Amore, tormented and without rest, yet happy, "perchè speran di venire, Quando che sia, alle beate genti." Paradise is the Emperor's court as it will be hereafter, when Maria, or the Immaculate Sect, shall have brought forth Christ, the anointed heir of the empire, who shall execute the great judgment on Babylon or Rome, and elevate all who have faithfully served him to peace and honor in his court. The Professor shall explain these things in his own words.

It will be allowed, I suppose, that in these two expressions — "Il Mondo presente," "Il Tempo presente," the two words mondo and tempo are equivalent in sense, and may be considered synonymous. Now, in the Purgatorio, Dante asks a spirit for what reason "il mondo fosse così privo di virtù, e gravido di malizia." And he makes the spirit answer him, Ben puoi veder," &c. You may easily perceive that bad government is the cause from which proceeds the guiltiness of the world. When Rome had two luminaries (the Emperor and the Pope), who pointed out to us the two ways, that of the world, or political well-being, and that of God, or spiritual felicity, then Rome produced the good time; but since one has destroyed the other (the Pope has eclipsed the Emperor), the exact contrary has taken place; for the people, perceiving their spiritual guide only intent on stealing that temporal good which their own appetites desire, follow readily the bad example of their head, and glut themselves with the things of this life, having no regard whatever to spiritual good. The Church of Rome, therefore, is the cause of such a depravation. She has perverted the two governments, as well that which is her own as that which she usurped, whereby she has fallen into the filth of all wickedness, and pollutes not only herself but whoever leans on her." In another part of the Purgatory, he says yet more clearly, "Il capo reo lo mondo torce." Hence the idea of Dante is evident, and expressly contained in his words. Rome, when good, had produced the good time. Rome, when bad, produced the bad time; because the bad head, in which the time is reflected, gave the example of depravity. Now all the Inferno of Dante has for its principal element the bad time, the same which Boccaccio mentions as the source of all the Tartarean streams described by the poet. The Ghibelline bard represents it in the fourteenth canto, under the aspect of a vast Colossus, composed of various metals corresponding to the various fictitious ages, golden, silver, copper, and iron. But in what direction is situated this bad time, all whose productions are poured into hell? In what place is it mirrored, as a perfect likeness? "E *Roma* guarda siccome suo speglio."

In the Inferno, Dante tells us that the Evangelist, who wrote the Apocalypse, beholding "Colei che siede sopra l'acque," saw a figure of the corrupted papacy. She is the great harlot, "quæ sedet super aquas multas," and those waters are figures of nations "et aquæ quas vidisti, ubi Meretrix sedet, populi sunt et gentes." The waters, therefore, produced by the bad time, which mirrors itself in corrupted Rome, are figures of corrupted nations, "la gente che sua guida vede." Let us follow the course of these waters, and see where they discharge themselves. They are poured, we shall find, into the lake of the abyss, where Satan dwells, "in su che Dite siede." This lake is surrounded by a great wall, and the wall by a vast intrenchment; the latter is twenty-two miles in circuit, the former eleven. Now the outer intrenchment of the walls of Rome (whether real or imaginary) is said by the contemporaries of Dante to be exactly twenty-two miles round, and the walls themselves were, and still are, about eleven. It is obvious, therefore, that the bad time is intended to behold, as a mirror, that bad place, which is the receptacle of those waters, or nations; in other words that figurative Rome, "in su che Dite siede!" The waters return to their great fountain; this is a physical fact, used allegorically: the perverted nations to the source of their iniquities: this is the meaning of the allegorical image.

The characteristic vice of the Papal Court was avarice.

A thousand writers tell us so, and Dante among the rest. The Demon of Avarice, when he sees Dante descend through Hell, cries out to him, "Pap' è Satan, Pap' è Satan, Aleppe." All commentators explain "Aleppe," as prince, from the Hebrew Aleph, just as Gioseppe comes from Joseph. For this reason, the demon cries, "The Pope is Satan, Prince of this Hell." Before we pursue the demonstration, we must make one remark on this verse. It has driven the commentators mad; they give it up as unintelligible: now we understand what it means. The two measurements, spoken of above, were always thought to be mentioned at random; now we perceive the evident allusion. Observe, too, they are the only measurements to be found in all the Inferno, and they are derived from no geographical dimension, nor any Scriptural doctrine: now we see at once from what quarter they are derived. And by the help of these passages, we may understand the origin of many other allusions to Rome and its Sovereign.

The Lake of the Abyss, central point of the region of wickedness governed by the Demon Gerione, is surrounded by moats, and a chain of successive bridges leads to the great wall of this Lake. Dante likens these motes to those which surround a fortified city, and the bridges to those which lead into such a city, and the damned spirits crossing the first bridge, to those who cross the bridge of Castel Santangelo at Rome, "e vanno a S. Pietro." We cannot, in this place, explain whom the demon of fraud, called Gerione, "qui tribus unus erat," is intended to represent: but only let us keep in mind that Dante's

Satan is also "tribus unus." Now can we fully declare the purport of those bridges over which the Demon presides: only let us keep in mind an etymology, sufficiently common, "Pontifex a pontibus faciundis."

The famous 734 towers of the Roman walls, mentioned by Pliny, were in the time of Dante, nearly half remaining. These towers caused many allusions to those of Babylon: and such allusions there are in Dante. The wall that encloses the Abyss is crowned with far-seen towers, "Montereggion di torri si corona." There, in that thick gloom, "A lui parve veder molte alte torri." He asked, "What city is this? What land is this?" His guide answered him, "Sappi, che non son torri, ma giganti," who were towering, "di mezzala persona," over that wall which was eleven miles round. Dante perceives the first to be a giant, and his head appeared, "Come la pina di S. Pietro a Roma."

Let us now set together six distinct points which bear relation to each other, and have one common direction. The trench which surrounds the lake of the abyss, has the precise dimensions of the intrenchment at Rome. The wall which surrounds the abyss, in which Satan resides, has the precise dimensions of the Roman walls within which the Pope resides. The Demon of Avarice exclaims, "Pape," &c. The corrupt time, which sends forth into the abyss its wicked nations, made so by itself, "Roma guarda," &c. The damned passing under the first bridge leading to the abyss, are compared to those who go to St. Peter's at Rome: on the wall of the abyss, to which that bridge leads, appear giants resembling towers, and the head of the first seemed to Dante as the cupola of St. Peter's at Rome. But who is the giant, whom Dante first perceived on the wall of the abyss, where he imagined he saw many towers? Who is he whose head seemed like "the cupola of St. Peter's?" He is Nimrod, the builder of the tower of Babylon. "Hic turrificus simul et terrificus Nemroth, turres in novissimâ Babylone construens." So speaks Petrarch of the Roman Court, which sometimes he called Hell, and almost always Babylon: for he never affixes any other date to his confidential letters, than "dalla gemina Babilonia," considering it perhaps as at once terrestrial and infernal: and in his answer to a friend, who had expressed surprise at this bold indication, he says, "Subscriptionibus epistolarum mearum miraris, nec immerito, non nisi geminam Babyloniam cum legeris. Desine immirari. Et sua Babylon huic terrarum tractui est; a quibus condita incertum, a quibus habitata notissimum, certa ab his a quibus jure optimo nomen hoc possidet. Hic Nemroth potens in terra contra dominum, ac *superbis turribus* cœlum petens. Hic pharetrata Semiramis (the Babylonian harlot). Non hic Cerberus horrendus, non imperiosus Minas?"—*Ep.* 8, *sin. tit.* Numberless writers of the time, and even historians, were in the habit of calling the Papal Court by this name: and it was doubtless to make more evident the signification of this abyss, the receptacle of waters springing from one "che Roma guarda," that Dante placed in the first rank there the builder of the tower of Babylon, whose head appeared to him long and bulky, like the dome of St. Peter's.—*Cap.* V. entitled, "*Principale Allegoria del' Inferno di Dante.*"

Our next extract relates to the scene of the chariot. It is taken from the eleventh chapter of Signor Rossetti's work, which is headed "Carattere Dommatico e Politico del Poema di Dante."

Dante has placed nearly in the middle of his Comedia a majestic representation, eminent above the rest, and standing out in clear light, like an obelisk in the centre of a large square; into this representation he has gathered all the effect of opposing lights and shades, for it partakes of the Inferno and Paradiso, between which it is situated, and brings them, so to speak, into contact. This scene, prepared by everything that has come before, and illustrated by every thing that follows, naturally arrests all the attention of the reader, as it concentrated all the art of the author. This scene, in short, presents to us the heavenly Beatrice in immediate opposition to the infernal Meretrice. There the virtuous lady is set over against the abandoned woman: they meet as two inveterate enemies, as Holiness and Sin. On the right explanation of this scene depends in a great measure the interpretation of the entire Comedia, for this is the secret knot in which the principal mystery is enclosed. We are about to disentangle this hard knot, but we shall not be able to loosen it entirely, until our labors are further advanced. We begin by asking, Is that abandoned woman a real person? Certainly not. She is an allegorical figure of the Pope. Dante declares it, and all agree in this. Shall we say then that the virtuous lady, introduced for the sole purpose of contrasting with the other, is to be considered a real character? Suppose you had before you a picture of some great master: such is the wonderful effect of the mingled lights and shades, that you yield to the illusion, and believe you see nature itself. Afterwards, when you look again and again, you perceive it is a picture, and not a reality. You see that what you considered shadow is only color contrived to imitate shadow, and not the real thing. But when you have become fully convinced of this, would it ever come into your head that the light, beside the painted shadow, is not itself the work of art, but a real, natural light, like that of the sun? Or what degree of judgment should we allow to a critic, who should maintain, that of these two expressions, the Iron Age and the Golden Age, one indeed was metaphorical and denoted the depravation of human society, with its attendant miseries, while the other signified real gold, excavated from mines, and wrought by workmen? Yet how does the case differ? In one and the same picture, Dante represents to us two women, one dissolute, another immaculate, each related to the other as her opposite. If in the first we have discovered the Anti-Christ and Anti-Cæsar, under a generic name of Babylon or its ruler, we ought at least to presume that in the other is typified Christ and Cæsar, under the generic name of Jerusalem or its sovereign. But let us not trust this presumption; let us not leave that best commentary on Dante, the Apocalypse. Both these allegorical females were taken from that book, and the forms of language with which the Evangelist represented them, in order to express their contrast, are nearly identical with those employed by Dante. Let us examine the sacred text. "Veni, et ostendam tibi damnationem Meretricis magnæ," &c.—*Apoc.* xvii. Here we have the Meretrice described by Dante. "Veni et ostendam tibi sponsam uxorem Agni," &c.—*Apoc.* xx. And here is that very Beatrice, whom Dante has painted on the great and lofty mountain, where he was placed to behold her: here is she, who descended from heaven in all the brightness of God, and "Parata sicut sponsa viro suo," &c., was solemnly hailed, "Veni, sponsa de Libano," like the mystic bride of Canticles. It is true Dante dared not call her Jerusalem, in open language; yet after his fashion he does call her so, and that in more places than one. Here is an instance. Describing himself at the foot of the lofty mountain, on whose summit he afterwards sees this Lady-City, he tells us,

> "Già era il sole all' orizonte giunto
> Lo cui meridian cerchio coverchia
> Jerusalem col suo più alto punto."—*Purg.* 11.

And the meridian circle in which he found himself covers with its high point exactly the top of that mountain, on which the New Jerusalem afterwards revealed herself, and which he indicates by this circumlocution. Every reader naturally turns his thoughts to the real Jerusalem in the arctic hemisphere, while Dante intends to speak of the figurative city in the antarctic. The antithetical spirit, which we shall find so marked and constant in him, led him to place in diametrical opposition the old Jerusalem to the New, "Paratam, sicut sponsam," (*Purg.* 11), as John saw it in the Spirit. August is her equipage, minutely described to us. She advances, preceded by all the books of the Old Testament, all the Sacraments personified. She pauses, surrounded by the four Gospels personified. She is followed by the Acts of the Apostles, the Apostolic Epistles, and the Apocalypse, equally personified. Are these attendants of Beatrice all real persons? No; and yet you hear them, see them, touch them. Let Dante alone — this is his art. The chariot on which the blessed lady proceeds is more beautiful than that of the sun: on the left are the four cardinal virtues, on the right the three theological virtues, all personified. But the sacred chariot is suddenly, by the poisonous breath of the dragon rising from beneath, transformed into a seven-headed, ten-horned monster. And lo! as soon as the chariot has become an image of the dragon Satan, and unworthy of Beatrice, there arises audaciously, "like a rock of Babylon," the shameless Meretrice, who dashes forward to plunge into the forest, the opposite of that garden in which her rival remains. Let us reflect on this. The heavenly lady retains all the venerable and august attendants with whom she appeared; all the theological and cardinal virtues, all the books of the old and new testament, all the sacraments, &c. And what does the other? The thief, who stole away the chariot, without the holy books, without the sacraments, without the virtues, hurries away with the beast on which she sits, and with a king of the earth, her paramour, "Meretrix magna cum quâ fornicati sunt reges terræ." In short her possessions are all infernal, not heavenly. Now, when we know that this abandoned creature is a symbol of Babylon and its ruler, we are forced to exclaim — What a dark idea of the Pope possessed the imagination of Dante? A Pope destitute of all that properly constitutes a Pope! A Pope without holy books, without sacraments, without cardinal and other virtues. Can we think that Dante held such a phantom to be a true Pope? But if not, who was, in his mind, the true Pontiff? Since it is evident that in these two women the Ghibelline poet meant to represent a contrast of extremes, and as it were the highest good and the highest evil personified, we may substitute for these apocalyptic ladies the two apocalyptic ages, the wretched age of impious Babylon, and the happy age of holy Jerusalem; or otherwise, the age of gold and that of iron, which do not differ from the Babylonish time and its opposite. The age of gold includes in itself all perfection, as well doctrinal as political, that is a pure worship and a rightful government; which to a Ghibelline implied the beatitudes imparted by an excellent Emperor and an excellent Pontiff. The age of iron is diametrically opposed to the other in both respects. Having established this, we are at liberty to say that this golden age, expressed as the Lady of Blessing, or Lady Beatrice, produces the two beatitudes which are the objects of human aspiration, that of mortal life and that of immortal, in such completeness, that we are put in possession of a terrestrial Paradise here, and a celestial Paradise hereafter. She will make us attain the earthly blessedness, by means of the moral and intellectual virtues, called cardinal, as a good Emperor ought to do. She will make us attain the heavenly blessedness, by means of the holy Christian virtues, called theological, as a good Pontiff ought to do. But these two abstract perfections, reduced to one concrete figure, form exactly the Donna Beatrice, who blesses by a double beatitude; and on this account the poet placed the cardinal virtues on her left, and the theological on her right, in the picture he has drawn of her. According to this Analysis, it appears that the imaginary Lady of Blessing, in whose eyes Dante contemplated lofty mysteries, "Or con uni or con altri reggimenti," includes in herself the temporal and spiritual government, so as to possess, we repeat, in the same moment the perfect and true essence of an excellent Emperor and an excellent Pope.

Who assures us then that this interpretation is correct? We might answer, Inductive Criticism; but we will rather say, Dante himself. Let Dante come to interpret himself, and let his words be not only heard but maturely considered, since they are worthy of all hearing and consideration. He has explained all this in the commentary he has left us on his poem, yet no one has hitherto understood him. "Duo igitur fines providentia illa inenarrabilis homini posuit intendendos; beatitudinem scilicet hujus vitæ, quæ in operatione propriæ virtutis consistit, et per Terrestrem Paradisum figuratur; et beatitudinem vitæ æternæ, quæ consistit in fruitione divini aspectûs, ad quam virtus propria accedere non potest, nisi divino lumine adjuta, quæ per Paradisum Celestem intelligi datur." Then having explained the several functions of a Pontiff and an Emperor, as the appointed guides to these several beatitudes, he continues, "Papa et Imperator, cum sint relativa, reduci habebunt ad aliquod Unum, in quo reperiatur iste respectus superpositionis absque differentialibus aliis." — *De Monarch. sub fin.* And he has reduced them to one, "in quantum homines," not taking into account at present the Holy Trinity, which, by his own confession, is also included in the Lady of Blessing, but only the Emperor and the Pope. Let us reflect on this.

We know from history that the Patarini were in the habit of charging the Pope with robbery and spoliation of the Church of Christ. We know that the Ghibellines accused him of having stolen and usurped the seat of Cæsar. Dante exhibits to us an allegorical representation, in which the Meretrice steals from Beatrice the "divine and august" chariot, bearing the characters of that Christian Church, and that Imperial Throne. If, after this evident allegory, any one persists in saying that this Lady of Blessing is not such as analysis demonstrates, but really and truly Madonna Beatrice Portinari of Florence, daughter of Messer Folco Portinari, a Florentine, and wife of Messer Simone de' Bardi, a Florentine, we are entitled to ask in what chronicle it is recorded for our instruction, that the Pope stole the Church and Empire from the daughter of Messer Folco, the wife of Messer Simone. What does Dante call the Empire, deprived of its Emperor?

> "Nave senza nocchiero in gran tempesta." — *Purg.* vi.

What does he call the chariot, deprived of Beatrice?

> "Nave in fortuna
> Vinta dell' onde, or da poggio, or da orso." — *Purg.* xxx.

What comparison does he apply to Beatrice? He likens her to the admiral of that ship. To whom does he compare the Emperor? To the pilot of that ship. Let us hear the two parallel similes.

> "Quale Ammiraglio che di poppa in prora
> Viene a veder la gente che ministra
> Per gli alti legni, ed a ben far la incuora,
> In su la sponda del carro sinistra
> Vidi la Donna che pria m' appario." — *Purg.* xxx.

"Siccome vedemo in una nave che diversi uffici e diversi fini a un solo fine sono ordinati; così è uno che tutti questi fini ordina, e questo è il nocchiero, alla cui boce tutti ubbidir deono. Perchè manifestamente vedere si può che a perfezione dell' umana spezie conviene uno essere quasi nocchiero, che abbia irrepugnabile ufficio or commandare. E questo ufficio è per eccellenza Imperio chiamato, e chi a questo ufficio è posto è chiamato Imperatore." In one, the Emperor is a pilot giving orders to the crew, who are working the ship; — in the other, Beatrice is an admiral, encouraging all her men, from stern to prow of the vessel. This Beatrice comes on in a triumphal car, resembling that which Rome saw driven by Augustus; and before her is chanted the Virgilian verse,

> "Manibus date lilia plenis,"

written for the presumptive heir of the throne of Augustus. Towards this mystical Beatrice, as the ultimate aim of his mystical journey, the bard of the imperial Roman monarch, Virgil, conducts the bold Ghibelline, Dante, who has told us in his last words,

> "Lustrando superos et Phlegetonta, jura monarchiæ cecini."

If now we turn to consider the sacred symbols of this lady, we shall see them in such clear light, that even the most blind understanding must be struck with them. Here are some. She comes in triumph with a numerous attendance of angels, into the terrestrial paradise, and she is saluted with the verse,

> "Hosanna benedictus qui venis,"

(the "filio David being omitted,) which was chanted before Christ when he made his triumphant entry into Jerusalem. She utters these words, "Modicum et non videbitis me," the very words of Christ. The angels sing to her, "In te Domine speravi," words addressed to Christ. She is compared, with several wiredrawn and far-fetched parallelisms, to Christ on Mount Tabor, with the three disciples, Peter, James, and John, and the two prophets, Moses and Elias. She is compared again to Christ raising the dead. She comes from east to west on the emblematic chariot, an evident type of the Church, which came also from east to west. She is surrounded with all the saintly company before mentioned, the biblical books, the sacraments, the virtues, &c., all which things relate to Christ and his religion. She is not only declared to be the Holy Trinity, but in particular is designated as the Second Person. This is the poet's method of doing it. In order to make us comprehend that this allegorical form is a male being figuratively transformed into a female, just as her opposite was, he gives her John for a forerunner, also changed into a woman. He tells us in the Vita Nuova how he saw two ladies approach, one preceding the other.

Here are the words: "The name of this lady, the first who came, was Giovanna; and soon after her I saw, as I looked, the admirable Beatrice draw nigh." Her name Giovanna is from that John who went before the true light, saying, "Ego vox clamantis in deserto." But for what Lord was the way prepared here, unless it be Beatrice, whom this Giovanna preceded? Biscioni makes a judicious remark on this passage: "Dante intends to allude particularly to the office of the Baptist. We all know that St. John was the precursor of the Incarnate Word." But if the precursor is represented with a change of sex, we ought to infer a similar change in the person who follows: so that Madonna Giovanna and Madonna Beatrice become the exact correspondents of the Holy Baptist and the Baptized Divinity. Jesus Christ is called the Wisdom of God, and on this account Dante paints him as a woman: but in the course of this painting, he introduces "Hosanna," &c., and by various similitudes explains to us that it is the portrait of Christ, although he cannot expressly call it such. In the last analysis then it appears, that these two opposed women, set in direct contrast by Dante, are the same he found in the Apocalypse, corrupt Babylon and New Jerusalem. In these two figures, which shadow forth, in personification, the ideas of Good and Evil, two cities are represented to us with separate political governments: on one side, Papal Rome, with its head and its government,—on the other, Imperial Rome, with its head and government; the same object, that is, under two aspects, and largely accompanied by symbols, characters, and indications just like the two allegorical women in the Apocalypse. We find there, that in the famous Millennium, Christ in person will be the visible head of the New Jerusalem, and will unite in himself the two characters of Supreme Ruler and Religious Head. Hence Imperial Rome, or New Jerusalem, comprehends all imaginable excellence; because Christ will, in person, produce there the two beatitudes: first the earthly, and then the heavenly, imaged in the terrestrial and celestial Paradise. It is easy for any one to perceive who such a figurative Christ would be for the Ghibellines, and whom they would expect to take upon him spiritual and temporal rule, for the purpose of redeeming the human race from the double slavery of Anti-Christ and Satan, the perverters of the Empire and the Church. It is evident, therefore, for what reason the two characters are united in Beatrice, who constitutes the "aliqua substantia in quâ Papa et Imperator habent reduci ad unum." The very same expression is actually applied to a Roman Emperor in the poem,

> "Una Sostanza,
> "Sopra la qual doppio lume s'addua." — *Parad.* vii.

Throughout we have the same two opposite parties expressed in various figures: Papal Rome and Imperial Rome; or Babylon the unholy, with Anti-Christ, and his wicked, anarchical, miserable people; and Jerusalem, with Christ, and his virtuous, peaceable, happy people. Hence the denominations of False City and True City; City of Evil Living, and City of Holy Living; or, more briefly, City of Death, and City of Life. These two opposites again, taken as persons, became, in Dante's apocalyptic poem, Meretrice and Beatrice, because the Apocalypse had represented them as two women. Hence two kinds of love, the bad and the good; and two classes of lovers, the wicked paramours of impious Babylon, and the holy lovers of Beatrice-Jerusalem. Also, as in the Apocalypse, Babylon is called the "habitation of devils," the receptacle of every unclean spirit; and New Jerusalem is shown as the dwelling-place of angels, the abode of every pure spirit; so, in the poem of Dante, these two cities, or Papal and Imperial Rome, became Hell, with a tri-une Lucifer, and devils and damned spirits; Paradise, with a tri-une God, and angels and blessed spirits. We have already seen how full of allusions to Papal Rome is the Inferno of Dante; we shall see, in its turn, that there are at least as many in the Paradiso to Imperial Rome.

Our readers have now a tolerable notion of the Professor's mode of argument. It is impossible, we think, to deny the praise of great ingenuity to the passages we have just cited. The justice of some of his remarks is sufficiently obvious. That there is much allegory in the Divina Comedia no one can be hardy enough to controvert, after the express assertion of the poet himself.

"O voi ch' avete gl' intelletti sani,
Mirate la dottrina, chè s' asconde
Sotto il velame degli versi strani."

The only questions then are, What is the character of the allegorical part? and what is its extent? Here again the first of these questions seems to be answered by Dante himself. In his Epistle to Can Grande, he says, "Sciendum est quod istius operis (poematis sc.) non est simplex sensus; immo dici potest *polysensum*, hoc est, plurium sensuum. Nam primus sensus est quod habetur per litteram, alius est qui habetur per significata per litteram. Et primus dicitur litteralis, secundus vero allegoricus. His visis manifestum est quod duplex oportet esse subjectum circa quod currant alterni sensus. Et ideo videndum est de subjecto hujus operis, prout ad litteram accipitur; deinde de subjecto, prout allegorice sententiatur. Est ergo subjectum totius, literaliter tantum accepti, status animarum post mortem. Si vero accipiatur ex istis verbis, colligere potes, quod, secundum allegoricum sensum, poeta agit de Inferno isto, in quo, peregrinando ut viatores, mereri et demereri possumus. Si vero accipiatur opus allegorice, subjectum est homo, prout, merendo et demerendo, per arbitrii libertatem, Justitiæ premianti et punienti obnoxius est." Does it not appear from this simple statement, that the principal allegory in the Commedia is of a moral nature, representing the struggles of man with himself, the wretched condition to which his vices condemn him, the glorious difficulties which attend his ascent upon the mountain of virtue, and that perfect peace which, when the good fight has been fought, awaits the religious mind in the enjoyment of unlimited love towards God and man? Rossetti, however, who thinks a man cunning in direct proportion to the openness of his language, believes this very passage to be written in *gergo!* and to contain for adepts a declaration that Italy and the Imperial court are the real subjects of the poem. By this scheme of interpretation anything may be made of anything: we continue to adhere to the plain words of Dante, although we by no means contend that there may not be several partial allegories of a political complexion scattered through the poem, as the "*Polysensum*" seems to intimate, and as Signor Rossetti's book has, we confess, made appear more probable to us than before. The second question, What is the extent of allegory in Dante? answers itself for those possessed of poetical feeling.* Moral and

* Lest the exclusion of Signor Rossetti from this number should seem harsh to any reader of these remarks, who has not also read

political ideas, however they may have contributed to the first formation of the plan in Dante's understanding, however much they may have strengthened his purpose and animated his feelings towards the execution of it, yet would assuredly not have been permitted to encroach on the ground already consecrated to the free activity of his imagination, and the deep tenderness of his affections. If Signor Rossetti were to write a poem, he would no doubt remind us, in every line, of some interior meaning, because that meaning would never be absent from his thoughts. The poetry would be to him an insignificant mask, and to indulge any feeling for

his book, we feel bound to mention an emendation of Petrarch proposed by that gentleman, which, we think, will set the matter beyond doubt. Having got some strange crotchet into his head about "Luce" being a sacred word among the sectarians, he proposes to alter the well-known line,

"Ove il bel volto di Madonna luce,"

into Ov' è il bel volto di *Madonna Luce;* literally, "where the pretty face of Mrs. Light is!" After this specimen, it is useless to quote his obstinate preference of the prosaic and indeed ridiculous reading, "porta *i fiori*" in Dante's noble description of the tempestuous wind. He takes no sort of notice of the imitated passage in Ariosto, where we never heard of "fiori" having been suggested by any commentator. The alteration, "Pap' è Satan, Pap' è Satan, Aleppe," does violence to the language no less than to the poetry. Besides, it was useless even for his own purpose.

it, considered apart from its prosaic object, would be in his opinion a ridiculous folly! But widely different is the method of creative minds. Their vision reaches far, and embraces all objects within their horizon, without ever passing over those in their immediate neighborhood. To every man, worthy the name of poet, the first object is always the Beautiful. No allegory, however wise and profound, can distract him from it. He may study such meanings as a diversion, a piece of by-play; but they never interfere with the grand purpose to which his "spiritual agents are bent up." They are limited then, not by speculations about the prospects of any party, Guelf or Ghibelline, but by the poet's own sense of harmonious fitness, that inward testimony, which affords to creative intellects a support during their work of thought, not very dissimilar from that which conscience supplies to all men in their work of life.

If we have been compelled to enter our protest against the uncertainty and exclusiveness of the new theory, when applied to the writings of the "gran padre Alighier," we must express a still more decided aversion, when it would embrace the two others of the great Italian triumvirate.

Petrarch, indeed, we are assured by our undaunted theorist, affords a far richer harvest of facts in corroboration of the new doctrine, than his great predecessor. These riches, however, like the rest of the Professor's wealth, are held out rather to feed our imagination with hopes for the future, than to satisfy us in present coin. We have little doubt he may hereafter write a very pretty Comento Analitico on the Canzoniere, but we have still less, that his arguments will prove utterly invalid and sophistical. At present he has given us no sort of evidence that Petrarch was a heretic, and a proper member of the supposed Setta. His language indeed, against the Papal court, is even more vehement than that of Dante; but its virulence is unconcealed, and far from incompatible with the severest notions of orthodoxy. It should be remembered too, although Signor Rossetti would have us forget it, that, in *almost* every instance, these denunciations are uttered against the court of Avignon, and that the word Babylon, when applied to that court, has a peculiar reference to the Jewish captivity. Far from being a proof of feelings inimical to the See of Rome, this tone of indignant complaint may be considered as fresh from the heart of a pious

Italian Catholic. So little does Petrarch appear to have been judged for these expressions by his own contemporaries, as Signor Rossetti would now judge him, that the Holy See actually forced its patronage upon him, and he was considered by the devout of that day as an eminent theologian. Yet his life was open to all. A frequent guest in the palaces of the great; a commissioned defender of the rights of senates; a correspondent of eminent men in church and state; the friend of Colonna; the advocate of Rienzi; famous throughout Europe for eloquence and learning, yet more than for the poetry which has raised him high among the immortals; with so many eyes upon him, and so many envious of his fortune, he would have been an easy victim, had he dealt in the secret manœuvres which Signor Rossetti supposes. We cannot consider a vague story that Pope Innocent once suspected him of magic, as carrying any weight in the balance against the immunity and even favor, so far as he would accept it, which he enjoyed under three successive pontiffs. Besides, a far more extensive alteration of *gergo* than that which is represented to have taken place in the time of Dante, would have been necessary to bring the sentiments of Petrarch into community with those of the Florentine Fuorusciti of 1311. The politics of Italy underwent, in the fifty years that separated the death of Dante from that of his successor, a revolution of no slight moment. The Ghibelline princes of the North loosened or broke off their connection with the Imperial court. No one now dreamed of universal monarchy, vested in the Cæsars, as a panacea for all political evils. Least of all would Petrarch give into such a chimera, who considered all Germans as "brutal knaves,"* and whose burst of patriotic indignation is so well known :

> "Ben provide Natura al nostro stato,
> Quando de l'Alpi schermo
> Pose fra noi, e la Tedesca rabbia."

At one time, it is true, Petrarchi with the other "magnanimi pochi a cui il ben piace," entertained hopes from the promised intervention of Charles IV. His hortatory epistle to that sovereign, entitled "De Pacificandâ Italiâ," is one of his best Latin compositions. His interview with him at Mantua, when, four years after the date of that epistle, Charles actually entered Italy, is recorded in an eloquent letter. A passage in the reply of Charles to Petrarch, as quoted

* Epist. sine tit. 15.

by De Sade, affords great cause of triumph to Rossetti. "En voyant tant d'obstacles, et si peu de forces, mon esprit auroit hésité, si l'Amour, ce puissant mobile des cœurs, ne les avoit fait disparoitre. L'Amour s'est assis sur mon char avec moi, en me presentant des triomphes, des couronnes, et une place parmi les astres."* He quotes, in illustration of this, some sonnets and canzones, in which obscure historical allusions occur, amongst others the famous "O aspettata in ciel beata e bella Anima," addressed, as is commonly said, to Jacopo Colonna, bishop of Lombes, Petrarch's intimate friend, but, according to Rossetti, who takes not the slightest notice of the received opinion, secretly designed for the Pontiff of the Setta d'Amore. He rests much on the concluding lines, "che non pur *sotto bende* Alberga Amor, per cui si piagne e ride."

But leaving this trifling guesswork, let us turn

* Is it not reasonable to suppose that "Amour," in this place, is used only in its general sense of benevolence? But if a more recondite meaning is required, we may plausibly conjecture that an allusion was intended to Petrarch, as a poet of Love. By that time his Italian verses were as much known, though perhaps hardly as much admired, as his Latin compositions. "Favola fù gran tempo." And he expressly tells us that, in his interview with Charles at Mantua, he found that prince acquainted with the minutest circumstances of his life.

to another point,—the passion for Laura. We are well content to let the whole question be decided by the judgment which any candid man would pronounce on this part of it. Not only, according to Rossetti, Laura never existed; but Petrarch's grief for her death is not meant to be grief; it is, on the contrary, a high state of inward exultation, employing—Heaven knows why or wherefore—an exterior language of seeming complaint! Now by this our patience is wellnigh exhausted. We have borne much from Signor Rossetti, but we consider this as an outrage upon common sense. Others have doubted the existence of Laura; but no one, however dead to poetry, or inattentive to facts, ever dreamed of suspecting a joyful intention in the melancholy strains of the second half of the Canzoniere. For our own parts, we agree with Ginguené, that in the present state of the question, a man must be an immoderate sceptic, who can refuse to admit the personality of Laura as an historical fact. If ever passion was real, we believe that was. It bears every character and note of truth. It was peculiar, certainly; some peculiarities attach to it as incidents of the time, and of these we shall presently speak more at large; some again, which arose from the character of the man. But if Love and Grief ever spoke by a human voice, they murmured on the banks of Sorga, and in the "vie aspre e selvagge" to which their devoted victim fled. The evidence for this does not rest on the poems alone, although, to any mind, undebauched by the jargon of a system, these must carry the fullest conviction. We know more of the habits, thoughts, and passions of Petrarch, than is our fortune with almost any other eminent man of modern times. His letters are a faithful and perpetual record of what he felt and did. Even his philosophical works are rich with the history of his own heart. He is too vain, too dependent on the affection of others, not to commit to writing the minutest turns in that troubled stream of passion, which hurried him onward from place to place, from one pursuit to another, until he found at last in the grave that desired repose, which neither the solitudes of Vaucluse and Arqua, nor the princely halls of the Visconti, had been able to bestow. How any one can read those numerous passages in his private correspondence, in which he speaks of Laura, without feeling the impossibility of his passion having been a political allegory, we cannot at present understand. Perhaps Signor Rossetti's future writings may give us some idea of it. Let him exert his abilities to discover the latent *gergo* in such accents as these : " The day may * perhaps come " —it is Petrarch speaking to one of his intimate friends — " when I shall have calmness enough to contemplate all the misery of my soul, to examine my passion, not however that I may continue to love her, but that I may love Thee alone, O my God! But at this day, how many dangers have I still to surmount, how many efforts have I yet to make ! I no longer love as I did love, but still I love. I love in spite of myself, but I love in lamentations and tears. I will hate her — no — I must still love her." Let the Professor tell us how he imagines real love would speak in such circumstances, and whether it

* I use the eloquent translation given by the author of Jacopo Ortis, in his excellent Essays on Petrarch. The following passage, which Foscolo has quoted from a MS. sermon of a Dominican friar, must be rather embarrassing to Signor Rossetti: " Ma pur Messer Francesco Petrarca, che è oggi vivo, ebbe un' amante spirituale appellata Laura: peró, poichè ella morì, gl' è stato più fedele che mai, e a li data tanta fama, che è la sempre nominata, e non morírà mai. E questo e quanto al corpo. Po' li ha fatto tante limosine, e fatte dire tante Messe e Orationi con tanta devotione, che s'ella fosse la più cattiva femina del mondo l'avrebbe tratta dalle mani del Diavolo, benchè si raxona, che la morì pur santa."

could borrow a more pathetic tone than this, or than we hear in the dialogues with St. Augustin, which are entitled, "De secreto conflictu curarum mearum."

The Professor's promises respecting Boccaccio are, as usual, more abundant than his performances. Yet there is some curious matter on this subject. The "Vita di Dante" is claimed for the all-absorbing *gergo;* by which the additional advantage is gained of being enabled to reject its biographical authority; the Filocolo contains, we are informed, "all the degrees, all the proceedings of the ancient sect, and relates in detail all its principal vicissitudes, especially that change of language, rendered necessary by imminent dangers. It is a hieroglyphical comment on the Commedia, and a companion to the Vita Nuova." We have not room to give the long and intricate explanation of it, which our readers will find in the chapter "Pellegrinaggi Allegorici, one of the most entertaining in the book. But the Decameron itself is not secure from this levelling theory. "Ogni minimo racconto e mistero, e spesso ogni minima frase è gergo: lascivie nella faccia esterna, ma nell' interno grembo assai peggio." Certainly, if this statement were correct, it might form the subject of a pretty problem, whether it were more perilous to understand the secret meaning of the Decameron, or to remain satisfied with the letter. Atheism within, impurity without! our morals are sadly in danger either way. One thing at least is certain, that the grace and delicacy of those exquisite stories will be materially injured by a theory which turns them all into masonic text books. Perhaps Signor Rossetti will inform us in his next edition, whether the great plague itself was a stratagem of the secret society. Laura did not die of it; Neifile and her blithe companions did not fly from its terrors; why should any body be supposed to have suffered, when the easy alternative is left us of explaining all extant accounts into convenient *gergo?*

We trust we have not expressed ourselves with any disrespect towards Signor Rossetti, whose talents and industry we freely acknowledge, and from whose further researches we expect much amusement and some benefit. Whatever becomes of this theory, much curious matter will be set before us in the course of its development. His example will induce others to study the great master, "Il Maggior Tosco," and to study him with the aid of those best of commentators, the contemporary writers. The enthusiastic ardor, which he shows in defence of his favorite idea, will be appreciated by the candid and sincere, even while their cooler judgment may force them to reject his conclusions. If indeed half, or one third of his abundant promises should ever be confirmed by future performances, it might become rather a difficult matter to make that resistance good. But the learned Professor must pardon us, if we retain our scepticism until he has adduced his proofs. We will yield to facts, but not to conjectures. At present he has given us no more; a heap of odd coincidences, and bewildering dilemmas, but certainly not enough to establish on a solid foundation the brilliant fabric he wishes to erect. There are two fatal errors in the Professor's mode of reasoning. He sees his theory in everything; and he will see no more in anything. Now, were he to establish to our full conviction the principal point of his argument, namely, that a sect did exist such as he has described it, and that the great luminaries of modern civilization were active members of that sect, it would by no means follow so easily as he seems to imagine, that they never were guided by any other motive, and never used the language of love or of religion in their simple acceptation. Nothing appears so absurd to him as that a number of learned men should spend their leisure in composing love poems. Out of pure kindness to their memories, he brings various instances of what he considers their nonsense and ridiculous exaggerations, and asks, with a fine air of indignation, how we can refuse to admit a theory, which elicits reason from that nonsense, and pares down those exaggerations to a level of ordinary understanding? Unfortunately there are some people still in the world, (we do not suppose we stand alone,) who are inclined to prefer the nonsense of Petrarch to the reason of Rossetti. The poems, whose literal sense he assures us is so unintelligible and preposterous, have contrived, by no other sense, to charm the minds of many successive generations. For our own part, we confess, so far from seeing anything inexplicable in the fact, that the resurgent literature of Europe bore a peculiar amatory character, we should consider the absence of that character a circumstance far more unaccountable. Not to insist on the Teutonic and Arabian elements of that civilization, which bore its first and lavish harvest on the fields of Provence, sufficient causes may be found in the change of manners occasioned by Christianity, to explain the increased respect for the female character, which tempered passion with reverence, and lent an ideal color to the daily realities of life. While women were degraded from their natural position in society, it could not be expected that the passions which regard them should be in high esteem among moralists, or should be considered capable of any philosophical application. The sages of the ancient world despised * love as a weakness.

* Plato, it is well known, inculcated the expediency of personal attachment as an incentive to virtue. He seems to have seen clearly the impossibility of governing man otherwise than through his affections; and the necessity of embodying our conceptions of beauty and goodness in some object worthy of love. But Plato had little influence on social manners. Many admired his eloquence, and many puzzled themselves with his metaphysics; but the peculiarities of his ethical system were not appreciated by the two great nations of antiquity. His kingdom was not of that world. It began only when the stone was rolled away from the sepulchre, and the veil of the temple was rent in twain. Platonism became the natural ally of Christianity. Not unjustly did the Old Fathers consider him a "vox clamantis in deserto;" an Elias of the faith

Calm reason, energetic will — these alone could make a man sovereign over himself; the softer feelings were fit only to make slaves. And they, who thought so, thought well. The Stoic κατορθωμα, was, in those circumstances, the noblest object of human endeavors. To it we owe the example of Rome among nations; of Regulus and Cato among individuals. But with Christianity came a new era. Human nature was to undergo a different development. A Christendom was to succeed an empire; and the proud αὐταρκεια of male virtues was to be tempered with feminine softness. Women were no longer obliged to step out of the boundaries of their sex, — to become Portias and Arrias, in order to conciliate the admiration of the wise. They appeared in their natural guise, simple and dignified, "As one intended first, not after made Occasionally." This great alteration of social manners produced a corresponding change in the tone of morality. The Church too did its utmost for the ladies. The calendar swelled as fast from one sex as from the other. Children

to come. In the same spirit Mr. Coleridge has said, "he is a plank from the wreck of Paradise cast on the shores of idolatrous Greece."

were taught to look for models of heroism, not, as heretofore, in the apathetic sublimity of suicidal patriots, but in the virgin martyrs whose burnings and dislocations constitute the most interesting portion of legendary biography. The worship of the Virgin soon accustomed Catholic minds to contemplate perfection in a female form. And what is that worship itself, but the exponent of a restless longing in man's unsatisfied soul, which must ever find a personal shape, wherein to embody his moral ideas, and will choose for that shape, where he can, a nature not too remote from his own, but resembling in dissimilitude, and flattering at once his vanity by the likeness, and his pride by the difference?

This opens upon us an ampler view in which this subject deserves to be considered, and a relation still more direct and close between the Christian religion and the passion of love. What is the distinguishing character of Hebrew literature, which separates it by so broad a line of demarcation from that of every ancient people? * Undoubtedly the sentiment of

* It would be a prize of inestimable value to a philosopher, if we possessed any monument of the religion of the ancients. Their

erotic devotion which pervades it. Their poets never represent the Deity, as an impassive principle, a mere organizing intellect, removed at infinite distance from human hopes and fears. He is for them a being of like passions with themselves, requiring heart for heart, and capable of inspiring affection because capable of feeling and returning it. Awful indeed are the thunders of his utterance and the clouds that surround his dwelling-place; very terrible is the vengeance he executes on the nations that forget him; but to his chosen people, and especially to the men "after his own heart," whom he anoints from the midst of them, his

mythology we know. Their philosophy we know. But of their *religion* we are entirely ignorant. The class of believers at Rome or Athens was not the class of authors. The reverential Theism of Plato and Cicero was a sentiment much fainter than that which must have agitated a true believer in the golden-haired Apollo, or the trident-shaking ruler of stormy seas. The recluses of Iris and Cybele must have felt many of the same passions, which ruffle the indifferent calm of a modern convent. What a pity that we cannot compare the forms assumed by the feelings of those idolatrous Polytheists, with those presented in the present day by Roman Catholic populations! We might find, perhaps, the same prayer breathed before a crucifix, which had been uttered ages before, beside the solitary fire of Vesta; the same doubt started, the same struggles made, the same noble extravagance of human self-devotion, the same sad declension of human frailty!

"still, small voice" speaks in sympathy and loving-kindness.* Every Hebrew, while his breast glowed with patriotic enthusiasm at those promises, which he shared as one of the favored race, had a yet deeper source of emotion, from which gushed perpetually the aspirations of prayer and thanksgiving. He might consider himself alone in the presence of his God; the single being to whom a great revelation had been made, and over whose head an "exceeding weight of glory" was suspended. His personal welfare was infinitely concerned with every event that had taken place in the miraculous order of Providence. For him the rocks of Horeb had trembled, and the waters of the Red Sea were parted in their course. The word

* Need we recall to our readers the solemn prelude of the Mosaic Law, the First and Great Commandment, as it was termed by One, who came to destroy in one sense, but in another to fulfil and establish that Law? "Hear, O Israel, the Lord thy God is One God. And thou shalt *love* the Lord thy God, *with all thy heart*, and *with all thy soul*, and *with all thy strength.*" These words have made the destiny of the world. Spoken, as they were, to a barbarous horde in an age before the first dawn of Grecian intellect, yet fraught with a power over the heart of man beyond the utmost reach of Grecian philosophy, they may be considered as the greatest of miracles, or, to speak more wisely, as the best manifestation of that Natural Order, in which the moral, no less than the material elements are regulated and maintained.

given on Sinai with such solemn pomp of ministration was given to his own individual soul, and brought him into immediate communion with his Creator. That awful Being could never be put away from him. He was about his path, and about his bed, and knew all his thoughts long before. Yet this tremendous, enclosing presence was a presence of love. It was a manifold, everlasting manifestation of one deep feeling, — a desire for human affection. Such a belief, while it enlisted even pride and self-interest on the side of piety, had a direct tendency to excite the best passions of our nature. Love is not long asked in vain from generous dispositions. A Being, never absent, but standing beside the life of each man with ever watchful tenderness, and recognized, though invisible, in every blessing that befell them from youth to age, became naturally the object of their warmest affections. Their belief in him could not exist without producing, as a necessary effect, that profound impression of passionate individual attachment, which in the Hebrew authors always mingles with and vivifies their faith in the Invisible. All the books of the Old Testament are breathed upon by this breath of life. Especially is it to be found in that beautiful collection, entitled the Psalms of David, which remains, after some thousand years, perhaps the most perfect form in which the religious sentiment of man has been embodied.

But what is true of Judaism is yet more true of Christianity, " matre pulchrâ filia pulchrior." In addition to all the characters of Hebrew Monotheism, there exists in the doctrine of the Cross a peculiar and inexhaustible treasure for the affectionate feelings. The idea of the θεανθρωπος, the God whose goings forth have been from everlasting, yet visible to men for their redemption as an earthly, temporal creature, living, acting, and suffering among themselves, then (which is yet more important) transferring to the unseen place of his spiritual agency the same humanity he wore on earth, so that the lapse of generations can in no way affect the conception of his identity ; this is the most powerful thought that ever addressed itself to a human imagination. It is the που στῶ, which alone was wanted to move the world. Here was solved at once the great problem which so long had distressed the teachers of mankind, how to make virtue the object of passion,* and to secure at once the warmest enthusiasm in

* It is a thought for meditation, not for wonder, that the same principle which worked out the exaltation of human virtue into a holiness of which ancient times had no model, wrought likewise a development of human crime, equally unknown to antiquity. The life of Fenelon was contemporaneous with the revocation of the Edict of Nantes. In human things pain ever borders upon pleasure, evil upon good, and the source of one is often the source of the other. The destiny of the race must be accomplished in no other manner than the destiny of individuals, to whom good never comes unmixed. Sufficient for us, if that good predominate; if the progress of the species, as well as of the individual, be towards the Higher and the Better? Let us not with the fanatical Encyclopedists see nothing in the Prince of Peace, but the sword which he sent upon the earth. But let us not, on the other side, with some inconsiderate apologists of Revelation, be content with the flimsy answer, that to ascribe the spread of intolerance to the spread of religion is to confound use with abuse, proximity with causation. No such confusion is made. The question is not, whether some precepts of the Christian legislator are not directly contravened by acts of fanatical oppression. On this no doubt can exist. But the true question is, whether there are not principles in human nature, which render a system of Monotheism, especially such a Monotheism as the Christian, a source of unavoidable persecution. It seems to us that this question must be answered in the affirmative. That mighty novelty, the love of God, which we have traced in its beneficial effects on all the virtues, had yet a separate tendency to enfeeble some which regard our fellow-beings. That love, if admitted at all, was by its nature exclusive and absorbing. Its object was the Highest, the Only Reality: it required the whole heart; it took the heart from its home on earth, to pillow it upon the clouds of Heaven. The

the heart with the clearest perception of right and wrong in the understanding. The char-

charities of father, husband, and child, were invigorated by it only so far as the objects of these happened to coincide with what was considered a far higher aim. Even then, though the act might not differ, the motive did. Love to God, said the eloquent preachers, is as the gravitation of the planets to their sun: let it once cease to actuate the creature, and he falls into erroneous disorder. It must be the sole, or at least the principal motive of every thought, and word, and deed. But motives unexercised become naturally feeble. Those who would love their neighbor only for the love of God, if they obeyed this difficult precept, came to love their neighbor not at all. But yet more, where these duties appeared contrary, was the overruling character of the new element perceived. To sacrifice the dearest affections to Christ was the most sacred of obligations; and while in some instances this was done with a bleeding heart, others perhaps may have made the discovery, that a more easy gratification of sensibility was to be found in devotion, than in the practice of an ordinary, but laborious virtue. Again, with love came jealousy. The Heathens had no religious wars; for it hurt no man that different deities should be worshipped with different rites. But, under the rule of One, rivality of worship was an insult to be avenged in blood. And Conscience applauded the promptings of Pride. For what were the sufferings of a finite creature, in comparison with injury done to the Most High? Heretics were burned for the pure and simple love of God; for it was a worthier thing by all the difference between infinite and finite, to do pleasure to Him, than to spare pain to a mortal. Besides, the flames that consumed the body might save the soul; and what were the pangs of a few minutes weighed with the bliss of an immortality? At all events, they would save the souls of others, by preventing the further diffusion of heretical venom. What therefore the love of God imperatively urged, and the love of man

acter of the blessed Founder of our faith became an abstract of morality to determine the judgment, while at the same time it remained personal, and liable to love. The written word and established church prevented a degeneration into ungoverned mysticism, but the predominant principle of vital religion always remained that of self-sacrifice to the Saviour. Not only the higher divisions of moral duties, but the simple, primary impulses of benevolence, were subordinated in this new absorbing passion. The world was loved " in Christ alone." The brethren were members of his mystical body. All the other bonds that had fastened down the Spirit of the Universe to our narrow round of earth, were as nothing in comparison to this golden chain of suffering and self-sacrifice, which at once riveted

did not restrain, was a most palpable duty. We have traced with fidelity the dark lines of this picture. Let it teach us charity to our ancestors, humility for ourselves. The Reformation made an end of intolerant principles. Luther, who wished to monopolize, destroyed them. A Protestant, uncertain himself of the truth, may check his impulse to punish a fellow-creature who has a different idea of it. But it is only perhaps by an illogical humanity, that a Roman Catholic, believing in an infallible criterion of faith, apart from which none meet salvation, can resist, at the present day, those conclusions which armed St. Dominic against the peace of human society.

the heart of man to one, who, like himself, was acquainted with grief. Pain is the deepest thing we have in our nature, and union through pain has always seemed more real and more holy than any other. It is easy to perceive how these ideas reign in the early Christian books, and how they continued to develop and strengthen themselves in the rising institutions of the Church. The monastic spirit was the principal emanation from them ;* but the same influence, though less apparent, was busily circulating through the organization of social life.* Who can read the eloquent com-

* Especially as seen in its effects upon women. The Spouses of Christ were not so in metaphor alone. Often they literally *fell in love* with the object of their worship. Voluntarily immured from the sources of domestic affection, their hearts opened with glad surprise to a new and unsuspected substitute. The sexual complexion which distinguishes the writings of the female mystics, might lead us to hazard a conjecture, that the adoration of the Virgin arose, in the minds of the other sex, as a natural counterpoise in feeling to this passionate adoration of the Redeemer. It might be curious, in this point of view, to compare the writings of St. Bernard with those of St. Teresa on one side, and with the Platonic love-poems on the other.

† Pascal, the most successful of those reasoners who have attempted to establish the divine origin of Christianity on its conformity to the human character, endeavored, with almost unexampled heroism, to set his conduct in exact accordance with his principles. His constant struggle, therefore, was to hate himself,

positions of Augustin, without being struck by their complexion of ardent passion, tempered, indeed,

and to do good from no motive of affection towards his neighbor. God, he thought, was the only end of a rational creature: all other aims were abominable, because contrary to nature. Consistently with these opinions, he sought to detach his friends and relations from himself. "Je ne suis la fin de personne," he would say, "il est injuste qu'on s'attache à moi." A society established on such grounds appeared to him the ideal commonwealth, to which man ought to tend, and in proportion to his attainment of which, his happiness would increase. It would be, in short, heaven; and, it must be confessed, nothing could be more unlike earth. In considering the life of this extraordinary man, we should not forget that since his accident at the Pont de Neuilly, he was subject to perpetual delusions of sight. Always, whether he sat or walked, he saw, yawning at his side, the gulf from which he had escaped. From a brain so overwrought, an imagination so constantly and gloomily excited, one would hardly expect a strong development of intellect. Yet in that time, and no other, he produced the Pensées and the Lettres Provinciales. Well might he exclaim, "Quelle chimère que l'homme!" Is it to mock us that reason and frenzy go hand in hand; sentiments the most glorious, with consequences the most fatal? Consider the life of Luther. Is it intelligible except on the supposition of frequent insanity? Yet to what heights of mind did Luther reach! Who has agitated so powerfully the intellects of generations beyond him! "*Ανευ μανιας*," said Plato, "*ουδεις ποιητης*." The experience of more than two thousand years since his day, might almost warrant an enlargement of that aphorism into a paradox, which perhaps, according to F. Schlegel's definition of paradoxes, may be only a "startling truth:" that without madness none have been truly great. Sober judgments achieve no victories; they are the pioneers of conquering minds.

and supported by the utmost keenness of intellect? At a later period in Church history, when religion began to languish under the pompous corruptions of the Romish schoolmen, a refuge was afforded it by those writers denominated Mystics, who seem to have prepared the general Reformation, which they wanted courage to accomplish.

Their works are now generally neglected, although remarkable for much curious observation of the turns and courses of feeling. One of them, however, the celebrated Imitation of Christ, by Thomas à Kempis, has escaped the fate of the rest; and a perusal of it will be sufficient to convince us that the influence of Christianity, in elevating the idea of love to the position it occupied at the dawn of our new civilization, was not merely indirect or collateral. A passion from which religion had condescended to borrow her most solemn phrases, her sublimest hopes, and her most mysterious modes of operation, could not fail of acquiring new dignity in the eyes of Catholic Christians. It was to be expected that in this, as in all things, the Visible would vindicate its rights, and the sentiments whose origin was in the constitution of earthly nature, would lay hold on an earthly object as their natural possession.*

* Will it be considered serious trifling, if, in illustration of the argument in the text, we compare the expression of religious feeling in the mouth of Pascal, "Mon âme ne peut souffrir tout ce qui n'est pas Dieu," with the expression of natural love, precisely similar, and perhaps borrowed, which Voltaire has given to Amenaïde, "Et je ne puis souffrir ce qui n'est pas Tancrède?" The age of Louis XIV. might confirm our argument by many more important examples. Catholicism was then in an attitude of defence. The trumpets of Luther and Calvin had sent alarm through the fortress; the warders were at their posts, and every resource of warfare was in readiness. We can judge well, therefore, of the genius of the place. We will but allude to the celebrated controversy on "pur Amour;" but we cannot resist an inclination to quote a passage from Bossuet, because he was on that occasion, as everybody knows, a rigid opponent of mysticism, and his authority is therefore the more valuable. "Là s'entendrait la dernière consolation de l'Amour Divin, dans un endroit de l'âme si profond et si retiré, que les sens n'en soupçonnent rien, tant il est éloigné de leur région: mais pour s'expliquer sur cette matière il faudrait un langage que le monde n'entendrait pas."

But the effect, although not immediate, of the Protestant Reformation, was to banish these expressions from the ordinary language of theology, and to change the tone of religious opinion hardly less in Catholic than in Reformed States. In the latter, during the course of last century, religion began to assume the aspect of what may be called Revealed Deism. In their joy at discarding superstition for a more rational creed, men forgot that they were substituting a weaker motive for a stronger. They tried to satisfy philosophers at the expense of their kind. Their Christianity might be very simple and rational, but it had no

But we cannot anticipate that Signor Rossetti will be brought to acknowledge this secondary influence of Christianity, since it is evident he ascribes little historical importance to its immediate operations. We cannot understand the reasonableness of a theory, which represents religious feeling as less efficient in the Middle Ages than we find it at present. According to all analogy one might conjecture, *à priori*, that a literature, which was the outgrowth of Christian civilization, would in its first beginnings be full and running over with abundant manifestations of its origin. When the Christian feelings and thoughts, long familiar to men's inward bosoms,

revolutionary power on the heart. It was not *the* Christianity which changed the aspect of the world. It was the same mistake in religion which is committed in ethics by those exaggerated Utilitarians, who would substitute utility as a motive of action for those primary aims implanted in us by the wisdom of nature. But among the English sectarians, and those of the Established Clergy who are denominated Low Church, some of the old spirit remained. Two energetic lines of our Calvinistic poet indicate, to an attentive reader, the great secondary cause to which we owe the original triumph of Christianity:

> "Talk of morality! Thou bleeding Lamb,
> The true morality is love to thee."

In the same spirit, hundreds of years before, Augustin had summed up his ethical system in one sublime sentence, "Beatus qui Te amat, et amicum in Te, et inimicum propter Te!"

but, in the absence of literature, incapable of permanent expression, first discovered those arts of imagination which are the natural, appointed exponents of our deeper emotions, should we not expect a voice of many songs would immediately break forth, announcing in joy and power the rise of a new world from that barbaric chaos into which the old had been resolved? Genius ever nourishes itself with Religion. A new spiritual truth is a pearl of great price to a soul gifted with spiritual power. It is the business of the Poet to number, and measure, and note down every form and fleeting appearance of human feeling. Gladly, and with an earnest thankfulness, he perceives any new chamber of the heart; but with what gratitude, with what exultation, with what bewilderment at these new effluences of celestial knowledge, must not the Poet have approached for the first time that sacred ark, in which the treasures of the Gospel had been safely borne through the diluvial times of Northern domination? And in the pomp of Catholic superstition, the slow and solemn chants, the white-robed processions, the incense, and the censers, and the golden baldacchins, with ever-burning lights, and images, and pictures, in whose rude forms a prophetic eye might even then discern the future arts of Raffaelle and Michelangiolo, "Like the man's thought, hid in the infant's brain;" in this ceremonial worship, so framed to attach the imagination and the senses, was there nothing to make a poet pause and adore? The Beautiful was everywhere around men, waiting, and, as it were, calling for their love. Is it wonderful that the call was heard? Is it wonderful that the feeling of reverence for that august name, the Church, — for its antiquity, its endurance, its unity, its widespread dominion, and yet more ample prospects of indefinite magnificence, should, in that day, have been often irresistible in the minds of imaginative men, since even in these latter times, some are yet to be found, who, induced by no other motives, have abandoned the cold precincts of a more intellectual creed, to fall down before the altars of their forefathers, exclaiming, "Sero te amavi, pulchritudo tam antiqua et tam nova, sero te amavi!" Now, when a learned Professor comes to tell us that writings, apparently composed under the influence of religious impressions, are, in reality, composed in quite a different spirit, and does not at the same time show us other writings equal to these in merit, but really inspired by the genius of Catholicism, we are constrained to tell him, "Quodcunque ostendi mihi sic, incredulus odi." We have before us a plain intelligible cause, acting in a known manner, and in a direction made clear to us by experience. We have also an effect, apparently adequate to that cause, and resembling the effects we have known produced by it, with such difference, however, as we should have predicted from the partial alteration of circumstances. Now if this effect be shown to belong to some other cause that we never dreamed of, we are entitled to ask, where then is the result of the first? For that remains before us. It cannot be got rid of. We are certain it has been in action. The traces of that agency must exist somewhere, and from their nature must be obvious. If the Dante of the Divina Commedia was no Catholic; if the Petrarch, who mourned at Valchiusa, never felt the hallowing force of religion; if the splendors of Romish worship never fascinated the numberless lovers of the Beautiful, who sang in Provence, Italy, and Castile, where, we ask, are those other mighty spirits, equal in worth and power to these we have mentioned, in whom the predominant religion may have exhausted its capacities of enlightening and exalting? If none such can be produced (and it is notorious that none can), the theory must be false, for it is inconsistent with the phenomena it pretends to explain.

We defy any man, of competent abilities, to read the poems of Dante, without a conviction that he is reading the works of a religious poet.*

* La Martine has said, "this is the age for studying Dante." Rossetti says the same; but with how different a meaning! The one thinks of the Catholic, the other of the Patriot. Rossetti does not perceive that what he supposes to be true of the age of Dante, is strictly true of the present, viz: that Italians judge of everything by a political criterion. We have known many able and worthy Italians, both in exile and in their own land, but none who could see a yard out of the atmosphere of their local liberalism. They talk of poetry, but they mean politics. This explains not only the fashionable Dantismo, but a much more curious phenomenon, their extravagant admiration of Alfieri. We once met an intelligent Italian, not unacquainted with the literature of our country, who expressed to us his determination never to read Shakspeare, because he was so firmly convinced of Alfieri's infinite superiority to every dramatic writer that had written or could write, that he considered it loss of time to peruse any other! We are very heretical on this subject. We agree with Mr. Rose (Letters from the North of Italy), that never did a man set up for a poet with so small a capital as Alfieri. There is some poetic material in his "Life;" but none that we could ever discover in his plays. How much poetic genius, indeed, can we suppose a

The spirit of Catholic Christianity breathes in every line. The Ghibelline, indeed, hates the Papal party and Papal usurpations ; he makes no secret of it ! no words can express more plainly or more energetically than his, a just and courageous indignation against all ecclesiastical tyranny. But the man is a devout Catholic, and respects the chair of the Apostle, while he denounces those who sat upon it. The sword of Peter, not the keys of Peter, is the object of his aversion. The same voice, he would tell us, that said "Put up thy sword," in the garden by the mount of Olives, said also, "Tu es Petrus, et super hanc petram fundabo Ecclesiam meam." When Rossetti would have us believe that in those fervent thoughts, those rich descriptions, those deep-drawn aspirations, which have hitherto been thought to convey Dante's profound sense of spiritual things, there is really nothing but a covert expression of political projects ; that Paradise is not* the sojourn of blessed souls through an

man to possess, who writes a drama in French prose in order to translate it into the verse of his own language !

* That reference to man's present life, which Dante himself mentions (Epist. to Can Della Scala), and which we readily allow, is not liable to the objection here made. We say this to prevent cavils. The subjects are homogeneous, and differ only in degree.

eternity spent in the love of God, but a future prosperous condition of the German Court; that Hell is not the awful place, where hope is left forever by all who enter therein, nor Purgatory the intermediate world of trial, where in purifying pains the "spirits happily born" rejoice "to make themselves beautiful;" but the one is the bad state of Italy under a corrupt government, and the other a secret club at Florence, which looks forward to the triumph of its machinations; when we are called upon to believe this, we cannot but feel that not only the dignity and magnificence of the poem are materially lowered by such an hypothesis, but the very foundations of our belief in testimony are affected. If the Divina Commedia is the work of a heretic, whose Paradise was entirely limited to this world, so may also be the Confessions of Augustin or the Thoughts of Pascal.* The former, indeed, has often struck us as

The good man's hopes of heaven are but prolongations of his earthly reward. The kingdom within, that cometh not with observation, contains, as it were in germ, the kingdom without, that shines from one part of heaven to the other.

* Even in such an extravagance he would not have the merit of originality. Father Hardouin, in his posthumous treatise "Athei detecti," gives a long list of atheists, in which the names of Jansenius, Arnauld, and Pascal, are conspicuous. Yet Hardouin, like Rossetti, professed submission to the Catholic Church, and died

bearing no little resemblance in spirit to the compositions of the Florentine bard. In both there is a freshness, an admiring earnestness, about their expression of Christian ideas, which shows the novelty of those ideas to the frame of European thought. This is indeed much more evident in Augustin, because he wrote six centuries earlier, and wrote in Latin, so that the discrepancy between the new wine and old bottles is perpetually betraying itself. The Ciceronian language is far too effete a frame to sustain the infused spark of

with all the appearance of belief. At the close of last century the same mania seized on two men, to whose opinions it was more conformable, Marechal and Lalande, one of whom published a Dictionary of Atheists, and the other a Supplement to the Dictionary, in which Atheism was shamelessly imputed to writers of all sorts, on the most futile pretences. Lalande, indeed, carried this so far, that he inscribed the name of Delille for a misprint in a single line, and then hastened in great glee to inform his old instructor of the discovery he had made. "Mon ami" answered the venerable Poet, "il faut que vous soyez fou, pour voir dans mes vers ce que je n'y ai jamais mis, et de ne pas voir dans le ciel ce que tout le monde y voit." There is a closer resemblance between Hardouin and Rossetti than the general extravagance of their theories. The Jesuit did not leave Dante alone. He saw proofs in the Divina Commedia that it was not what it appeared. But his conclusions were less revolutionary than those of our modern Hardouin. He contented himself with ascribing the Commedia to some person or persons unknown; and respected the historical character of the Poet, while he destroyed the evidences of his genius.

heavenly fire. It heaves beneath those active stirrings with the throes of a convulsive weakness. In Dante, on the other hand, the form and spirit perfectly correspond, as if adapted to each other by preëstablished harmony. But in earnestness and apparent sincerity, we know not any difference between the bishop of Hippo and the exile of Ravenna. If the one is an impostor, so may be the other. Or why stop there? Why not at once startle the world with the information, that theology has been always a masonic trick? That the passions of which we have been speaking never had any real existence, and it is therefore worse than useless to look for their effects? There needs only one bold application of the Professor's principles, and the whole edifice of religion comes crumbling to the ground. He seems to consider that, in every instance, probabilities are against a man's meaning what he says. Earnestness, solemnity, lofty thoughts, sublime imaginations, all these should only make us suspect mischief, and look out for a hidden meaning. Veracity, according to him, left the earth with Astræa. We do Signor Rossetti the justice to suppose he has not maturely deliberated on the consequences to which his principles conduct him.

From one passage, indeed, in his book, unless we have mistaken a meaning so dimly intimated,* we conjecture he holds ulterior opinions, which he thinks it imprudent to communicate. But, although cautious enough to be illogical in resisting the conclusions of his own premises, when speculating on sacred subjects, there is no reason to anticipate any pause in his devastating progress along the fields of profane history. Already we have intimations that the later poets of Italy are no more exempt from his transforming powers, than their predecessors of the fourteenth century. Nor will it surprise us to find him quite at home in the territories of romance. Doubtless, if he is acquainted with the Spanish language, we shall have valuable results of his inquiries in that quarter. Perhaps our old friend, Don Quixote, may turn out a disguised Ghibelline; and honest Sancho may be only the knight himself in his everyday countenance, a sort of exterior man,

* "Io stesso che per pertinacia di studio ho scorto ciò che altri sapeva per communicazione segreta, avrei potuto io mai svelarlo, se fossi in Italia rimaso? Nè anche fuori di lâ avrei alzato la cortina del tutto, contentando mi di sollevarne un solo lembo, come già fatto avea, se necessità di difesa non mi avesse fatto ardita la mano. Ma anderò io sempre innanzi? No, *Esce di sotto a un velo una voce che grida, Noli me tangere; ed io mi inchino e mi arretro.*" —p. 450.

much in the same way as, we have seen, Laura and Fiammetta were only faces or vestments of their own lovers. Many a profound meaning, we doubt not, lies hid in the windmills. And woe to those who think the virago Maritornes no better than she should be!

But we will not take leave of the ingenious Professor with a jest. We wish him well in his further progress. We wait patiently for his promised proofs, and till they appear, shall not dismiss our old prejudices on these subjects, lest we find nothing in their room but a dismal void. Signor Rossetti is very sensitive to criticism; but we trust he will believe our remarks at least to have been made in fairness and love of truth. He will not, perhaps, be the worse for bearing in mind some gentle warnings we have given. Let him moderate his pretensions, and enlarge his views. He may succeed possibly in establishing the principle, hypothetically assumed by him, as a *vera causa;* but that he should prove it to be the sole or the chief actuating principle, to which all the historical phenomena in question are to be referred, we believe, for the reasons already stated, to be altogether impossible.

EXTRACT FROM A

REVIEW OF TENNYSON'S POEMS.

PUBLISHED IN THE ENGLISHMAN'S MAGAZINE, 1831.

It is not true, as the exclusive admirers of Mr. Wordsworth would have it, that the highest species of poetry is the reflective; it is a gross fallacy, that because certain opinions are acute or profound, the expression of them by the imagination must be eminently beautiful. Whenever the mind of the artist suffers itself to be occupied, during its periods of creation, by any other predominant motive than the desire of beauty, the result is false in art. Now, there is undoubtedly no reason why he may not find beauty in those moods of emotion, which arise from the combinations of reflective thought; and it is possible that he may delineate these with fidelity, and not be led astray by any suggestions of an unpoetical mood. But though possible, it is hardly probable: for a man whose reveries take a reasoning turn, and who is accustomed to measure his ideas by their logical relations rather than the congruity of the sentiments to which they refer, will be apt to mistake the pleasure he has in knowing a thing to be true, for the pleasure he would have in knowing it to be beautiful, and so will pile his thoughts in a rhetorical battery, that they may convince, instead of letting them flow in a natural course of contemplation, that they may enrapture. It would not be difficult to show, by reference to the most admired poems of Wordsworth, that he is frequently chargeable with this error; and that much has been said by him which is good as philosophy, powerful as rhetoric, but false as poetry. Perhaps this very distortion of the truth did more in the peculiar juncture of our literary affairs to enlarge and liberalize the genius of our age, than could have been effected by a less sectarian temper. However this may be, a new school of reformers soon began to attract attention, who, professing the same independence of immediate favor, took their stand on a different region of Parnassus from that occupied by the Lakers,* and one, in our opinion, much less liable to perturbing currents of air from ungenial climates. We shall not hesitate to express our conviction, that the cockney school (as it was termed in derision from a cursory view of its accidental circumstances) contained more genuine inspiration, and adhered more steadily to that portion of truth which it embraced, than any *form* of art that has existed in this country since the days of Milton. Their *caposetta* was Mr. Leigh Hunt, who did little more than point the way, and was diverted from his aim by a thousand personal predilections and political habits of thought. But he was followed by two men of very superior make; men who were born poets, lived poets, and went poets to their untimely graves. Shelley and Keats were indeed of opposite genius; that of the one was vast, impetuous, and sublime, the other seemed to be "fed with honey

* This cant term was justly ridiculed by Mr. Wordsworth's supporters; but it was not so easy to substitute an inoffensive denomination. We are not at all events the first who have used it without a contemptuous intention, for we remember to have heard a disciple quote Aristophanes in its behalf: — '*Ουτος ὀυ τῶν ἥθαδων τῶνδ' ὧν ὁρᾶθ' ὑμεῖς ἀεὶ, ἀλλὰ* ΛΙΜΝΑΙΟΣ. "This is no common, no barn-door fowl: No, but a Lakist."

dew," and to have "drunk the milk of Paradise." Even the softness of Shelley comes out in bold, rapid, comprehensive strokes; he has no patience for minute beauties, unless they can be massed into a general effect of grandeur. On the other hand, the tenderness of Keats cannot sustain a lofty flight; he does not generalize or allegorize nature; his imagination works with few symbols, and reposes willingly on what is given freely. Yet in this formal opposition of character there is, it seems to us, a groundwork of similarity sufficient for the purposes of classification, and constituting a remarkable point in the progress of literature. They are both poets of sensation rather than reflection. Susceptible of the slightest impulse from external nature, their fine organs trembled into emotion at colors, and sounds, and movements, unperceived or unregarded by duller temperaments. Rich and clear were their perceptions of visible forms; full and deep their feelings of music. So vivid was the delight attending the simple exertions of eye and ear, that it became mingled more and more with their trains of active thought, and tended to absorb their whole being into the energy of sense. Other poets seek for images to illustrate their conceptions; these men had no need to seek; they lived in a world of images; for the most important and extensive portion of their life consisted in those emotions which are immediately conversant with the sensation. Like the hero of Goethe's novel, they would hardly have been affected by what is called the pathetic parts of a book; but the *merely beautiful* passages, "those from which the spirit of the author looks clearly and mildly forth," would have melted them to tears. Hence they are not descriptive, they are picturesque. They are not smooth and *negatively* harmonious; they are full of deep and varied melodies. This powerful tendency of imagination to a life of immediate sympathy with the external universe, is not nearly so liable to false views of art as the opposite disposition of purely intellectual contemplation. For where beauty is constantly passing before "that inward eye, which is the bliss of solitude;" where the soul seeks it as a perpetual and necessary refreshment to the sources of activity and intuition; where all the other sacred ideas of our nature, — the idea of good, the idea of perfection, the idea of truth, are habitually contemplated through the medium of this predominant mood, so that they assume its color, and are subject to its peculiar laws; there is little danger that the ruling passion of the whole mind will cease to direct its creative operations, or the energetic principle of love for the beautiful sink, even for a brief period, to the level of a mere notion in the understanding. We do not deny that it is, on other accounts, dangerous for frail humanity to linger with fond attachment in the vicinity of sense. Minds of this description are especially liable to moral temptations; and upon them, more than any, it is incumbent to remember, that their mission as men, which they share with their fellow-beings, is of infinitely higher interest than their mission as artists, which they possess by rare and exclusive privilege. But it is obvious that, critically speaking, such temptations are of slight moment. Not the gross and evident passions of our nature, but the elevated and less separable desires, are the dangerous enemies which misguide the poetic spirit in its attempts at self-cultivation. That delicate sense of fitness which grows with the growth of artist feelings, and strengthens with their strength, until it acquires a celerity and weight of decision hardly inferior to the correspondent judgments of conscience, is weakened by every indulgence of heterogeneous aspirations, however pure they may be, however lofty, however suitable to human nature. We are therefore decidedly of opinion that the heights and depths of art are most within the reach of those who have received from nature the "fearful and wonderful" constitution we have described, whose poetry is a sort of magic, producing a number of impressions, too multiplied, too minute, and too diversified to allow of our tracing them to their causes, because just such was the effect, even so boundless and so bewildering, produced on their imaginations by the real appearance of nature. These things being so, our friends of the new school had evidently much reason to recur to the maxim laid down by Mr. Wordsworth, and to appeal from the immediate judgment of lettered or unlettered contemporaries to the decision of a more equitable posterity. How should they be popular, whose senses told them a richer and ampler tale than most men could understand, and who constantly expressed, because they constantly felt, sentiments of exquisite pleasure or pain, which most men were not permitted to experience? The public very naturally derided them as visionaries, and gibbeted *in terrorem* those inaccuracies of diction occasioned sometimes by the speed of their conceptions, sometimes by the inadequacy of language to their peculiar conditions of thought. But it may be asked, does not this line of argument prove too much? Does it not prove that there is a barrier between these poets and all other persons so strong and immovable, that, as has been said of the Supreme Essence, we must be themselves before we can understand them in the least? Not only are they not liable to sudden and vulgar estimation, but the lapse of ages, it seems, will not consolidate their fame, nor the suffrages of the wise few produce any impression, however remote or slowly matured, on the judgment of the incapacitated many. We answer, this is not the import of our argument. Undoubtedly the true poet addresses himself, in all his conceptions, to the common nature of us all. Art is a lofty tree, and may shoot up far beyond our grasp, but its roots are in daily life and experience. Every bosom contains the elements of those complex emotions which the artist feels, and every head can, to a certain extent, go over in itself the process of their combination, so as to understand his expressions and sympathize with his state. But this requires exertion; more or less, indeed, according to the difference of occasion, but always some degree of exertion. For since the emotions of the poet, during composition, follow a regular law of association, it follows that to accompany their progress up to the harmonious prospect of the whole, and to perceive the proper dependence of every step on that which preceded, it is absolutely necessary *to start from the same point*, i. e. clearly to apprehend that leading sentiment of the poet's mind, by their conformity to which the host of suggestions are arranged. Now this requisite exertion is not willingly made by the large majority of readers. It is so easy to judge capriciously, and according to indolent impulse! For very many, therefore, it has become *morally* impossible to attain the author's point of vision, on account of their habits, or their prejudices, or their circumstances; but it is never *physically* impossible, because nature has placed in every man the simple elements, of which art is the sublimation. Since then this demand on the reader for activity, when he wants to peruse his author in a luxurious passiveness, is the very thing that moves his bile, it is obvious that those writers will be always most popular who require the least degree of exertion. Hence, whatever is mixed up with art, and appears under its semblance, is always more favorably regarded than art free and unalloyed. Hence, half the fashionable poems in the world are mere rhetoric, and half the remainder are, perhaps, not liked by the generality for their substantial merits. Hence, likewise, of the really pure compositions, those are most universally agreeable which take for their primary subject the usual passions of the heart, and deal with them in a simple state, without applying the transforming powers of high imagination. Love, friendship, ambition, religion, &c., are matters of daily experience even amongst unimaginative tempers. The forces of association, therefore, are ready to work in these directions, and little effort of will is necessary to follow the artist. For the same reason, such subjects often excite a partial power of composition, which is no sign of a truly poetic organization. We are very far from wishing to depreciate this class of poems, whose influence is so extensive, and communicates so refined a pleasure. We contend only that the facility with which its impressions are communicated is no proof of its elevation as a form of art, but rather the contrary. What, then, some may be ready to exclaim, is the pleasure derived by most men, from Shakspeare, or Dante, or Homer, entirely false and factitious? If these are really masters of their art, must not the energy required of the ordinary intelligences that come in contact with their mighty genius, be the greatest possible? How comes it then, that they are popular? Shall we not say, after all, that the difference is in the power of the author, not in the tenor of his meditations? Those eminent spirits find no difficulty in conveying to common apprehensions their lofty sense and profound observation of nature. They keep no aristocratic state, apart from the sentiments of society at large; they speak to the hearts of all, and by the magnetic force of their conceptions, elevate inferior intellects into a higher and purer atmosphere. The truth contained in this observation is undoubtedly important; geniuses of the most universal order, and assigned by destiny to the most propitious era of a nation's literary development, have a clearer and a larger access to the minds of their compatriots than can ever open to those who are circumscribed by less fortunate circumstances. In the youthful periods of any literature there is an expansive and communicative tendency in mind, which produces unreservedness of communion, and reciprocity of vigor between different orders of intelligence. Without abandoning the ground which has always been defended by the partisans of Mr. Wordsworth, who declare with perfect truth, that the number of real admirers of what is really admirable in Shakspeare and Milton is much fewer than the number of apparent admirers might lead one to imagine, we may safely assert that the intense thoughts set in circulation by those "orbs of song" and their noble satellites "in great Eliza's golden time," did not fail to awaken a proportionable intensity of the natures of numberless auditors. Some might feel feebly, some strongly; the effect would vary according to the character of the recipient; but upon none was the stirring influence entirely unimpressive. The knowledge and power thus imbibed became a part of national existence; it was ours as Englishmen; and amid the flux of generations and customs we retain unimpaired this privilege of intercourse with greatness. But the age in which we live comes late in our national progress. That first raciness and juvenile vigor of literature, when nature "wantoned as in her prime, and played at will her virgin fancies" is gone never to return. Since that day we have undergone a period of degradation. "Every handicraftsman has worn the mask of poesy." It would be tedious to repeat the tale so often related of the French contagion and the heresies of the Popian school. With the close of the last century came an era of reaction, an era of painful struggle to bring our over-civilized condition of thought into union with the fresh productive spirit that brightened the morning of our literature. But repentance is unlike innocence; the laborious endeavor to restore, has more complicated methods of action than the freedom of untainted nature. Those different powers of poetic disposition, the energies of Sensitive,* of Reflective, of Passionate Emotion,

* We are aware that this is not the right word, being appropriated by common use to a different signification. Those who think the caution given by Cæsar should not stand in the way of urgent occasion, may substitute "sensuous;" a word in use amongst our elder divines, and revived by a few bold writers in our own time.

which in former times were intermingled, and derived from mutual support an extensive empire over the feelings of men, were now restrained within separate spheres of agency. The whole system no longer worked harmoniously, and by intrinsic harmony acquired external freedom; but there arose a violent and unusual action in the several component functions, each for itself, all striving to reproduce the regular power which the whole had once enjoyed. Hence the melancholy which so evidently characterizes the spirit of modern poetry; hence that return of the mind upon itself and the habit of seeking relief in idiosyncrasies rather than community of interest. In the old times the poetic impulse went along with the general impulse of the nation; in these it is a reaction against it, a check acting for conservation against a propulsion towards change. We have indeed seen it urged in some of our fashionable publications, that the diffusion of poetry must be in the direct ratio of the diffusion of machinery, because a highly civilized people must have new objects of interest, and thus a new field will be open to description. But this notable argument forgets that against this *objective* amelioration may be set the decrease of *subjective* power, arising from a prevalence of social activity, and a continual absorption of the higher feelings into the palpable interests of ordinary life. The French Revolution may be a finer theme than the war of Troy; but it does not so evidently follow that Homer is to find his superior. Our inference, therefore, from this change in the relative position of artists to the rest of the community is, that modern poetry in proportion to its depth and truth is likely to have little immediate authority over public opinion. Admirers it will have; sects consequently it will form; and these strong under-currents will in time sensibly affect the principal stream. Those writers, whose genius, though great, is not strictly and essentially poetic, become mediators between the votaries of art and the careless cravers for excitement.* Art herself, less manifestly glorious than in her periods of undisputed supremacy, retains her essential prerogatives, and forgets not to raise up chosen spirits who may minister to her state and vindicate her title.

* May we not compare them to the bright but unsubstantial clouds which, in still evenings, girdle the sides of lofty mountains, and seem to form a natural connection between the lowly valleys spread out beneath, and those isolated peaks above that hold the "last parley with the setting sun?"

One of the faithful Islâm, a poet in the truest and highest sense, we are anxious to present to our readers. He has yet written little and published less; but in these "preludes of a loftier strain" we recognize the inspiring God. Mr. Tennyson belongs decidedly to the class we have already described as Poets of Sensation. He sees all the forms of nature with the "eruditus oculus," and his ear has a fairy fineness. There is a strange earnestness in his worship of beauty which throws a charm over his impassioned song, more easily felt than described, and not to be escaped by those who have once felt it. We think he has more definitiveness and roundness of general conception than the late Mr. Keats, and is much more free from blemishes of diction and hasty capriccios of fancy. He has also this advantage over that poet and his friend Shelley, that he comes before the public unconnected with any political party or peculiar system of opinions. Nevertheless, true to the theory we have stated, we believe his participation in their characteristic excellences is sufficient to secure him a share of their unpopularity. The volume of "Poems, chiefly Lyrical," does not contain above 154 pages; but it shows us much more of the character of its parent mind, than many books we have known of much larger compass and more boastful pretensions. The features of original genius are clearly and strongly marked. The author imitates nobody; we recognize the spirit of his age, but not the individual form of this or that writer. His thoughts bear no more resemblance to Byron or Scott, Shelley or Coleridge, than to Homer or Calderon, Firdúsí or Calidasa. We have remarked five distinctive excellences of his own manner. First his luxuriance of imagination, and at the same time, his control over it. Secondly, his power of embodying himself in ideal characters, or rather moods of character, with such extreme accuracy of adjustment, that the circumstances of the narration seem to have a natural correspondence with the predominant feeling, and, as it were, to be evolved from it by assimilative force. Thirdly his vivid, picturesque delineation of objects, and the peculiar skill with which he holds all of them *fused*, to borrow a metaphor from science, in a medium of strong emotion. Fourthly, the variety of his lyrical measures, and exquisite modulation of harmonious words and cadences to the swell and fall of the feelings expressed. Fifthly, the elevated habits of thought, implied in these compositions, and imparting a mellow soberness of tone, more impressive to our minds, than if the author had drawn up a set of opinions in verse, and sought to instruct the understanding rather than to communicate the love of beauty to the heart.

We shall proceed to give our readers some specimens in illustration of these remarks, and if possible, we will give them entire; for no poet can be fairly judged of by fragments, least of all, a poet like Mr. Tennyson, whose mind conceives nothing isolated, nothing abrupt, but every part with reference to some other part, and in subservience to the idea of the whole.

THE END.

CAMBRIDGE: PRINTED BY H. O. HOUGHTON.

www.ingramcontent.com/pod-product-compliance
Lightning Source LLC
LaVergne TN
LVHW021134110826
845150LV00005B/1030

* 9 7 8 1 4 2 5 5 4 9 3 1 2 *